P9-AGA-426

DO-AHEAD
ENTERTAINING

◆

DO-AHEAD
ENTERTAINING

COOKING
IN ADVANCE
FOR ANY
OCCASION

MALABAR HORNBLOWER

THE GLOBE PEQUOT PRESS
Chester, Connecticut

Library of Congress Cataloging-in-Publication Data
Hornblower, Malabar.
Do-ahead entertaining: cooking in advance for any occasion/
Malabar Hornblower.—1st ed.
Includes index.
p.   cm.
ISBN 0-87106-685-8
1. Make-ahead cookery.   I. Title.
TX652.H648 1988
641.5′55—dc19   88-22609
                                                        CIP

Manufactured in the United States of America
First Edition/First Printing

CONTENTS

THE STEPS TO SUCCESSFUL ENTERTAINING
How to Make It All Appear Effortless   1

ENTERTAINING FOUR   13

ENTERTAINING SIX   73

ENTERTAINING EIGHT

ENTERTAINING LARGE GROUPS

TO H. K. B. AND W. B. S.
A. W. B. AND S. B. B.

ACKNOWLEDGMENTS

Living with, or knowing, a cookbook writer is not necessarily all happiness and light. Meals tend to be late, erratic, nutritionally unbalanced—and often, because of the recipes' experimental nature, not all that might be desired. Yet no food writer, at least not I, can go it alone. We need our families and friends for their patience, encouragement, support, criticism, love, endurance, and, most important, appetites. It is no exaggeration to say that, without them, there would be no cookbooks.

Let me give my thanks, then, to many people: to my late husband, Harry, who encouraged me from the very beginning with his love of good food, humor, kindness, and wisdom; to my children, Stephen and Rennie, who not only tasted and advised but also helped with many of the pedestrian chores intrinsic to food preparation; to my stepchildren, Hank, Hatzy, Gusty, and Eleanor; and to the many friends who were called in, often at the last minute, to consume and criticize. Finally, let me thank Diane Nottle, whose astute editorial eye and organizational skills helped me produce this book.

THE STEPS TO SUCCESSFUL ENTERTAINING

◆

HOW TO MAKE IT ALL APPEAR EFFORTLESS

I was an only child. Perhaps that explains my lifelong determination to be always in the center of things and never to miss any of the action.

Certainly this determination has always been true when it comes to entertaining. From day one, from my first small dinner party in my first one-room studio apartment, it profoundly affected my attitude toward having guests in my home. I simply didn't want to be out in the kitchen, away from my friends and the fun. Nor do I today.

My initial solution to this problem, which I call "absentee-host-ism," were casseroles and salads, hot French bread, and standard, easy desserts or the occasional esoteric creation that struck my fancy, such as Alice B. Toklas's Prunes in Port. (Even then I was an avid reader of cookbooks, and some of her recipes were, to say the least, very different.)

None of the dishes I served in the old days were particularly good or particularly bad. The casseroles, designed to be "new" and "sophisticated," would have a glimmer of some inexpensive cut of meat—helpful to the beginner's budget—and be laden with vegetables and such oddities as olives and capers. The salads would be the usual mix of greens, though with decent nonbottled dressings. And the desserts were created to satisfy even the most critical craving for sweet.

But what did all these dishes have in common? What unconscious theme was their raison d'être?

They all could be prepared *ahead of time* and either heated, or dressed, or served chilled from the refrigerator. During the party, they did not require my prolonged presence in the kitchen. I could enjoy the company of my guests and partake of their conversations.

By degrees I expanded this do-ahead concept, adventuring beyond the limitations of casserole cookery. I was fortunate enough in the late sixties to be associated for four years with the Time-Life Books *Foods of the World* series, which gave me an international food education second to none. In our test kitchens, I was able to observe the luminaries of the food world who were helping to compile our books: James Beard, Michael Field, Pierre Franey, Jacques Pépin, José Wilson, Elisabeth Lambert Ortiz, Florence Lin, and Grace Chu. Over the years, my knowledge and expertise grew, and soon I was sharing with others, teaching and writing about food.

But always my theme was the same: preparing ahead so I could enjoy later.

Do-Ahead Entertaining is the second of two cookbooks that I have written, which are devoted exclusively to menus and recipes designed to aid the host and hostess in generating an atmosphere of easy hospitality while providing their friends with top-tasting food. Most of the recipes can be executed sufficiently in advance so that the host and hostess are free to be with the guests, disappearing only for a short time into the kitchen.

Do-Ahead Entertaining is divided into chapters according to the number of guests being fed and feted: four, six, eight, and "large groups" (ten or more people). It is presented in menu form, but the menus are not hard and fast. They should be read as my suggestions for dishes that are compatible with each other. You, as host, should always take into consideration your preferences and those of your guests. Substitutions can always be made. At the request of some of my readers, I have designed a few menus for specific occasions, such as "A Graduation Luncheon for Sixteen" and "A Rehearsal Dinner for Twenty-four," but there is no reason to limit those particular menus to such events if you feel they would serve well for other occasions.

Some of the recipes contained in this book, like the paella, are well-known. I have included them because they are particularly suited to the do-ahead premise. But, in giving a recipe for paella, I have tested and worked over many versions of the same dish until I have come up with what I believe to be the best. Some recipes are my own creations. Some come from friends. And still others are the result of being served a dish that so impressed me that I was inspired to try to duplicate it. (Whenever I taste something I like at home or abroad, I take note of the dish, guess at the ingredients, and, when I get home, try to re-create it. I always try to point out these "inspired" recipes in my introduction to each menu.)

◆

There are two hard and fast rules for successful home entertaining. First and foremost, the event should appear effortless. And, secondly, in order to appear effortless, the event should be as carefully orchestrated as any symphony, as carefully planned as any battle.

In order to help you attain this goal, I have listed in sequence the steps that you should take, along with a few thoughts that might make the occasion a particular success.

◆

1. PLAN THE EVENT

The first secret to successful entertaining is defining and acknowledging the advantages and limitations of the space available to you. Given a clear understanding of what you have, then the kind of events you can hold become obvious. Comfortable, easy entertaining can always be managed. It is the tone and nature that has to be adjusted.

When I was married for the first time, my husband and I lived in an apartment in New York City with a kitchen the size of a breadbox. It had about two feet of counter space and such limited shelving that everything had to be stacked inside, or on top of, the other. And to reach the topmost shelf, I had to stand on a chair; we didn't have room for a stepladder. I learned to have on hand only the cooking tools that were absolute necessities. There was no room for the superfluous.

Abutting the kitchen was a "dining area" barely large enough to contain a table that sat three.

When I married for the second time and moved to a Boston suburb, I went from the ridiculous to the sublime. The kitchen seemed the size of a football field with counter space stretching out to infinity. There was even room enough for a dining table at which I could seat eight. Shelves and closets were so ample that I had storage for every possible appliance.

If our kitchen sounds enormous, our dining room was even larger. It held two dining tables that, when extended, could seat ten and twelve people respectively without crowding.

Because the space in my suburban home was literally limitless, entertaining was much more formal and, therefore, quite rigorous and demanding. For more than eight guests, I needed, and hired, help. At the other extreme, entertaining in my New York apartment had to be informal out of necessity; there was no room for large sit-down dinners. With more than one guest, I was forced to give a buffet, and the guests had to sit in the living room, balancing plates on their laps. I never hired help—although I could have used an extra pair of hands to clear dishes and wash up—because there wasn't enough room in the kitchen for me and a helper at the same time.

Very few people will ever undergo such extremes of entertaining, but take a lesson from me:

Make a careful appraisal of your home. Tour your rooms. Look over what you have and let your imagination fly! Don't be restricted by what you've done in the past. If you can't comfortably fit eight at a dining table for a sit-down meal, consider other options. Look at your kitchen, your dining "area," your living room, your den or family room, your back porch, or your terrace, even your backyard, and see how—and if—they can be used in some inventive, alternative dining capacity. Instead of feeding everyone in just one room, perhaps you can set up small dining tables throughout the house. Don't worry about isolating your guests. Have them switch tables and dinner partners at dessert so that they get a chance to talk to other people. To increase your seating capacity in one or more rooms, consider renting or buying collapsible table tops. These handy devices rest on top of small tables (such as card tables), transforming them into circular tables seating eight. They are not very expensive and fold up for easy storage. There are also collapsible rectangular metal tables available.

If all else fails, and you're talking large numbers, there are always buffets. It may mean plates-on-laps, or one-handed eating, but if the food and company are good, who cares?

In your appraisal of the house, consider your kitchen very carefully. Can it handle large numbers? If it is small, and you have limited space, forget crowds and entertain smaller groups more often. Moreover, plan a menu that is easy to execute at the last moment. In other words, don't serve a roast loin of pork for eight, which takes up a lot of oven room and demands valuable counter space for carving, when you need the same space for finishing off the vegetables and tossing the salad.

Once you have decided upon the size and nature of the event . . .

2.   PLAN YOUR GUEST LIST

Drawing up a good guest list is something of an art. It is important that the guests be compatible, and it is equally important that they be comfortable among each other. Many people are shy. Throwing a guest into a room full of total strangers can ruin the evening for him. He freezes. He wants out. (Others, of course, are very gregarious and have no problem meeting new people.) But if he sees a familiar face or two, confidence returns, and all is well.

In planning a party, I always try to see that each guest knows at least one other person present, even if it's just a dinner for six. I call this my "Guest Security Blanket." As the occasion increases in size, I increase the ratio of guests to friends. It inevitably makes for a much better, happier party. And at very large gatherings, such as cocktail parties, it is the guarantee of success.

Don't make up a guest list comprised of people that you "owe." Such a grouping immediately sets the wrong tone and the obligatory nature of the event shines through. Remember: Entertaining should be fun. Have several smaller events, and pay back one or two friends at a time.

Try to match your guests by interests, not necessarily occupations. A room full of brokers or bankers doesn't make magic; it makes for shoptalk. But if three of the guests are travel demons or great readers, they have something in common, and undoubtedly they'll lighten up the evening with heated discussions on the newest "in" novel or the comparative joys of scuba diving in the Red Sea or the Great Barrier Reef. (This shouldn't faze the others; they'll either join in, listen, or find different things to talk about.) The point is, conversation will be lively, and that's just what you want.

Try to avoid too many maternal or paternal types in one sitting, unless all your guests are young parents and are fascinated by parenthood. Parent-talk can drive nonparents mad—or at least to the point of swearing off children. A dinner that revolves around Getting Baby Into Kindergarten just doesn't make entertaining history.

Try for an assortment of personality; invite some witty people (everybody loves a teller of good jokes), some provocative people, some beautiful or stylish people (other guests will flock to them like moths to a light), perhaps even a local celebrity if you can dig one up. If you must, invite the Town Bore, but try to lose him in the throng.

But don't, for heaven's sake, include two or three people on the same guest list for a large party if you know they abhor each other. Tensions can be palpable and can destroy an otherwise pleasant occasion.

Once a compatible guest list is drawn up . . .

3. PLAN YOUR MENU

In planning a menu, consider the season. Light food is much more pleasant in summer, while hearty fare is very satisfying in winter. (Would you want to eat a stew on a hot summer's evening?)

Consider the season, too, in your selection of fresh ingredients. Don't plan a tomato and basil salad if local and luscious tomatoes are unavailable. Thanks to efficiency of air freight, more and more produce is available year-round. I won't knock the blueberries and asparagus we get from Mexico today; but I will say most emphatically that local blueberries and asparagus in season are so much better.

If you are aware of any of your guests' food idiosyncrasies or allergies, take note of them and plan accordingly. I find nothing worse than watching a guest help himself to a teaspoonful of a seafood dish, smiling bravely while holding back the tears, all because he will suffer the most terrible food poisoning if he consumes one tender, innocent scallop.

When you have planned your menu . . .

4. MAKE A SHOPPING LIST

An organized shopping list can save lots of wear and tear and time.

Divide your list into three categories: "staples," "fresh," and "freshest."

"Staples" may be bought well in advance to be gotten out of the way. Wine and liquor should be considered staples. (If you are giving a cocktail party, consult with a bartender on the quantity of various alcoholic beverages, mixers, and soft drinks you will need. Don't guess. It's terrible to run out, and only a pro really knows what people are currently drinking. Some years it's white wine; others it's vodka.)

"Fresh" ingredients—those that have a day or two of staying power or those that will be used in recipes prepared well in advance—should be bought as early as possible without sacrificing quality.

"Freshest" ingredients—those with a limited shelf-life, like French bread, salad greens, and flowers—should be bought the afternoon before or the morning of the event. Try to keep this list small. Too much time spent shopping too close to the event makes for shattered nerves.

A word here about flowers. Decorate your house and table discriminately with flowers. Don't spend a fortune unnecessarily. The temptation is to fill all available space with pretty posies. But sometimes such efforts are wasted. No one, but no one, notices flowers at a large, crowded party except perhaps the first arrivals. At sit-down dinner parties, flower arrangements on tables are very charming, but they can be done in moderation and with an eye to the budget. Instead of a $30 centerpiece, buy three or four pots of perky primroses or begonias or whatever catches your eye, and set them on a platter in the middle of the table. Or float a single blossom in a fingerbowl in front of each diner. Or make a freeform arrangement of fruits, vegetables, or nuts in the center of the table. (They won't go to waste; you can eat them the next few days.)

After you have complied your shopping lists . . .

5. SEE TO THE TECHNICAL
NEEDS OF THE PARTY

Do you have enough tables or chairs? Linens? Glassware and china? The necessary cooking utensils (perhaps you do not own an 8-quart casserole)? Do you want to borrow, buy, or rent? Remember, you do not want to run out of anything!

If you are giving a cocktail party, be doubly certain that you have enough glasses. Consult with a professional bartender. He will know how many highball, old-fashioned, and wine glasses you need for a specific number of guests. (People always seem to abandon their glasses at parties, and you don't want to be in the kitchen washing dirty glasses when you run out of clean.) Rent glasses if you don't have enough, or if you think you'll be doing a lot of entertaining in the future, buy some cheap ones. Department stores are always having specials on inexpensive and quite attractive barware. Please don't succumb to the temptation of plastic unless the occasion is very informal, and I mean VERY (like a large picnic). I am a plastic snob, and—no question—plastic is tacky.

Place your ice order now, or make a mental note to buy it the afternoon of the party. (Bartenders allow about one pound per person.)

Consider whether you will need help at the bar, cooking, or serving.

If you are giving a large party, you definitely need help. You are not supposed to be in the kitchen, playing the cook, or carrying hors d'oeuvres around, playing the waitress. You are supposed to mingle among your guests, making introductions and ensuring that people-circulation is good and that no one is stuck with the Town Bore. If you're giving a cocktail party, don't have your husband be the bartender. He's supposed to circulate too. And, never, never, let your guests pour for themselves unless you want to find yourself with one or two inebriated souls whose heavy hands have taken their toll.

Hired help doesn't mean Jeeves, the condescending English butler. You can hire your nephew, or the teenager down the street, or call your local college or university and find some student who's all too eager to make an extra buck or two. (Comfort yourself with the knowledge that you're helping him make it through college!)

Don't put off hiring help to the last moment, though. There are not always many people available. It's strange how often all the parties seem to be on the same night, and, if you're poky about getting around to doing the hiring, nobody—or only the truly inept ones—will be left for you. I have been known to confirm that the help I want is available BEFORE I commit to the date itself.

Don't forget to plan where your guests are going to leave their coats, hats, and, should the sun not shine on you, boots and umbrellas. You may want to rent a coat rack and extra hangers.

This is also the time to consider the condition your home is in. Are your table linens clean? Do they need to be ironed? Will the andirons need polishing? Does the rug in the dining room need cleaning? Do those green, leafy plants in the living room look pretty pathetic and need replacing?

Figure out what needs to be done and how far in advance of the party they can be done. Make another list to remind yourself of these chores, if necessary, and do the chores at the appropriate time.

As the day approaches, so does . . .

6. SHOPPING

Follow your carefully constructed shopping lists, buying "staples," "fresh," and "freshest" on the designated days.

Remember, you are not infallible. You may have forgotten something. Double-check yourself.

As you fill the larder, you can start . . .

7. DO-AHEAD COOKING

The more cooking that can be done ahead, the more relaxed you will be and the more you will enjoy your own party. The menus in this book are designed with your needs in mind. Each recipe is divided into two parts: that which can be done ahead (and it tells you how far ahead); and that which can only be done at the time of final preparation (and it tells you how much time will be needed then).

Cook what you can ahead. Plan the timing for the "final preparation." Many recipes instruct you to remove certain dishes from the refrigerator "one hour before final preparation." This is to bring the dish to room temperature, which can be very important when it comes to timing the execution of the dish. An ice-cold marinating roast, just out of the refrigerator, will take much longer to cook than one already at room temperature.

A day or two before the party, you can . . .

8. PREPARE YOUR HOME

Of course, you want your home looking nice and fresh. Set a time to do it, and get it done. Threaten your children with dire punishments if they mess up the sofa pillows or leave soda cans in the family room. They should understand that this inconvenience they're undergoing is only temporary.

If you are giving a cocktail party, this is the hour to remove extraneous furniture that might hamper the flow of your guests from bar to buffet to friends. Get rid of anything they might trip over, like small tables or awkward standing lamps. Few people sit at cocktail parties. Remove large, cumbersome chairs.

It may look ridiculous, but set up your bar, arranging the glasses and bottles in the most convenient manner for the bartender. Figure out where you are going to place the ice and in what, because you don't want it to melt all over your floor. You will probably want some kind of large plastic container, like a garbage can, to hold the bulk of it, and a smaller ice bucket for the top of the bar. Decide in what container you are going to place the chilled white wine to keep it cold. A large plastic or glass salad bowl, packed with shaved ice, often does the trick pretty neatly.

If you're giving a dinner party, don't wait until the last moment to set the table, unless you live in a dust bowl where everything will promptly be covered with grime. Arrange your table and get the feel of how it will look when your guests arrive.

Don't forget to have enough candles on hand. Candlelight radiates warmth and is very conducive to congenial dining. John Carafoli, a good friend with a deft hand at decorating, once did away entirely with traditional candlesticks. Instead he substituted several dozen votive candles, placed in ribbed glass containers, and scattered them, seemingly at random, across the whole table. (The idea came to him when he was setting his table a day or two before his party, and he had the time to experiment with lighting.) The effect was so stunning that he didn't need any other form of decoration on the table.

Select and check your china, making certain that it is clean. Check your glassware too. Run it through a wash if it's not crystal-clean and shiny. If you're using silver and it's dirty, polish it. Get out your serving pieces.

This is the time to make the final decisions about flowers and table decorations. With your rooms clean and your table set, you will have a good idea of what you really need.

This is also the day to check the clothes you will be wearing. Are they clean, do they need pressing, is there any last-minute item that you need to buy?

And don't forget the guest bathroom. Have extra towels on hand and a fresh bar of soap. (Many of us, of course, don't have guest bathrooms, so if you will be using your kids' bathroom or your own, for heaven's sake tidy it up!)

9. ALL THAT REMAINS NOW IS THE DAY OF THE EVENT

- Shop for your "freshest" ingredients. Wash and prepare the salad greens. Arrange the flowers.
- Plan the sequence of the recipes' "final preparations," and execute them accordingly.
- Make certain you have enough ice on hand.
- If you have hired help, be sure to give them complete, concise instructions. (It never hurts to write a list for them.) Show them around the kitchen and the house so they'll feel comfortable with their surroundings.

• Take a long, relaxing bath or shower. Save time for leisurely dressing. You want to look your best.

• Then, answer the doorbell, secure in the knowledge that you will be enjoying the occasion just as much as your guests.

Given that spirit, the evening will be truly gala.

ENTERTAINING
FOUR

Dinners for four, by their very nature, are apt to be intimate and informal occasions. They almost demand their host's continual presence, for if the guests don't know each other, conversation and spontaneity may become forced and leaden.

If I am entertaining such a small group, I prefer to bring them right into my kitchen for dinner, leaving the dining room for larger numbers. I realize, of course, that we are living in the Age of Compact Kitchens, and not everyone is fortunate enough to have space for seating four right in the kitchen. But if you can, I urge you to. And if you can't, try to design an informal setting, for informality breeds conviviality and ease. For example, if you plan to seat your guests at a large dining room table, don't scatter them equidistant from each other. Sit them companionably at one end. Or forget the dining room entirely, and set up a table in the living room or den.

Unless you are trying to impress the Boss or some such V.I.P., don't feel compelled to bring out the best linen, cutlery, and crystal. They generate insecurity among small groups. (I learned this lesson the hard way, of course. My first small party was very formal, with all the trimmings I could muster. It was inevitable: one guest spilled his red wine, the other managed to knock over the salt, and the third dropped his buttered butter knife (who needs one anyway?) on the new carpet. I am sure if the table had been set with a checkered cloth, or mats, and paper napkins instead of the brightest white linen, none of this would have happened.)

Make your guests feel a part of the entertainment. Enlist their help, if you want, in bringing food to the table or whipping cream or pouring beverages. That way, everybody will keep busy, feel useful, and—without question—be convinced that not only was the food superior, but that it was a very special evening indeed.

A LANDMARK VEAL DINNER FOR FOUR

Veal Dumont

Braised Leeks

Sautéed Mushrooms with Scallions

Hot Garlic Bread

Four-Fruit Sherbet

We are all profoundly influenced by our mothers' ways in the kitchen.

My mother was a superb cook. She knew it and reveled in it. Seldom would she let anyone else enter her domain. Once in a while I tried to cook for her, but she would only turn up her nose at my comparatively inept endeavors.

The evening I first made Veal Dumont for her changed everything. I had learned about this simple and delicious dish when I was just out of college, flying thirty thousand feet in the air over India, between Colombo, Sri Lanka, and Bombay. My seatmate was a loquacious Frenchwoman, Marie Dumont, who passed the time with me talking food, all manner of food. She described her favorite veal dish so alluringly that I remembered all her instructions without notes, word for word. I made it for dinner a few months later when I returned to my parents' home in New York City.

Mother sat down at the table without much enthusiasm for what was on the plate in front of her. She cut into the meat almost despondently and put the fork into her mouth with a gesture akin to resignation. She chewed a minute, then swallowed. Then she took another bite. Suddenly her eyes lit up. She turned to me, looking incredulous.

"This is good," she said. "This is delicious."

At long last I had earned her culinary respect. It was a moment I have cherished these many years.

While veal is very expensive these days, a little goes a long way. (But if you prefer, boneless, skinless chicken breasts, pounded thin, may be substituted for the veal to reduce the cost of the entree.) Veal Dumont is so easy to prepare that it can be done in its entirety in virtually ten minutes, if you prefer not to prepare it ahead. I urge you to use an imported Swiss-style cheese such as Gruyère or even Jarlsberg, which have so much more flavor than their American counterparts.

For dessert, the Four-Fruit Sherbet is particularly refreshing. Make a game of it, though, and try out your friends' palates. Ask them to identify the fruits. I'll wager not many will be able to name all four. To recoup a bit for the veal's extravagance, you might even make them bet for money.

VEAL DUMONT

(MAY BE PARTIALLY PREPARED UP TO 24 HOURS IN ADVANCE)

8 to 12 thinly sliced veal scallops (about 1½ pounds)
2 tablespoons unsalted butter
2 tablespoons oil
½ teaspoon salt
Freshly ground black pepper
6 tablespoons sour cream
6 tablespoons grated Gruyère or Jarlsberg cheese (about ¼ pound)
2 tablespoons minced fresh parsley

Place the slices of veal between sheets of wax paper and pound them thin with a cleaver, mallet, or rolling pin.

In a large skillet, over moderately high heat, combine the butter and oil and bring them to a foam. Sprinkle the veal with salt and pepper, then sauté a few slices at a time, about 20 seconds on each side, or until just barely cooked through. As the pieces of meat are done, transfer them to a cookie sheet, jellyroll pan, or baking dish. Repeat until all the slices are done. Cover with plastic wrap and refrigerate until 1 hour before final preparation.

TIME ALLOWANCE FOR FINAL PREPARATION: 10 MINUTES

Preheat the oven to 450 degrees.

Spread a dollop of sour cream on top of each piece of veal. Sprinkle with grated cheese. Heat the veal in the oven for 5 minutes. If the cheese topping has not browned slightly during that time, place the veal briefly under the broiler.

Sprinkle with the minced parsley and serve immediately.

SERVES 4

BRAISED LEEKS

(MAY BE PARTIALLY PREPARED UP TO 24 HOURS IN ADVANCE)

4 large leeks, about 1 ½ inches in diameter
1 to 2 cups chicken stock
3 tablespoons unsalted butter, cut into small pieces
Salt and freshly ground black pepper to taste

Preheat the oven to 350 degrees.

Trim off the roots and the green section of the leeks' leaves, leaving white stalks 5 to 6 inches long. One-half inch from the root end, slice straight through the stalk lengthwise up to the greenish top. Spread the leaves apart and wash them thoroughly under cold water. Pat dry with paper toweling and compress the leeks into their original shape.

Place the leeks side by side in an ovenproof baking dish small enough to contain them compactly in one layer. Add enough chicken stock to cover them barely. Dot the leeks with the butter, and sprinkle them with salt and pepper to taste. (The amount of salt should be adjusted according to the saltiness of the stock.) Cover the baking dish tightly with aluminum foil. Bake for 1 hour.

Remove the baking dish from the oven and allow the leeks to cool. Reserve them in a cool corner of the kitchen if you are preparing them within 4 hours of the dinner. Otherwise, refrigerate them until 1 hour before final preparation.

TIME ALLOWANCE FOR FINAL PREPARATION: 35 MINUTES

Preheat the oven to 450 degrees.

Discard the aluminum foil cover. Bake the leeks for 15 minutes. Turn them over with a pair of tongs, and bake them another 15 minutes.

Serve immediately, spooning a little broth over each serving.

SERVES 4

SAUTÉED MUSHROOMS WITH SCALLIONS

◆

(MAY BE PARTIALLY PREPARED UP TO 4 HOURS IN ADVANCE)

6 tablespoons unsalted butter
1 pound mushrooms, ends trimmed, quartered
¼ cup thinly sliced green scallion leaves (reserve white portions for another use)

In a large skillet equipped with a tight-fitting lid, melt the butter over low heat. When it is completely melted, remove the pan from the heat and swirl the melted butter around so that it completely coats the bottom of the pan.

Place the mushrooms in the skillet and give them a vigorous shaking to coat them with as much of the remaining butter as possible. Cover the skillet with its lid and set the pan aside in a cool corner of the kitchen.

TIME ALLOWANCE FOR FINAL PREPARATION: 10 MINUTES

Set the mushroom-filled skillet over moderately high heat. Keeping the lid on, steam the mushrooms for 3 to 4 minutes, shaking the pan occasionally to redistribute them. Remove the lid, stir the mushrooms, lower the heat, and cook 1 minute longer. The mushrooms should be cooked through but still firm.

Transfer the mushrooms immediately to a heated serving dish. Garnish them with the scallion greens.

SERVES 4

FOUR-FRUIT SHERBET

◆

(MAY BE PREPARED UP TO 2 DAYS IN ADVANCE;
MUST BE PREPARED AT LEAST 3 HOURS IN ADVANCE)

2 cups water
2 cups sugar
⅓ cup strained fresh lemon juice
1 cup strained fresh orange juice
¾ cup pineapple juice
1 large, very ripe banana, peeled

Make a simple syrup by combining the water and sugar in a saucepan. Set the pan over moderate heat and, stirring frequently, heat the liquid until the sugar has dissolved.

Combine the lemon, orange, and pineapple juices with 1¼ cups of the simple syrup in a large bowl. Pour 1 cup of the simple syrup into the bowl of a food processor fitted with a steel blade. Add the banana, broken into large pieces, and whirl until smooth. Add half the fruit juice and syrup mixture, whirl again, then return the contents of the processor to the juice and syrup mixture remaining in the large bowl. Mix until well blended. Cover with plastic wrap and refrigerate until well chilled, at least 2 hours.

Pour the four-fruit mixture into the container of a hand-cranked or electric ice cream freezer, and freeze according to the manufacturer's directions. When the sherbet is frozen, remove it from the machine and pack it into a tightly covered freezer container.

TIME ALLOWANCE FOR FINAL PREPARATION: 20 MINUTES

Remove the Four-Fruit Sherbet from the freezer 15 minutes before serving to allow it to soften slightly. (The fruit flavors are more pronounced when the sherbet is not icy cold.)

With an ice-cream scoop, make attractive balls of the sherbet and present them in a large serving dish or individual dessert plates.

SERVES 4

NOTE: The remaining simple syrup may be tightly covered and stored in the refrigerator for a future use.

SUCCULENT SALTIMBOCCA FOR FOUR

Cream of Carrot Soup

Chicken Saltimbocca

Green Rice

Mixed Green Salad with Cherry Tomatoes Vinaigrette

Assorted Fruit and Cheeses

Creating a special dinner for a few guests can be more difficult than planning a party for twenty. Roasts and stews generally feed more than four—unless the host chooses to present a minuscule roast or half a recipe for stew—and, as the focus of the meal, such entrees simply don't appear as festive as they should.

One solution is chicken breasts, which can be enhanced in any number of ways and are unfailingly popular to boot.

Saltimbocca—the literal translation from the Italian is "jump in the mouth"—is traditionally made with veal. But this version, using chicken breasts crisply pan-fried and dressed in parsley butter, is equally appealing with its internal surprise of ham and mozzarella cheese. Assembling the chicken may sound difficult, but it really isn't, because all the messy work can be done the night before, and the flaws, if any, are very easy to disguise.

For a change, the vegetables are presented almost imperceptibly: carrots in the soup, spinach mixed in with the rice. Both dishes can be prepared well in advance and simply reheated. A mixed green salad punctuated with cherry tomatoes acts as a nice foil to the richness of the entree, while a special cheese or two, such as a goat cheese or a St. André, accompanied by fruit, rounds off the meal nicely.

All in all, this menu provides for an intimate evening with only a brief interruption while the host is in the kitchen.

CREAM OF CARROT SOUP

◆

(MAY BE PARTIALLY PREPARED UP TO 4 DAYS IN ADVANCE)

2 tablespoons unsalted butter
1/2 cup coarsely chopped onions
1 medium potato (about 1/2 pound), peeled and thickly sliced
1 pound carrots, peeled and thickly sliced
1 teaspoon dried tarragon
2 cups chicken stock
1 cup heavy cream
Salt and freshly ground black pepper to taste
2 tablespoons minced fresh chives

In a 2- to 3-quart saucepan, melt the butter over low heat, and sauté the onions until they are wilted, about 5 minutes. Add the sliced potato and carrots, tarragon, and chicken stock. Bring the liquid to a boil over high heat, then lower the heat and simmer, partially covered, until the potatoes and carrots are very tender, about 15 minutes.

Remove the pan from the heat and allow the vegetables and stock to cool slightly. Transfer the contents of the pan in batches to a blender or food processor fitted with a steel knife; puree until smooth. Pour the pureed base into a container with a tight-fitting lid and refrigerate until time for final preparation.

TIME ALLOWANCE FOR FINAL PREPARATION: 10 MINUTES

Pour the pureed vegetable base into a 3-quart saucepan. Stir in the heavy cream. Over medium heat, reheat to just below the boiling point. Taste for seasoning and add salt and pepper as needed. Pour into heated individual bowls or mugs, sprinkle with chives, and serve immediately.

SERVES 4

CHICKEN SALTIMBOCCA

◆

(MAY BE PARTIALLY PREPARED UP TO 24 HOURS IN ADVANCE;
MUST BE PARTIALLY PREPARED AT LEAST 2 HOURS IN ADVANCE)

4 whole chicken breasts, halved, skinned, and boned (8 half breasts)
8 thin slices imported ham, such as prosciutto
8 (1-ounce) slices mozzarella cheese
¾ cup flour
½ teaspoon salt
Freshly ground black pepper
2 eggs, beaten
3 tablespoons milk
2 cups soft bread crumbs, preferably homemade
¾ cup unsalted butter
⅓ cup minced fresh parsley
3 tablespoons oil

With a mallet, cleaver, or rolling pin, pound the chicken breasts between sheets of wax paper until they measure approximately 5 by 6 inches. (They will be quite thin and may even tear slightly in some spots; don't worry.) Depending on the shape of the ham slices, either fold them in half or trim them smaller than the chicken pieces.

Arrange a ham slice in the center of each breast, including any trimmings. Center a slice of cheese on top of the ham. Tuck opposite ends of the chicken just slightly over the ham and cheese, then roll the breast up lengthwise, pressing the edges together firmly. Repeat with the remaining chicken. (Some chicken breasts are more cooperative than others when it comes to being rolled; don't be discouraged. The meat is very adhesive and once the rolls are floured, dipped, and breaded, all the goofs will be completely disguised and the results quite professional-looking.)

Spread the flour, salt, and pepper out on a piece of paper toweling or a sheet of wax paper, blending the ingredients with your fingers. Beat the eggs with the milk in a shallow bowl and set it next to the flour. Spread the bread crumbs out on another piece of toweling or wax paper next to the egg mixture.

Coat one chicken roll on all sides first in the flour, shaking off any excess, then in the egg, then in the bread crumbs, making certain it has a generous coating of the latter. Transfer it to a small platter. Repeat with the remaining chicken rolls. Cover the platter with plastic wrap and refrigerate the chicken for at least 2 hours. Do *not* bring the rolls to room temperature before the final preparation.

TIME ALLOWANCE FOR FINAL PREPARATION: 20 MINUTES

In a small skillet, melt ½ cup of the butter over low heat. Add the minced parsley and set aside.

In a 14-inch skillet, combine the remaining ¼ cup butter with the oil and, over moderately high heat, bring the mixture to the foaming stage. Fry the chicken rolls approximately 10 minutes, turning them frequently so they brown evenly on all sides. Lower the heat and continue turning; cook them 5 minutes more. (If you do not have a skillet large enough to contain all the chicken pieces in one layer, cook them in 2 batches. Transfer the first batch, when it is done, to a low oven to keep warm while you prepare the second batch.)

Briefly reheat the melted parsley butter.

Transfer the Chicken Saltimbocca to a heated platter and drizzle the warm parsley butter over the top.

SERVES 4

GREEN RICE

◆

(MAY BE PREPARED UP TO 6 HOURS IN ADVANCE)

¾ cup long-grain rice
2 tablespoons olive oil
1 teaspoon minced garlic
½ cup thinly sliced scallions, including 2 inches of green leaves
½ pound spinach, stalks discarded, washed, and coarsely chopped
½ teaspoon salt
Freshly ground black pepper
3 tablespoons minced fresh dillweed

Cook the rice according to package directions, taking care not to overcook. The kernels should be separate and slightly firm. Remove from the heat and reserve.

In a medium-size skillet equipped with a tight-fitting lid, warm the oil over moderately low heat. Add the garlic and sauté until just soft, about 2 minutes. Toss in the scallions and sauté for 3 minutes, or until they have just begun to soften but are still bright green. Stir frequently. Add the spinach and toss well to coat the leaves with the oil. Cover tightly and steam for 5 minutes. Remove the lid, stir briefly, and cook an additional 3 to 4 minutes, uncovered, allowing any excess moisture to evaporate. Season with salt and pepper. Remove the skillet from heat and set aside to cool.

When the spinach is cool to the touch, add the dillweed and mix thoroughly. Combine the spinach and the reserved rice and toss to blend well. Transfer the mixture to the top portion of a large double boiler and set it aside in a cool corner of the kitchen until time for final preparation.

TIME ALLOWANCE FOR FINAL PREPARATION: 20 MINUTES

Fill the bottom of the double boiler with 2 inches of water. Place the double boiler over moderate heat, bring the water to a boil, and reheat the Green Rice for 15 minutes, stirring occasionally.

SERVES 4

MIXED GREEN SALAD WITH CHERRY TOMATOES VINAIGRETTE

(SALAD MAY BE PARTIALLY PREPARED UP TO 6 HOURS IN ADVANCE; VINAIGRETTE MAY BE PREPARED UP TO 3 DAYS IN ADVANCE)

MIXED GREEN SALAD
*4 to 6 cups assorted salad greens, such as arugula and watercress
(stems cut off), bibb and Boston lettuce, romaine, chicory, endive, red and
green cabbage, Chinese cabbage, and raddichio, washed and thoroughly
dried*
4 teaspoons thinly sliced scallions, including 2 or more inches of green leaves
¾ cup cherry tomatoes, hulled, washed, and halved

To make the salad: Line a salad bowl with paper toweling. Place the salad greens and scallions in the bowl, and toss with your hands to mix. Cover with a dampened linen towel and refrigerate until time for final preparation.

VINAIGRETTE
½ teaspoon Dijon-style mustard
¼ teaspoon salt
Freshly ground black pepper
2 tablespoons tarragon or red wine vinegar
1 clove garlic, peeled and halved lengthwise
6 tablespoons fruity, imported olive oil

To make the dressing: Place the mustard, salt, pepper, and vinegar in a jar with a tight-fitting lid, and stir until the mustard and salt are dissolved. Add the garlic pieces and the oil, cover tightly, and shake vigorously. Store the dressing in a cool corner of the kitchen until ready to use.

Before dressing the salad, remove the garlic pieces. (The longer the garlic remains in the dressing, the stronger its flavor, so you may want to remove it 1 or 2 hours after making the dressing.)

YIELD: ½ CUP DRESSING

TIME ALLOWANCE FOR FINAL PREPARATION: 5 MINUTES

Remove the toweling from the salad. Shake the vinaigrette vigorously and pour it over the greens. Using a salad fork and spoon, toss the greens until they are completely coated with the dressing. Add the cherry tomato halves and toss again.

SERVES 4

A WAY TO LOVE LIVER

Calf's Liver, Venetian Style

Red Potatoes with Dill Butter

Sesame Broccoli

Hot Gingered Peaches

Nobody seems to feel halfway about liver. You either love it or hate it. As a child I hated it with all the passion of youth until my mother tricked me into believing that, when accompanied by bacon, it was a totally new and delicious kind of liver. So, at the age of six, I started loving it, and it's been a lifelong love affair ever since. Now I love liver cooked in many ways.

The best liver is calf's liver; its flavor is sweet and delicate. Beef, pork, or lamb liver comes from older beasts and tastes much stronger. The trick to any good liver, however, lies in the cooking. Undercooked, it is soft and rather unattractively mushy; overcooked, it has an unpleasantly bitter taste. The best test for doneness is what I fondly call the "finger prod," and only experimentation will bring you real knowledge and success. Poke the surface as the liver is cooking. If it feels soft, the meat is too rare. If it's firm to the touch, it's overdone. If it feels resilient, it should be exactly right. At any rate, don't be put off. Venetian-style liver calls for onions as an accompaniment, and they're a major asset to the dish. If you don't judge the cooking time perfectly, the onions will help disguise the fact.

With the liver, serve simple boiled red-skinned poatoes embellished with dill butter and tender broccoli flowerets made all the sweeter with a drizzling of sesame oil.

And I have a surprise for dessert: pedestrian canned peaches jazzed up to new heights with the addition of sugar and rum and a brief baking in the oven. These Hot Gingered Peaches are a marvelous fail-safe for the unexpected guest. Always keep a can of peaches in the larder, and you will never be at a loss for the final touch to an impromptu meal.

CALF'S LIVER, VENETIAN STYLE

(MAY BE PARTIALLY PREPARED UP TO 2 HOURS IN ADVANCE)

4 tablespoons unsalted butter
1 cup thinly sliced onions
1/2 cup flour
1/2 teaspoon salt
Freshly ground black pepper
8 generous slices calf's liver, about 1/3 inch thick, gristle removed (about 1 1/2 pounds)
1/4 cup red wine vinegar
Parsley sprigs

In a medium-size skillet, melt 2 tablespoons of the butter over low heat. Add the onions and sauté, stirring occasionally, until they are soft, about 5 minutes. Remove the skillet from the heat and set it aside in a cool corner of the kitchen.

In a pie tin or on a paper towel, combine the flour, salt, and pepper and mix with your fingers to blend. Reserve for final preparation.

Remove the liver from the refrigerator 30 minutes before final preparation.

TIME ALLOWANCE FOR FINAL PREPARATION: 10 MINUTES

Preheat the oven to 250 degrees.

Place the skillet of onions over very low heat to warm. Stir occasionally.

In a large 12- to 14-inch skillet, melt the remaining 2 tablespoons butter over moderately high heat. When the butter is foaming, dust the liver slices in the seasoned flour and shake off any excess. Carefully lower four slices into the skillet. Cook 1 to 2 minutes on one side, then turn and cook another minute on the second side. This should produce a nice pink—but not rare or gray—liver. Poke the meat with your finger. If it feels mushy, the meat is underdone and should cook a minute or so longer; if it feels firm, it's overcooked. (You will know better next time.)

As the slices are cooked, transfer them to the warm oven to hold while you finish the remaining four slices.

When all the liver has been cooked and is in the oven, pour off any fat remaining in the large skillet. Deglaze the pan by pouring in the vinegar and scraping up any particles left clinging to the bottom of the pan. Allow the vinegar to boil down for 20 seconds. Turn off the heat. Return the pieces of liver to the skillet, add the onions, and toss gently to mix and to distribute the flavors. Serve immediately on heated plates, garnished with parsley sprigs.

SERVES 4

SESAME BROCCOLI

(MAY BE PARTIALLY PREPARED UP TO 8 HOURS IN ADVANCE)

2 tablespoons sesame seeds
6 cups broccoli flowerets including a few thin slices of the tender upper stems
2 tablespoons butter
1/2 teaspoon salt
1 teaspoon imported sesame oil

Place the sesame seeds in a small nonstick skillet over moderate to low heat. Shaking the pan frequently, toast them for 5 to 7 minutes, or until they are nicely brown. Transfer them to a small dish and hold until final preparation.

Fill a 2-quart stainless steel saucepan with water to within 2 inches of the rim. Bring it to a boil. Drop in the broccoli pieces. Bring the water to a boil again over high heat. Watch carefully. When the water just starts to bubble, start timing the cooking process for 1 minute. Do not overcook. The broccoli should be almost tender but still a vivid green. Drain immediately in a colander and place under cold water to refresh and cool. Cover the colander loosely with a linen towel and hold in a cool corner of the kitchen.

TIME ALLOWANCE FOR FINAL PREPARATION: 10 MINUTES

Melt the butter in a large skillet over moderately high heat. When it is foaming, add the reserved broccoli and salt. Stirring frequently, cook for 3 to 4 minutes, or until the broccoli is steaming hot but has not changed color.

Dribble the sesame oil over the broccoli, toss a few more times, and transfer to a heated serving dish. Garnish the broccoli with the toasted sesame seeds.

SERVES 4

HOT GINGERED PEACHES

(MAY BE PARTIALLY PREPARED UP TO 8 HOURS IN ADVANCE)

8 "homestyle" canned peach halves, syrup reserved
2 teaspoons ground ginger
4 teaspoons dark brown sugar
4 teaspoons butter
3 tablespoons dark rum
1 cup heavy cream, whipped

Arrange the peach halves, cut side up, in a shallow baking dish large enough to contain them in one layer. Reserve 1½ cups of their syrup, supplementing it with orange juice if necessary.

Sprinkle ¼ teaspoon ginger into each peach cavity, then ½ teaspoon brown sugar. Dot each with ½ teaspoon butter. Pour the reserved syrup into the baking dish. Cover with plastic wrap and reserve in a cool spot in the kitchen until time for final preparation.

TIME ALLOWANCE FOR FINAL PREPARATION: 35 MINUTES

Preheat the oven to 350 degrees.
Bake the peaches, uncovered, for 30 minutes, or until steaming hot.
While the peaches are baking, beat the rum into the whipped cream. Transfer it to a separate bowl to accompany the hot peaches.

SERVES 4

SAUCY FISH
FOR FOUR

*Steamed Haddock with
Mushrooms and Sauce
Madeleine*

Fresh Corn and Peppers

*Boiled Potatoes with Parsleyed
Butter*

Strawberry Fool

Some friends are better than others! I am referring to the special kind who are generous about sharing their recipes. This menu's Sauce Madeleine is a gift from such a friend, an elegant Swiss-born American currently living in Connecticut. She served it one gala evening over a fine fillet of poached red snapper. When I implored her for the recipe, she negotiated with all the expertise of a Swiss banker; she would give me her sauce recipe only in exchange for my Walnut Moss dessert (see page 181).

I agreed most happily, and, indeed, I think I got the better of the bargain. Her sauce (which I have named in her honor) is simplicity itself to prepare and so versatile that, with the substitution of different herbs, it can enhance any number of fish, fowl, or meat dishes. Today's recipe calls for spooning it over steamed haddock; try it another time over poached salmon—or even poached chicken—and substitute fresh cilantro for the dill.

The Fresh Corn and Peppers is a bright and cheery dish that, naturally, tastes best made with freshly picked corn. (But substitute frozen if local corn is out of season. Frozen is better than corn that has meandered to your market from Florida or California.)

For dessert, try the light, pretty, and easy Strawberry Fool. (I love some of the English names for desserts, such as trifles and fools. Unless you are familiar with them, you have no idea what you may be getting!) Traditionally, "fools" are made with stewed and pureed gooseberries, blackberries, or raspberries. Not-so-traditional strawberries, on the other hand, don't have to be stewed to achieve the proper consistency for a fool, so they are a quick and easier alternative. (They also seem to be perpetually "in season" these days, making them even more attractive when it comes to menu-planning.)

STEAMED HADDOCK WITH MUSHROOMS AND SAUCE MADELEINE

◆

(FISH MAY BE PARTIALLY PREPARED UP TO 6 HOURS IN ADVANCE; SAUCE MAY BE PREPARED 2 HOURS IN ADVANCE AND REHEATED, BUT IT IS BEST PREPARED JUST BEFORE SERVING; TIME ALLOWANCE FOR SAUCE IS 5–10 MINUTES)

4 teaspoons unsalted butter, softened
2 one-pound haddock fillets, skinned
2 teaspoons strained fresh lemon juice
Freshly ground black pepper
2 teaspoons minced fresh chives
¼ pound mushrooms, trimmed and sliced

Cut two 18-inch lengths of heavy-duty aluminum foil. Rub 1 teaspoon of the softened butter across each piece of foil in roughly the same shape and length as the haddock fillets. Place a fillet on each buttered section of the foil. Sprinkle each fillet with 1 teaspoon lemon juice, a grinding of pepper, and 1 teaspoon chives. Arrange one-half of the sliced mushrooms along the top of each fillet. Dot the fillets with the remaining 2 teaspoons of butter. Fold the ends of the foil over the head and tail portions of each fillet. Then bring the long sides together and fold them over and over each other several times until the fish "package" is flat and securely sealed. Repeat with the second fillet. Refrigerate the packages until 1 hour before final preparation.

TIME ALLOWANCE FOR FINAL PREPARATION: 25 MINUTES

Preheat the oven to 450 degrees.

Place the fish packages directly on the rack in the middle of the oven. Bake for 20 minutes. Unwrap the foil and drain off any accumulated juices. Transfer the fillets, intact, to a heated serving platter, and serve immediately, accompanied by Sauce Madeleine.

SERVES 4

SAUCE MADELEINE

2 teaspoons Dijon-style mustard
2 teaspoons tomato paste
1 cup heavy cream
3 tablespoons minced fresh dillweed

In a small saucepan, off the heat, combine the mustard and tomato paste. Stir until they are completely blended. Add the cream a few tablespoons at a time, always blending it in before adding the next amount. When all the cream has been incorporated, place the saucepan over medium heat and bring the mixture to a boil, stirring constantly. Continue boiling and stirring until the cream mixture is reduced by half and has thickened slightly. Add the dill, mix thoroughly, and spoon the sauce over the fish or pour it into a heated sauceboat to accompany the fish.

YIELD: ½ CUP SAUCE

FRESH CORN AND PEPPERS

(MAY BE PARTIALLY PREPARED UP TO 4 HOURS IN ADVANCE)

6 large ears of corn, shucked (or substitute a 10-ounce package frozen cut corn, thawed)
3 tablespoons unsalted butter
3 red peppers, cored, seeded, and coarsely chopped (about 1 pound)
¼ cup heavy cream
2 tablespoons minced fresh parsley

Run a fork lengthwise down and around each ear of corn to slit open the kernels. With a sharp knife, immediately cut the corn from the cob into a large bowl to collect the juices along with the kernels. Reserve.

In a large skillet equipped with a tight-fitting lid, melt the butter over low heat. Add the chopped peppers and sauté them until soft, about 3 minutes. Do not overcook them. Remove the pan from the heat, add the cut fresh corn (or thawed frozen), and toss to mix. Cover the skillet with the lid and hold in a cool corner of the kitchen until final preparation.

TIME ALLOWANCE FOR FINAL PREPARATION: 7 MINUTES

Uncover the skillet and dribble the cream over the corn and peppers. Stir to mix. Place the skillet over medium heat, cover, and cook 3 to 5 minutes, sitrring occasionally, until the corn is tender and steaming hot. Serve immediately, garnished with the minced parsley.

SERVES 4

STRAWBERRY FOOL

◆

(MAY BE PARTIALLY PREPARED UP TO 6 HOURS IN ADVANCE)

1 pint strawberries, washed and hulled
1 tablespoon grated orange rind
½ to ¾ cup sugar
1 cup heavy cream, well chilled

Select 4 perfect strawberries and reserve. Place the remaining berries, orange rind, and ½ cup sugar in the bowl of a food processor fitted with a steel knife. Whirl the berries until smooth, about 30 seconds. Taste for sweetness and add more sugar if desired. Transfer the puree to a bowl, cover with plastic wrap, and refrigerate until final preparation.

TIME ALLOWANCE FOR FINAL PREPARATION: 5 MINUTES

In a chilled bowl, whip the cream until soft peaks form. Fold the cream into the strawberry puree, but don't completely blend it in. Leave pretty swirls of pink.

Divide the fool among four parfait or wine glasses and top each serving with one of the reserved strawberries.

SERVES 4

HEARTY INTERNATIONAL DINNER FOR FOUR

Steak with Green Peppercorn Sauce

Andalusian Potatoes

Broiled Cheddar Tomatoes

Fennel and Arugula Salad with Basil Vinaigrette

Hot Apple Crisp

I have given many a dinner party with all sorts of delicacies designed to entrance my guests, but it's when my guests see a nice fat steak, or steaks, ready for the fire that their eyes light up with a rare sparkle. It is at such times that I have the slight suspicion that people are tired of the spicy sautéed shrimp, the dainty medallions of veal, the stunning pink salmon, and the carefully fabricated homemade pasta stuffed with lobster that nutrition dictates is better for their health.

So occasionally I break with current thinking and indulge my guests with hearty red meat. But I can't simply go the steak-potatoes-and-caesar-salad route. It has to be a little different, a little intriguing. After all, our meals are the product of the eighties: They have to be special.

Today's menu, for example, takes the all-American fare of steak, potatoes, tomatoes, and apples and adds a few international flourishes. The steak isn't just broiled or grilled; it has a peppercorn sauce more often than not associated with France. The potatoes are fried, but with a Spanish twist. The Fennel and Arugula Salad is pure Italian. Only the tomatoes and the dessert are all-American with deep orange cheddar cheese as a topping on the broiled tomatoes, and a hot apple crisp.

"Plain" fare, perhaps, but with a real sparkle.

STEAK WITH GREEN PEPPERCORN SAUCE

(MAY BE PARTIALLY PREPARED UP TO 4 HOURS IN ADVANCE)

1 (2-pound) boneless sirloin steak, about 1¼ inch thick
1 tablespoon green peppercorns, packed in brine
2 tablespoons unsalted butter
¼ cup minced shallots
½ cup dry white wine
½ cup heavy cream
Salt and freshly ground black pepper
2 tablespoons minced fresh parsley

The steak should be cooked just before serving. However, in order to save time, there are a couple of preliminary steps that may be taken.

Trim the steak of any excess fat. Using the skillet in which you will fry the steak, render the fat over low heat until you have 2 to 3 tablespoons. Discard the remaining chunks of fat. Remove the skillet from the heat and set aside. Refrigerate the steak until 1 hour before final preparation.

Rinse the green peppercorns in cold water and place them on paper toweling to drain. Reserve for final preparation.

TIME ALLOWANCE FOR FINAL PREPARATION: 15 MINUTES

Heat the skillet containing the rendered fat over moderately high heat until it is very hot. Carefully place the steak in the skillet and sauté for 3 minutes. Turn the steak over and sauté for another 3 to 4 minutes. This timing should produce a rare steak. Prod its surface with your finger. The softer the meat feels, the rarer it is. (When it is firm to the touch, it will be well done.) When the meat is cooked to your preference, transfer it to a heated serving platter and cover it with a tent of aluminum foil to hold in the heat.

Discard any fat remaining in the skillet. Lower the heat and add the butter. When it has melted, toss in the shallots and sauté them, sitrring frequently, over low heat until they are just wilted, about 4 minutes. Add the wine, increase the heat to moderate, and deglaze the pan by scraping up any particles left clinging to the bottom. Add the cream and cook, stirring, until the liquid has reduced by half. Mix in the peppercorns and cook 1 minute longer. Taste for seasoning and add salt and pepper according to taste.

Carve the steak crosswise into ½-inch-thick slices and arrange the slices on four heated dinner plates. Spoon some of the sauce over each portion, and garnish with the minced parsley.

SERVES 4

ANDALUSIAN POTATOES

◆

(MAY BE PARTIALLY PREPARED UP TO 6 HOURS IN ADVANCE)

1½ pounds new or red potatoes
3 tablespoons unsalted butter
2 large leeks (about 1 pound), roots and upper green leaves cut off, thoroughly cleaned
½ red pepper, cored and seeded, coarsely chopped
1 tablespoon oil
½ teaspoon salt

Place the potatoes in a large saucepan, cover them with water, and bring to a boil. Lower the heat to moderate and cook the potatoes 15 to 25 minutes (depending on the size), or until they are just tender when pierced with the tip of a knife. Do not overcook. Drain, then fill the pan with cold water so that the potatoes stop cooking. When the potatoes are cool enough to handle but still warm, skin them and cut them into ½-inch cubes. Put the potatoes in a bowl, cover with plastic wrap, and set aside in a cool corner of the kitchen.

In a medium-size skillet equipped with a tight-fitting lid, melt 2 tablespoons of the butter over moderately low heat. Cut the leeks lengthwise into quarters, then crosswise into ¼-inch slices. Place the leeks in the skillet, toss briefly to coat them with butter, cover, and steam for 15 minutes. Remove the cover, add the chopped pepper, and cook 2 more minutes, stirring frequently. Remove the skillet from the heat and cool. When the pan is no longer hot to the touch, cover it and set it aside until time for final preparation.

TIME ALLOWANCE FOR FINAL PREPARATION: 25 MINUTES

Melt the remaining tablespoon of butter with the oil in a 12-inch heavy skillet over moderate heat. Add the diced potatoes and fry, stirring occasionally, until they are hot and just beginning to color, about 15 to 20 minutes. Add the reserved leek and pepper mixture and continue to fry, stirring frequently, until the leeks are hot, about 3 minutes. Season with salt and serve immediately.

SERVES 4

NOTE: These potatoes are not meant to resemble crispy, brown, American pan-fried potatoes. They should remain somewhat soft, with just a faint touch of color.

BROILED CHEDDAR TOMATOES

◆

(MAY BE PARTIALLY PREPARED UP TO 4 HOURS IN ADVANCE)

4 large tomatoes (about ½ pound each), washed
4 tablespoons dry sherry
4 teaspoons minced fresh dillweed
Freshly ground black pepper
¼ cup mayonnaise
¼ cup finely grated sharp cheddar cheese

Generously butter an ovenproof baking dish large enough to hold 8 halved tomatoes compactly.

Split each whole tomato in half horizontally. Place the halves, cut side up, in the baking dish. With the tines of a fork, prick each half in several spots on the cut surface. Dribble ½ tablespoon sherry over each half, then sprinkle each with ½ teaspoon dillweed. Grind a sprinkling of pepper on top. Cover the tomatoes loosely with plastic wrap and set them aside in a cool corner of the kitchen.

Combine the mayonnaise with the cheese in a small bowl and mix well. Cover with plastic wrap and reserve.

TIME ALLOWANCE FOR FINAL PREPARATION: 12 MINUTES

Preheat the broiler.

Place the tomatoes about 3 inches from the heat and broil for 4 minutes. Remove them from the oven and spread the tops with the mayonnaise mixture. Return the dish to the broiler and broil 2 to 3 minutes longer, or until the tomato tops are lightly browned and bubbling.

SERVES 4

FENNEL AND ARUGULA SALAD WITH BASIL VINAIGRETTE

(SALAD MAY BE PARTIALLY PREPARED UP TO 6 HOURS IN ADVANCE;
THE DRESSING MAY BE PREPARED 2 OR 3 DAYS IN ADVANCE)

FENNEL AND ARUGULA SALAD

2 large fennel bulbs (about 1 pound each), stalks trimmed
1 bunch arugula (or substitute ½ bunch watercress), washed, dried, and tough
  stems removed
4 ounces radishes, trimmed and sliced paper-thin
2 tablespoons minced red onion

To make the salad: Cut off the tough outer skin of the fennel bulbs and discard. Cut each bulb in quarters, then peel the onionlike layers apart. Cut each layer of "skin" into roughly 1-inch pieces.

Place the fennel with the arugula in a large salad bowl lined with paper toweling. Add the radish slices and the red onion. Toss to distribute the ingredients. Cover loosely with a linen towel and refrigerate until time for final preparation.

BASIL VINAIGRETTE

2 tablespoons red wine vinegar
Pinch of salt
½ teaspoon Dijon-style mustard
1 teaspoon dried sweet basil
Freshly ground black pepper
6 tablespoons fruity, imported olive oil

To make the dressing: In a small jar equipped with a tight-fitting lid, combine the vinegar, salt, mustard, and basil. Stir until the ingredients are well blended. Add the pepper and the oil. Cover the jar with its lid and shake vigorously. Store in a cool place until ready to use.

YIELD: ½ CUP DRESSING

TIME ALLOWANCE FOR FINAL PREPARATION: 5 MINUTES

Remove the toweling from the salad bowl. Shake the dressing vigorously. Pour it over the salad and toss with a salad fork and spoon until all the ingredients are well coated with dressing.

SERVES 4

HOT APPLE CRISP

(MAY BE PARTIALLY PREPARED UP TO 6 HOURS IN ADVANCE)

> 5 large Golden Delicious apples (about 2 pounds), peeled, quartered, cored, and thinly sliced
> 2 teaspoons grated orange rind
> 1/2 strained fresh orange juice
> 1/2 cup sugar
> 1/2 teaspoon freshly grated nutmeg
> 3/4 teaspoon ground cinnamon
> Pinch plus 1/4 teaspoon of salt
> 3/4 cup flour
> 1/3 cup "old-fashioned" oats (slow-cooking)
> 1/2 cup firmly packed dark brown sugar
> 6 tablespoons unsalted butter, softened
> 1/3 cup coarsely chopped walnuts
> 1 cup heavy cream, plain or whipped, optional

Place the apple slices in a 10-inch round (3-inch deep) baking dish or its equivalent. Add the orange rind, juice, sugar, nutmeg, cinnamon, and a pinch of salt. Toss to mix thoroughly and to coat all the apple slices with the orange juice so that they do not discolor. Lay a length of plastic wrap directly on top of the apples, pressing it down to conform to the contours of the apples. (In other words, do not seal the baking dish, but instead seal the apples themselves. You want to prevent air from coming in contact with the fruit.)

Set the apples aside in a cool corner of the kitchen until time for final preparation.

Place the flour, oats, brown sugar, and the remaining 1/4 teaspoon of salt in a small mixing bowl, and blend well. Reserve for final preparation.

TIME ALLOWANCE FOR FINAL PREPARATION: 70 MINUTES

Preheat the oven to 350 degrees.

Slice the softened butter onto the flour-oat mixture. Using two knives or your fingers, rub the butter into the dry ingredients until the mixture resembles coarse meal. Stir in the chopped walnuts. Sprinkle the topping evenly over the apples. Place the baking dish on a rack in the middle of the oven and bake 50 to 60 minutes, or until the juices are bubbling around the sides of the dish and the topping is crisp.

Serve hot (or at room temperature), accompanied by plain or whipped cream, if you wish.

SERVES 4 TO 6

CARIBBEAN CHICKEN FOR FOUR

Avocado with Herb Vinaigrette

Grilled Caribbean Chicken

Glazed Sesame Carrots

Red Potatoes with Parsleyed Butter

Baked Rhubarb and Strawberries

Folks are grilling year-round now. No matter the weather, whether they're in shorts or ski parkas, barbecue devotees can be found outside tending the faithful, often battered, backyard grill, turning ordinary fare into sublime repasts and flooding the neighborhood with wonderful aromas.

In New England, where I live, such devotion to barbecuing is indeed extraordinary, given our long, arduous winters and practically nonexistent springs. Much as I love grilled food, I tend to wait for the warm weather, when daylight lingers into evening. When that special day eventually arrives, I greet it as the harbinger of summer, and all of summer's delights, and somehow, the waiting makes it all the better.

One year that beautiful, balmy day arrived a bit early and unexpectedly. I had been planning to bake a marinated chicken. But because of the weather, the chicken underwent a glorious transformation and was grilled instead of baked. The recipe was inspired by a similar dish I had consumed several years earlier on the island of Tobago in the Caribbean, where cilantro grows wild and its pungent fragrance rides on the trade winds. Since cilantro, also known as "Chinese parsley" or coriander, is readily available now, I often use it in cooking and am continually delighted by the new nuances it gives old favorites. (If you can't find cilantro, substitute parsley. In this case the dish won't taste the same, but it will still taste good.)

While you're fussing with the charcoal, assuage your guests' burgeoning appetites with avocados filled with a parsley-and-chive-bedecked vinaigrette. Make sure the avocados are ripe—but not too ripe! With the grilled chicken, I like to serve sesame-flecked carrots and small red potatoes; they make a compatible threesome.

For dessert, I blend two of my springtime favorites, rhubarb and strawberries, cooking them only in sugar and their own inimitable juices. Top them with mounds of whipped cream, and you'll have a simple but sublime finish to a meal.

AVOCADO WITH HERB VINAIGRETTE

(HERB VINAIGRETTE MAY BE PREPARED 2 OR 3 DAYS IN ADVANCE; AVOCADO CAN ONLY BE PREPARED IMMEDIATELY BEFORE SERVING)

HERB VINAIGRETTE

2 teaspoons Dijon-style mustard
¼ teaspoon salt
Freshly ground black pepper
2 tablespoons strained fresh lemon juice
½ cup fruity, imported olive oil
1 teaspoon minced fresh parsley
2 teaspoons minced fresh chives

To make the vinaigrette: Place the mustard, salt, pepper, and lemon juice in a small bowl. With a wire whisk, slowly beat in the olive oil, tablespoon by tablespoon, so that the oil and lemon juice form an emulsion. Add the parsley and chives and store in a jar equipped with a tight-fitting lid. Just before serving, shake vigorously.

YIELD: ¾ CUP DRESSING

FINAL ASSEMBLY

8 Boston lettuce leaves, washed and dried
4 watercress sprigs, tough stems removed
2 ripe, but not overly ripe, avocados, split in half, seeds discarded

Arrange the lettuce leaves on four salad plates. Decorate each plate with a sprig of watercress. Arrange the avocados, cut side up, skins intact, on the lettuce beds. Fill each hollow with a portion of the Herb Vinaigrettte.

SERVES 4

GRILLED CARIBBEAN CHICKEN

(MAY BE PARTIALLY PREPARED UP TO 8 HOURS IN ADVANCE:
MUST BE PARTIALLY PREPARED AT LEAST 2 HOURS IN ADVANCE)

2 tablespoons grated gingerroot
3 tablespoons minced fresh chives
1/4 cup strained fresh lime juice
1 teaspoon grated lime rind
2 tablespoons oil
1/4 teaspoon salt
Freshly ground black pepper
1/2 teaspoon dried rosemary, crushed
1/4 cup minced fresh cilantro (or substitute parsley)
1 (3- to 4-pound) chicken, quartered

Make the marinade by combing the gingerroot, chives, lime juice and rind, oil, salt, and pepper in a small bowl. Blend well. Add the crushed rosemary and cilantro.

Place the chicken quarters, skin side up, in a shallow glass baking dish. (Do not use a metal pan as metal reacts badly with acid such as lime juice.) Spoon the marinade over the chicken, distributing it as evenly as possible. Cover loosely with plastic wrap and marinate for at least 2 hours or up to 8 hours. (If you are marinating the chicken longer than 2 hours, be sure to refrigerate it. Remove it from the refrigerator, however, 1 hour before final preparation.) Turn the chicken several times during the marinating period to make certain all the parts are well flavored with the marinade.

TIME ALLOWANCE FOR FINAL PREPARATION: 30 MINUTES
PLUS TIME NEEDED TO PREPARE COALS

Prepare a charcoal grill. You can begin cooking the chicken when the coals are red-hot but not flaming. Place a greased rack about 5 inches above the coals.

Drain and discard any marinating liquid from the chicken, but retain as many of the herbs as possible on the skin. turn the quarters every 5 minutes with tongs, and grill for a total of 20 to 30 minutes, depending on the weight of the chicken and the heat of the coals.

SERVES 4

GLAZED SESAME CARROTS

(MAY BE PARTIALLY PREPARED UP TO 24 HOURS IN ADVANCE)

2 tablespoons sesame seeds
1 pound carrots, peeled and cut into 1-inch lengths
1 clove garlic, peeled and quartered
2 tablespoons imported sesame oil
2 tablespoons honey
1 tablespoon light soy sauce

Place the sesame seeds in a small nonstick skillet over moderate to low heat. Toast them, stirring frequently, until they turn golden brown, about 5 minutes. Be careful that they do not burn. Remove the pan from the heat, transfer the seeds to a small bowl or saucer, and reserve them, uncovered, until final preparation.

Fill a 2- to 3-quart saucepan two-thirds full with salted water. Bring the water to a boil. Drop in the carrots and garlic quarters. When the water returns to a boil, lower the heat and simmer for 10 to 15 minutes, or until the carrots are just barely tender. (The timing depends on size of the carrots.) Drain the carrots and refresh them under cold water. Discard the garlic and transfer the carrots to a bowl. Cover them loosely with plastic wrap and refrigerate until 1 hour before final preparation.

TIME ALLOWANCE FOR FINAL PREPARATION: 15 MINUTES

Pour the sesame oil, honey, and soy sauce into a large skillet. Over low heat, stir until they are well combined. Raise the heat to moderately low, add the carrots, and sauté them, stirring occasionally, until they are completely heated through and shiny with the glaze, about 10 minutes. Just before serving, sprinkle the sesame seeds over the carrots.

SERVES 4

BAKED RHUBARB AND STRAWBERRIES

(MAY BE PREPARED 24 HOURS IN ADVANCE;
BEST PREPARED 1–2 HOURS IN ADVANCE AND SERVED SLIGHTLY WARM)

1 pound rhubarb
1 pint strawberries, hulled

¾ to 1 cup light brown sugar (depending on sweetness of the berries and
personal preference)
Pinch of salt
Freshly grated nutmeg
½ cup heavy cream, whipped

Preheat in the oven to 350 degrees.

Trim the ends of the rhubarb. If the stalks are thick, cut them into ½-inch slices. If they are thin, cut them into 1-inch pieces. Transfer them to an ovenproof casserole equipped with a tight-fitting lid.

Test one of the strawberries for sweetness and adjust the amount of sugar you add to the rhubarb and strawberry mixture accordingly. (Even if the strawberries are beautifully ripe and sweet, 1 cup of sugar is not excessive. However, you may prefer a more tart dish.) Add the strawberries, sugar, salt, and grated nutmeg to the rhubarb and toss to mix well. Cover the casserole and place in the oven to bake for 35 to 45 minutes, or until the rhubarb is tender when pierced with the tip of a knife but not falling apart.

If the dish is being prepared a day in advance, cover it and refrigerate; remove it from the refrigerator 1 hour before serving to bring it to room temperature. Otherwise, it may be cooked 1 to 2 hours ahead of serving time and held at room temperature. It can even be put in the oven just before you sit down to dinner and be served piping hot.

Serve with whipped cream.

SERVES 4

A SATISFYING SATÉ
FOR FOUR

Jellied Watercress Soup

Indonesian Pork Saté

Mango Chutney

Buttered Baby Lima Beans

*Mushroom Salad with
Raspberry Vinaigrette*

Upside-Down Apple Pancake

Some people think jellied soups should be consumed only in hot weather. There's nothing wrong with that notion, but I think they're good any time of year. Jellied soups are light and not so filling that the idea of anything more to eat becomes a burden. This menu's Jellied Watercress Soup, which combines the pleasantly tart crunch of watercress with a soothing base of jellied chicken broth, is a splendid prelude to the spicy Pork *Saté* that follows.

A lot of people don't like garlic or say that garlic doesn't like them. Those unfortunate souls probably won't be wild about Pork Saté. But for those who do like garlic, Pork Saté should satisfy their yearnings for pungency. Do remember, though, to use fresh garlic; stale, dried cloves will ruin a dish. Fresh garlic is much subtler and, curiously, packs less of a wallop and aftertaste. Furthermore, use a freshly opened can of imported Hungarian paprika. Domestic paprikas have no flavor and should be used only to garnish an otherwise bland-appearing dish. (Even imported paprikas can lose their flavor if they are old, however, so don't hold any opened cans longer than two months.)

Lima beans go nicely with the Park Saté, particularly if they're fresh from the garden. A salad of pristine white mushrooms with a vinaigrette redolent of raspberries adds a novel taste sensation and, with the addition of a few of the red berries for extra color, a visual delight. Do save room for the Upside-Down Apple Pancake, a soufflelike pancake made more interesting with rum-soaked apples. Your sweet tooth will be forever grateful.

JELLIED WATERCRESS SOUP

(MAY BE PREPARED UP TO 36 HOURS IN ADVANCE;
MUST BE PREPARED AT LEAST 4 HOURS IN ADVANCE)

2 envelopes unflavored gelatin
4 cups chicken broth, preferably homemade
1 bunch watercress
1 tablespoon strained fresh lemon juice
Freshly ground black pepper
1/2 cup sour cream
2 tablespoons minced fresh chives

Sprinkle the gelatin over 1 cup of the chicken broth in a small saucepan. Allow it to soften, then place the saucepan over low heat and stir until the gelatin is completely dissolved.

Pour the rest of the chicken broth into a medium-size mixing bowl. Add the broth and gelatin mixture and mix well. Refrigerate the chicken broth until it has solidified or jelled, about 2 to 4 hours depending on the temperature of your refrigerator.

When the broth has jelled, remove the tough stems from the watercress and whirl the leaves in a food processor fitted with a steel blade until they are nicely chopped. (The degree of fineness depends on personal preference.) Using a rubber spatula, transfer the chopped watercress to the bowl with the jellied chicken broth. Add the lemon juice and a few grindings of black pepper. Vigorously beat the watercress into the broth. (This will break up the jellied broth somewhat, but that is the texture and appearance you wish to achieve.) Cover the bowl with plastic wrap and refrigerate until final preparation.

TIME ALLOWANCE FOR FINAL PREPARATION: 5 MINUTES

Divide the jellied watercress soup among four soup or consomme bowls. Top each with a dollop of sour cream and a sprinkling of chives. Served chilled.

SERVES 4

INDONESIAN PORK SATÉ

(MAY BE PARTIALLY PREPARED UP TO 24 HOURS IN ADVANCE;
MUST BE PARTIALLY PREPARED AT LEAST 8 HOURS IN ADVANCE)

4 tablespoons olive oil
2 tablespoons imported Hungarian paprika
1 cup finely chopped onions
2 teaspoons minced garlic
½ cup minced fresh parsley
1 teaspoon salt
2 pounds boneless lean pork loin, cut into 1-inch cubes
Mango chutney

Make the marinade by combining the olive oil, paprika, onions, garlic, parsley, and salt in a large mixing bowl. Mix all the ingredients well. Add the pork cubes and toss to coat with the marinade. Cover the bowl with plastic wrap and refrigerate for at least 8 hours or up to 24 hours. Toss the pork several times during this period to redistribute the ingredients. Remove the pork from the refrigerator 1 hour before final preparation.

TIME ALLOWANCE FOR FINAL PREPARATION: 20 MINUTES

Preheat the broiler.

Thread the pork cubes onto four skewers. Rest the skewers on the parallel sides of a roasting pan to suspend the meat above the pan. Spoon any onion mixture remaining in the mixing bowl over the meat. Broil the pork about 3 inches from the broiler element for a total of 10 minutes, turning the skewers at least twice.

Spoon any pan juices and onions over the pork and serve one skewer to each diner. Present a bowl of mango chutney as an accompaniment.

SERVES 4

MUSHROOM SALAD WITH RASPBERRY VINAIGRETTE

(SALAD MAY BE PARTIALLY PREPARED 2 HOURS IN ADVANCE;
VINAIGRETTE MAY BE PREPARED UP TO 3 DAYS IN ADVANCE)

MUSHROOM SALAD

8 to 12 leaves radicchio (depending on size), washed and dried
12 ounces unblemished white mushrooms, ends trimmed
¼ cup whole fresh raspberries

To make the salad: Make beds of radicchio leaves on four salad plates. Thinly slice the mushrooms and arrange the slices decoratively on top of the radicchio. Cover reach plate tightly with plastic wrap and refrigerate until final preparation.

RASPBERRY VINAIGRETTE

1 egg yolk
½ teaspoon Dijon-style mustard
6 tablespoons fruity, imported olive oil
3 tablespoons raspberry vinegar
¼ teaspoon salt
Freshly ground black pepper
½ teaspoon sugar

To make the dressing: Drop the yolk into a small bowl. Using a whisk, beat in the mustard, then add the oil by tablespoonfuls, each time beating until the oil is emulsified. Whisk in the vinegar. Add the salt, pepper, and sugar and whisk vigorously for a few seconds.

Transfer the dressing to a small jar equipped with a tight-fitting lid, or cover the bowl tightly with plastic wrap. If you are holding the dressing longer than 2 hours, refrigerate it until 1 hour before using it.

YIELD: ½ CUP DRESSING

TIME ALLOWANCE FOR FINAL PREPARATION: 5 MINUTES

Remove the plastic wrap from the salads. Give a quick whisk or shake to the Raspberry Vinaigrette, then drizzle the dressing evenly over the mushrooms. Garnish with 4 or 5 raspberries per plate.

SERVES 4

UPSIDE-DOWN APPLE PANCAKE

(MAY BE PARTIALLY PREPARED UP TO 2 HOURS IN ADVANCE)

4 tablespoons butter
3 Golden Delicious apples, peeled, cored, and thinly sliced
¾ cup sugar
¼ teaspoon ground cinnamon
Pinch of salt
¼ cup dark rum
4 eggs, separated and at room temperature
3 tablespoons cornstach
½ cup half-and-half
½ teaspoon vanilla
½ cup heavy cream, whipped or plain

In a 10-inch enamel or cast-iron skillet with 2-inch-high sides, melt the butter over moderate heat. Add the sliced apples and sauté them, turning occasionally, for 15 minutes, or until they are soft but still holding their shape. Remove the skillet from the heat. Sprinkle the surface of the apples with ½ cup of the sugar, the cinnamon, salt, and dark rum. Allow to sit for at least 15 minutes or up to 2 hours. (If you are holding the apples longer than 15 minutes, lay a sheet of plastic wrap directly on the fruit to prevent discoloration.)

In a mixing bowl, beat the egg yolks until light.

In a small saucepan, combine the cornstarch, half-and-half, and remaining ¼ cup sugar. Stir over low heat until the sugar and cornstarch are dissolved. Beat the cornstarch mixture into the egg yolks. Add the vanilla. Cover the bowl with plastic wrap and refrigerate until final preparation.

TIME ALLOWANCE FOR FINAL PREPARATION: 25 MINUTES

Preheat the oven to 400 degrees.

In another bowl, beat the egg whites with a second pinch of salt until stiff. Add them to the cornstarch mixture, folding them in until they are well blended. (This is not a souffle; you do not have to be too worried about lightness.) Pour the batter over the apple slices, which are still in the original skillet, and bake for 15 to 20 minutes, or until the pancake is golden brown and somewhat puffed. (It will collapse quite quickly after being removed from the oven.)

Run a knife around the edge of the skillet. Scrape a spatula under the pancake to loosen it, then invert the pancake onto a cake plate. If some of the apples become dislodged, simply replace them on the top of the pancake.

Serve the pancake immediately, piping hot and cut in wedges, accompanied by cream, either whipped or plain.

SERVES 4

NOTE: Golden Delicious apples hold their shape very well in cooking and are strongly recommended for this recipe.

AN INDIAN MEAL FOR FOUR

Lamb Patties, Indian Style

Minted Carrot Puree

Rice Pilaf

Mango Chutney

Raita (Cucumber and Yogurt Salad)

Fresh Fruit or Fruit Sherbet

My parents spent most of their adult lives in India, and consequently Indian food played a dominant role in many of our meals. It is a marvelous and much-misunderstood cuisine: Indian food is not necessarily hot, and those white-sauced dishes flavored with curry powder, known indiscriminately in the United States as "curries," are simply not representative. Indian food calls for a subtle blend of spices particular to each dish, some hot, some "cool."

This menu offers an Indian dinner that should please any Westerner with its pleasant and mild blend of spices and herbs. I found the recipe for the Lamb Patties in an old notebook of my mother's many years ago, and it quickly became a family favorite.

With it, I suggest a delicately sweet minted carrot puree—mint is present in many Indian dishes—and a traditional rice pilaf. *Raita*, or cucumber and yogurt salad, is a longtime Indian favorite because it does much to soothe palates overstimulated by spices and chilies. If you can't locate fresh cilantro, substitute parsley, but the salad will have a different taste. Coriander, an ingredient in the

Lamb Patties, is the seed produced by the cilantro plant, and makes a very pungent spice when it is dried and ground to a powder.

If you're a little apprehensive about an all-Indian meal, don't feel that you must prepare the entire menu as suggested. Although these dishes go very well together, they may also be happily combined with Western foods.

LAMB PATTIES, INDIAN STYLE

(MAY BE PARTIALLY PREPARED UP TO 24 HOURS IN ADVANCE)

1½ pounds lean ground lamb
1 tablespoon grated gingerroot
4 tablespoons unsalted butter
½ cup finely chopped onions
1 teaspoon minced garlic
1 teaspoon ground coriander
1 teaspoon curry powder
1½ cups bread crumbs, preferably homemade
½ teaspoon salt
¼ teaspoon freshly ground black pepper
2 eggs
Cilantro or parsley sprigs

Break up the ground lamb into small chunks in a large mixing bowl. Sprinkle the grated ginger on top of them.

Melt 2 tablespoons of the butter in a small skillet and sauté the onions and garlic over low heat until wilted, about 5 minutes. Add the coriander and curry powder and cook another minute or two to release the flavors. Stir occasionally. Scrape the mixture over the lamb and mix well with a large wooden spoon or your fingers. Add ½ cup of the bread crumbs, salt, pepper, and 1 beaten egg. Beat the mixture briskly until all the ingredients are completely blended.

Spread the remaining bread crumbs on a piece of paper toweling. Place the remaining beaten egg close by in a shallow bowl or pie plate. Shape the lamb into four oval patties, 3 to 4 inches long and 1 inch thick. Dip each patty into the egg, coating it on all sides, then turn it over several times in the bread crumbs until it is well covered with crumbs. Reserve the patties on a plate. Cover them with plastic wrap and refrigerate until 1 hour before final preparation. (The longer the patties are held before cooking, the more their flavor develops.)

TIME ALLOWANCE FOR FINAL PREPARATION: 35 MINUTES

Melt the remaining 2 tablespoons butter in a skillet large enough to hold the patties without crowding. Over moderately low heat, cook them 15 minutes on each side. The lamb will be pink but not rare. Serve garnished with cilantro or parsley sprigs and accompanied by mango chutney.

SERVES 4

MINTED CARROT PUREE

(MAY BE PREPARED UP TO 24 HOURS IN ADVANCE)

6 sprigs mint, tied together
1 teaspoon sugar
1 pound carrots, peeled and cut in 1/2-inch slices
1 tablespoon packed mint leaves, stems discarded
2 tablespoons unsalted butter
1/2 cup heavy cream
1/2 teaspoon salt
Freshly ground black pepper

Fill a 2-quart saucepan with water to within 2 inches of its rim. Add the sprigs of mint, sugar, and carrot slices. Bring to a boil over high heat, then reduce the heat and simmer, partially covered, for 15 to 25 minutes, or until the carrots are very soft when pierced with the tip of a knife. The cooking time will depend on the size and freshness of the carrots. Drain the carrots and discard the mint sprigs.

Place the packed mint leaves in a food processor fitted with a steel knife. Whirl until the mint is finely minced. Add the carrots and whirl for 10 seconds, scraping down the sides as necessary with a rubber spatula. Add the butter and cream and whirl for 1 minute. Taste for seasoning, adding the salt and pepper to taste. The puree will not be absolutely smooth; it will have a slightly granular texture from both the carrots and the mint.

Transfer the puree to the top of a double boiler, cover, and refrigerate until 1 hour before final preparation.

TIME ALLOWANCE FOR FINAL PREPARATION: 20 MINUTES

Beat the puree briskly. Cover the pan and place it over boiling water. Lower the heat to moderately low and warm, stirring occasionally, for 15 minutes, or until it is steaming hot.

SERVES 4

RICE PILAF

◆

(MAY BE PREPARED UP TO 24 HOURS IN ADVANCE)

2 tablespoons unsalted butter
¼ cup finely chopped onions
1 cup long-grain converted rice
2 cups chicken stock, preferably homemade
½ teaspoon salt
2 tablespoons melted unsalted butter
¼ cup sliced almonds, toasted (optional)
2 tablespoons minced fresh parsley

In a 2-quart flameproof casserole with a tight-fitting lid, melt the 2 tablespoons butter over low heat. Add the onions and sauté them, stirring occasionally, until soft, about 5 minutes. Stir in the rice and toss until all the kernels are coated with the butter. Add the stock and salt, increase the heat to high, and bring to a boil. Stir the rice, lower the heat, and simmer the rice, covered, for 20 minutes. Allow it to rest, off the heat, for 10 minutes. If you are preparing the rice more than 6 hours in advance, refrigerate it in the covered casserole until 1 hour before final preparation. If not, simply hold it in a cool corner of the kitchen

TIME ALLOWANCE FOR FINAL PREPARATION: 30 MINUTES

Preheat the oven to 325 degrees.

Pour the 2 tablespoons of melted butter over the rice, add the almonds if you are planning to include them, and fluff the rice with a fork. Cover the casserole and place it in the oven. Heat the rice for 20 minutes, or until it is steaming. Just before serving, fluff again and sprinkle with the minced parsley.

SERVES 4

RAITA

(MAY BE PREPARED 4 HOURS IN ADVANCE;
MUST BE PREPARED AT LEAST 2 HOURS IN ADVANCE)

1 teaspoon ground cumin
Pinch of cayenne pepper (optional)
1 pint unflavored yogurt
1 small ripe avocado, peeled and cut into ½-inch cubes
1 teaspoon strained fresh lemon juice
¼ cup thinly sliced scallions, including 2 inches green leaves
2 cucumbers, peeled, seeded, and thinly sliced
3 tablespoons finely chopped fresh cilantro (or substitute parsley)

In a small skillet, preferably one with a nonstick surface, toast the ground cumin over low heat for 1 or 2 minutes, or until it just begins to darken and emits a pungent aroma. Stir occasionally so that the powder does not burn. Remove the pan from the heat, stir in the cayenne if desired, and add the salt. Mix briefly. Pour the spices into the container of yogurt and stir until well combined.

Place the avocado cubes in a small salad bowl. Sprinkle with the lemon juice. Add the scallions, cucumber, and cilantro and toss to mix. Finally pour the yogurt mixture over the vegetables and toss again to coat them thoroughly. Refrigerate the Raita for at least 2 hours to let the flavors develop and to chill it thoroughly. Serve chilled.

SERVES 4

A MEATLESS SUMMER'S DINNER FOR FOUR

Spaghetti with Fresh Tomato Sauce

Squash and Zucchini Salad with Lemon-Tarragon Vinaigrette

Hot Garlic Bread

Chocolate Walnut Pie

You don't have to be a vegetarian to enjoy a meatless meal. Consider all the dishes we consume with pleasure that don't actually contain meat: cheese fondue, vegetable souffle, pea soup, caesar salad, herbed omelets, risotto with mushrooms, and the wildly rich and wonderful fettucine alfredo, to name just a few of my favorites. (I realize that strict vegetarians would not consider these "meatless" as they contain anchovies and eggs, among other things, but I do.)

Like most Americans, I've always been meat-oriented. But one mid-August day, all that changed. I was contemplating the glories of the tomatoes in my garden. It was at the peak of the season, and glorious red spheres weighed down each plant. Having become a true and frugal New Englander, I was not only admiring the produce of my labors (I garden, it must be confessed, very reluctantly), I was wondering how I could use the greatest quantity for dinner that evening. (No tomato salad would make any kind of a dent in the number of tomatoes my garden offered.) Spaghetti, as an alternative, come to mind almost immediately. As I started to prepare a prosaic meat sauce and was peeling off the tomato skins, it suddeny occurred to me that an uncooked tomato sauce, laced with basil, would create a meal that was the essence of August, with the full, fruity taste of tomatoes fresh from the vine. The notion was heady. So were the results.

Just one word of warning: Should you make this recipe, use only vine-ripened tomatoes, picked from your own or a neighbor's garden, or purchased at a reliable produce stand. The thick-skinned woolly creations that we accept out of season just won't give the desired results.

Still working on the same theme—using the season's bounty in terms of the prolific squash family—I offer a delicate and pretty salad of yellow squash and zucchini. Choose small, tender vegetables; save the giants for something else.

For dessert, try this sinfully rich Chocolate Walnut Pie. I generally prefer fruit or fruit desserts in August, but somehow the chocolate is a very satisfying foil to the healthful entree and salad.

SPAGHETTI WITH FRESH TOMATO SAUCE

(MAY BE PARTIALLY PREPARED UP TO 6 HOURS IN ADVANCE)

1 teaspoon minced garlic
3/4 cup finely chopped fresh basil leaves
1/3 cup minced fresh parsley
1/3 cup plus 2 tablespoons olive oil
3 pounds tomatoes, peeled, seeded, and coarsely chopped
1/2 teaspoon salt
Freshly ground black pepper
1 teaspoon sugar
1 pound thin spaghetti

In a medium-size mixing bowl, combine the garlic, basil, parsley, 1/3 cup olive oil, tomatoes, salt, pepper, and sugar. Mix thoroughly with a fork. (If you prefer your sauce to have more of a pureed consistency, place the mixture in a food processor fitted with a steel blade, and whirl until blended to the desired consistency.) Cover the bowl with plastic wrap and refrigerate until 1 hour before final preparation.

TIME ALLOWANCE FOR FINAL PREPARATION: 10–15 MINUTES

Cook the spaghetti "al dente," (literally, "to the tooth"; that is, cooked through but still firm) according to the manufacturer's directions. It should take between 8 and 10 minutes. If it is fresh spaghetti, however, it will cook much more rapidly and should be done in 1 or 2 minutes.

Drain the spaghetti well. Return it to the pan in which you cooked it, or transfer it to a heated bowl, and toss it with the remaining 2 tablespoons olive oil. Spoon the sauce, which is at room temperature, over the spaghetti and serve.

SERVES 4

SQUASH AND ZUCCHINI SALAD WITH LEMON-TARRAGON VINAIGRETTE

(SALAD MAY BE PARTIALLY PREPARED UP TO 6 HOURS IN ADVANCE; VINAIGRETTE MAY BE PREPARED UP TO 3 DAYS IN ADVANCE)

SQUASH AND ZUCCHINI SALAD
1 pound yellow squash, ends trimmed
1 pound zucchini, ends trimmed
½ red pepper, cored, seeded, and cut in ¼-inch strips
½ cup thinly sliced red onion
1 cup cherry tomatoes

To make the salad: Cut the squash and zucchini crosswise into thirds. Cut each third in half lengthwise, then cut each portion into julienne strips about ¼ inch thick.

Fill a large frying pan two-thirds full with water. Bring the water to a boil. Add the squash and zucchini. Return the water to a boil and boil for exactly 1 minute. Drain the vegetables immediately, then refresh them under cold water to stop their cooking. Drain thoroughly, then spread them out on paper toweling to remove any excess moisture.

Place the vegetables in a salad bowl lined with paper toweling. Sprinkle the red pepper and onion on top. Cover the salad with a layer of paper toweling and refrigerate until final preparation.

LEMON-TARRAGON VINAIGRETTE
2 tablespoons strained fresh lemon juice
¼ teaspoon salt
½ teaspoon Dijon-style mustard
Freshly ground black pepper
½ teaspoon sugar
2 teaspoons minced fresh tarragon leaves (or ½ teaspoon dried tarragon)
6 tablespoons fruity, imported olive oil

To make the dressing: In a small jar equipped with a tight-fitting lid, combine the lemon juice, salt, mustard, pepper, and sugar. Stir until the mustard is well blended with the lemon juice, and the salt and sugar are dissolved. Add the tarragon and the oil. Cover the jar tightly with its lid and shake the contents vigorously. Set aside until ready to use.

YIELD: ½ CUP DRESSING

TIME ALLOWANCE FOR FINAL PREPARATION: 5 MINUTES

Remove the salad from the refrigerator and discard the paper towels. Shake the Lemon-Tarragon Vinaigrette vigorously and pour it over the vegetables. Toss with a salad fork and spoon to coat them well. Distribute the cherry tomatoes decoratively around the edges of the bowl.

SERVES 4

CHOCOLATE WALNUT PIE

(MAY BE PREPARED UP TO 24 HOURS IN ADVANCE)

3 ounces unsweetened chocolate
4 tablespoons unsalted butter
3 eggs
¾ cup dark brown sugar
¾ cup dark corn syrup
1 tablespoon flour
½ teaspoon salt
2 teaspoons vanilla
1 cup coarsely chopped walnuts
1 unbaked 9-inch pie shell
1 cup heavy cream, whipped

Preheat the oven to 350 degrees.

Place the chocolate and butter in the top of a small double boiler. Half-fill the lower section with water. Place the double boiler over moderately low heat until the chocolate and butter have just melted.

Meanwhile, beat the eggs until frothy. Add the brown sugar and continue to beat until the mixture has almost doubled in volume. Beat in the corn syrup, flour, salt, and vanilla. Add the melted chocolate and butter and mix until well blended. Stir in the nuts. Pour the mixture into the pie shell and bake for 50 to

60 minutes, or until a knife inserted in the center comes out clean. (Do not overbake; it is better to have the filling a little moist than too dry.)

Serve hot or at room temperature, accompanied by generous dollops of whipped cream.

YIELD: 1 9-INCH PIE

AN UNCONVENTIONAL BARBECUE FOR FOUR

Grilled Marinated Pork Loin

Baked Potatoes with Sour Cream and Chives

Tomato and Eggplant Casserole

Mixed Green Salad with Vinaigrette*

Simple Banana Ice Cream

Much as Americans love their barbecues and outdoor grilling, for the most part they are very conventional about the meats they use. I was too, until I started experimenting with a leg of lamb. It was apparent that a piece of meat intended to be roasted could not be barbecued over a charcoal grill unless it rotated on a spit, for it would char on the outside before the heat even came close to cooking the center. However, when the "roast" was boned and shaped in such a way as to render it flatter and thinner, it became a prime prospect for charcoal cooking. The success of the boned, butterflied leg of lamb on the grill prompted me to try other meats; this menu's grilled pork loin (also boned and butterflied) is one result. Aside from a few minutes spent whipping up the marinade, it is remarkably easy to prepare and, according to those who've tasted it, a delightful change from the usual barbecue fare.

Some meat packers now distribute vacuum-sealed boned loins and tenderloins of pork. This is a bonus since the cook doesn't have to cajole a harassed butcher into boning the cut. All the cook has to do is butterfly the meat, which is simplicity itself.

* See the recipe on page 24.

The Tomato and Eggplant Casserole combines two of my favorite vegetables. The recipe, designed to foil eggplant's chameleonlike urge to absorb surrounding flavors, forces it to stand on its own: a nice, earthy vegetable, somewhat reminiscent of wild mushrooms. Unlike many eggplant dishes, it does not swim in juices, and it's every bit as good at room temperature as it is when hot—another boon for the cook who likes to prepare food ahead of time.

An easy and wonderful banana ice cream rounds off the meal. So many ice cream makers are on the market that I am assuming everyone owns one, even if it is the simple sort that works in the freezer. Homemade ice creams are one of the great joys of the kitchen these days. Pity the previous generations who had to go to the corner drugstore or ice cream parlor instead.

GRILLED MARINATED PORK LOIN

(MAY BE PARTIALLY PREPARED UP TO 6 HOURS IN ADVANCE;
MUST BE PARTIALLY PREPARED AT LEAST 4 HOURS IN ADVANCE)

1 clove garlic, peeled and thickly sliced
1 inch gingerroot, peeled and thickly sliced
1 tablespoon fresh rosemary leaves (or 1 teaspoon dried), crushed
½ cup dry white wine
¼ cup oil
2 tablespoons light soy sauce
1 cup applesauce, preferably homemade
1 (2- to 2½-pound) boneless center-cut loin of pork

Drop the sliced garlic, gingerroot, and rosemary into a food processor fitted with a steel blade. Mince into fine pieces. Add the white wine, oil, and light soy sauce, and whirl briefly to mix. Then pour in the applesauce and whirl until blended.

Pour the marinade into a nonreactive baking dish large enough to contain the loin of pork after it is butterflied.

If your butcher is too busy to butterfly the meat, it is very simple to do yourself. Simply lay the loin on a flat surface and, with a sharp knife, make a lengthwise incision through the middle of the meat from one end of the loin to the other and to within half an inch of the opposite side. (You do not want to cut the loin in half.) Open the loin like a book, so that it is twice as wide but half as thick as before.

Place the loin in the marinade, turning it once or twice to coat it well. Cover the dish with plastic wrap and refrigerate it for 4 to 6 hours. Remove it from the refrigerator 1 hour before final preparation.

TIME ALLOWANCE FOR FINAL PREPARATION: 30 MINUTES
PLUS TIME NEEDED TO PREPARE COALS

Prepare a charcoal grill. When the coals are red-hot but not flaming, take the pork out of the marinade and place it on a greased rack about 5 inches above the coals, fat side down. Reserve the marinade. If your grill has a cover, cover the pork. If not, watch the coals carefully and try to prevent flaming by sprinkling them with water if flames rise.

The grilling time is based on the thickness of the pork. If the pork is approximately 1 inch at its thickest point, allow 8 minutes per side. If it is about 1½ inches thick, allow 10 minutes per side. Cook the pork on one side for the prescribed time, then turn and cook the other side for the same length of time. Check for doneness. (If you are uncertain about your timing, insert a meat thermometer when you think the pork is done. The meat thermometer should register an internal reading of 160 degrees.)

While the pork is grilling, pour the reserved marinade into a saucepan and bring it to a boil. Let it boil briskly for 10 minutes, or until it is reduced by half.

Transfer the pork to a heated platter and serve immediately, cutting the pork into ¼-inch-thick slices. Serve accompanied by the marinade gravy.

SERVES 4

TOMATO AND EGGPLANT CASSEROLE

(MAY BE PARTIALLY PREPARED UP TO 8 HOURS IN ADVANCE)

1 small eggplant (about 1 pound)
2 teaspoons salt
3 tablespoons olive oil
2 teaspoons minced garlic
1 teaspoon dried oregano
Freshly ground black pepper
2 large tomatoes (about 1 pound), peeled and sliced
½ cup bread crumbs, preferably homemade
½ cup freshly grated Parmesan cheese
2 tablespoons minced fresh parsley

Cut the eggplant crosswise into ¾-inch slices. Do not peel.

Sprinkle the slices with 1 teaspoon salt, put them in a colander over the sink, weight them down with canned goods or a heavy frying pan, and allow them to drain for 30 minutes. This will eliminate any bitter taste in the eggplant.

Warm the olive oil in a small skillet over low heat. Add the garlic and let it cook for about 3 minutes or until it has softened and emits a strong garlicky odor. Set aside.

Generously butter a large, shallow ovenproof baking dish equipped with a tight-fitting lid.

When the eggplant has drained sufficiently, wipe off any remaining salt and cut each slice in half, or in quarters if the slices are very large. Lay the pieces in one or two layers in the baking dish. Spoon the garlic and oil over them. Sprinkle with the oregano. Season with ½ teaspoon salt and pepper to taste. Arrange the tomato slices on top of the eggplant. Sprinkle with the remaining ½ teaspoon salt and more pepper. Spoon the bread crumbs and then the Parmesan cheese over the tomatoes, distributing both as evenly as possible. Cover the casserole with plastic wrap and refrigerate until 1 hour before final preparation.

TIME ALLOWANCE FOR FINAL PREPARATION: 60 MINUTES

Preheat the oven to 350 degrees.

Remove the plastic wrap from the casserole and cover it with its own lid. Place the dish in the oven and bake for 45 minutes. Remove the cover and place the casserole under the broiler for 5 minutes, or until the cheese is bubbling and lightly browned. Sprinkle with the parsley before serving.

SERVES 4

NOTE: This dish may be served hot from the oven or allowed to cool to room temperature.

SIMPLE BANANA ICE CREAM

(MAY BE PREPARED 24 HOURS IN ADVANCE BUT IS BEST
PREPARED WITHIN ½ HOUR OF SERVING)

½ cup water
½ cup sugar
4 large or 5 medium, very ripe bananas
3 tablespoons strained fresh lemon juice
1 cup heavy cream
4 tablespoons banana liqueur (optional)

Make a simple syrup by combining the water and sugar in a small saucepan and bringing them to a boil over moderate heat. Stir until the sugar is dissolved. Remove from the heat and cool.

When the syrup is cool, place the bananas in the bowl of a food processor fitted with a steel blade and pour the lemon juice over them. Process the bananas until they are smooth. With the machine still on, pour in the simple syrup, then the cream, and whirl until well blended. Transfer the mixture to a bowl, cover it with plastic wrap, and refrigerate until chilled.

TIME ALLOWANCE FOR FINAL PREPARATION: APPROXIMATELY 30 MINUTES,
DEPENDING UPON THE ICE CREAM FREEZER USED

Freeze the banana puree according to the instructions accompanying your ice cream freezer. When the puree is frozen, scoop 4 portions into individual dessert bowls. Serve plain or with the banana liqueur dribbled on top.

SERVES 4

AN ALL-SEASON DINNER FOR FOUR

Squash "Gazpacho"

Fillets of Sole with Dill Cream

Fried Sweet Potatoes

Mixed Green Salad with Cherry Tomatoes Vinaigrette*

Caramelized Baked Pears

It is a credit to this vast, productive land of ours that so many vegetables and fruits can be obtained year-round. They're not always as good as those harvested in season at local farms, but they offer a splendid range of choices never available before this age of air freight and refrigeration.

Even in coldest, darkest winter, "summer" (or yellow) squash and its close cousin, zucchini, can be found at produce counters. While the recipe for Squash "Gazpacho," this menu's appetizer, was developed during the abundance of one August, it works just as nicely with winter crops from California or Florida.

Fillet of sole, of course, knows no real season either, or so we think. Actually, the sole, or flounder, that we eat in the summer along the Atlantic coast is for the most part fluke. Once cold weather arrives, fluke promptly hibernates in the mud of the seabed and, consequently, we are forced to substitute winter flounder (or blackback) or gray sole. Whichever, these delicate flatfish, made all the more distinctive with their two eyes on the topside of their bodies, are at their best when accompanied by a tender sauce, such as this menu's wine-based, cream reduction.

Try pan-fried sweet potatoes with the fish. They too are available year-round, and pan-frying them is an unusual and pleasing treatment. Round off the dinner with a tangy salad and a light pear concoction that should satisfy any craving for a sweet.

* See the recipe on page 24.

SQUASH "GAZPACHO"

◆

(MAY BE PREPARED UP TO 6 HOURS IN ADVANCE)

1 clove garlic, peeled and sliced
1 cucumber, peeled, seeded, and cut in pieces
1 green pepper (about ½ pound), cored, seeded, and cut in pieces
1 small red onion (about ¼ pound), peeled and cut in pieces
2 tablespoons olive oil
3 tablespoons tarragon vinegar
1 summer squash (1 pound), peeled and cut in pieces
1 teaspoon salt
2 egg yolks
2 tablespoons minced fresh dillweed
Freshly ground black pepper
4 heaping tablespoons sour cream

Turn on the motor of a food processor fitted with a steel blade. Drop in the garlic slices and whirl until the garlic is finely minced. Drop in the cucumber, pepper, and onion pieces, a few at a time, and pulse until they all are finely chopped but not pureed. Pour in the oil and vinegar and whirl briefly. Add the squash and whirl until it is finely chopped. Finally drop in the salt, egg yolks, and dill, and whirl until the soup is frothy but still has a crunchy texture. Beware of overblending. Taste, and adjust the seasoning. Add a grinding of black pepper.

Transfer the soup to a bowl, cover with plastic wrap, and refrigerate until 30 minutes before final preparation.

TIME ALLOWANCE FOR FINAL PREPARATION: 5 MINUTES

Divide the soup evenly among four soup bowls. Garnish each bowl with a heaping tablespoon of sour cream.

Squash "Gazpacho" should be served at room temperature, not chilled.

SERVES 4

FILLETS OF SOLE WITH DILL CREAM

(SAUCE MAY BE PREPARED UP TO 2 HOURS IN ADVANCE;
FISH MUST BE PREPARED JUST BEFORE SERVING)

2 tablespoons finely chopped shallots
6 tablespoons minced fresh dillweed
1½ cups dry white wine
½ cup heavy cream
4 tablespoons unsalted butter, cut into 4 slices
Salt and freshly ground pepper to taste
4 tablespoons vegetable oil
4 to 8 fillets of sole (about 1½ to 2 pounds)

In a nonreactive saucepan such as stainless steel or enamel, combine the shallots, 4 tablespoons of the minced dillweed, and the white wine. Bring to a boil over moderately high heat and continue to boil until the liquid is reduced to about ¾ cup. This will take about 10 minutes. Add the heavy cream and continue reducing until the liquid has thickened slightly and about ½ cup remains, which will take 4 to 5 minutes. Remove from the heat and strain into a clean saucepan.

Over the lowest possible heat, whisk the butter, a slice at a time, into the reduction, adding the next slice only as the first is incorporated. The butter should not melt completely but should soften to form a creamy, only slightly thickened sauce. When all the butter has been incorporated, remove the pan from the heat and taste for seasoning, adding salt and pepper as needed. If you are not using Dill Cream immediately, hold it over hot water without letting the pan touch the water. (The temperature of the water should not exceed 140 degrees.)

TIME ALLOWANCE FOR FINAL PREPARATION: 10 MINUTES

In a large frying pan, heat the oil over moderately high heat. Season the pieces of sole with a sprinkling of salt and pepper. Add the fillets to the frying pan and sauté them, without turning, for 3 to 4 minutes, or until they turn opaque. (Sole is very fragile and can fall apart with too much handling. Since it is thin, cooking it on one side will suffice.)

With a large spatula, carefully remove the fillets from the pan, placing them on a heated serving platter, cooked side up. Spoon the Dill Cream over them and garnish with the remaining 2 tablespoons of dillweed.

SERVES 4

FRIED SWEET POTATOES

◆

(MAY BE PARTIALLY PREPARED UP TO 24 HOURS IN ADVANCE)

4 sweet potatoes (about 2 pounds)
2 tablespoons unsalted butter
2 tablespoons vegetable oil
¼ cup sugar
¼ cup dark rum
Salt and freshly ground black pepper to taste

Drop the sweet potatoes into a saucepan full of salted water. Bring the water to a boil over high heat, then lower the heat and simmer the potatoes, uncovered, until they are tender when pierced with the tip of a knife (about 20 minutes depending on size). Rinse them in cold water and remove their skins when they are cool enough to handle.

If you are preparing the sweet potatoes more than 4 hours in advance, wrap them individually in plastic wrap and refrigerate them until time for final preparation. Otherwise, hold them in a bowl of cold water in a cool spot in the kitchen until you are ready to proceed.

TIME ALLOWANCE FOR FINAL PREPARATION: 25 MINUTES

Remove the plastic wrap from the refrigerated potatoes, or drain those held in water. (Pat the water-held ones dry with paper toweling.) Cut the potatoes into ¼-inch-thick slices.

Meanwhile, in a large skillet, preferably one with high sides, combine the butter and oil over high heat. When the butter is foaming, lower the heat to medium-high and add the potatoes. Sauté the potatoes, turning them occasionally, until they are light brown (about 15 to 20 minutes). Sprinkle with the sugar and rum, turn a few more times, and sauté until the sugar has dissolved. Sprinkle with salt and pepper to taste. Serve immediately.

SERVES 4

CARAMELIZED BAKED PEARS

(MAY BE PARTIALLY PREPARED UP TO 3 HOURS IN ADVANCE)

6 Bosc or Anjou pears (about 3 pounds), peeled, cored, and quartered
2 tablespoons strained fresh lemon juice
½ cup sugar
4 tablespoons unsalted butter, cut into small pieces
½ cup heavy cream

Arrange the pears in one layer, closely packed, in a shallow baking dish. A 12-inch pie plate, if you have one, is a nice alternative as the pears can be arranged with their tips toward the center in a concentric circle.

Sprinkle the pears with the lemon juice, then generously dust with the sugar. Dot with the butter.

If you are not baking the pears immediately, cover them tightly with plastic wrap and hold in a cool corner of the kitchen until final preparation.

TIME ALLOWANCE FOR FINAL PREPARATION: 50 MINUTES

Preheat the oven to 450 degrees.

Remove the plastic wrap from the pears and bake them for 45 minutes, or until the sugar is bubbling and has caramelized. Remove the pears from the oven and dribble the cream over them. Tip the baking dish and repeatedly spoon the caramelized sugar and cream over the pears until the two are well mixed and the pears are slightly glazed.

Serve the pears warm, directly from the baking dish.

SERVES 4

THE SHANK OF THE LAMB FOR FOUR

Braised Lamb Shanks

Dried Beans, French Style

Asparagus Parmesan

Orange Jelly

How many times have I been in a supermarket or butcher shop, purchasing lamb shanks for dinner, when a curious customer has queried, "What are they?" or "How do you cook those things?" Far too often, it seems.

When one considers the wildly escalating cost of lamb these days, lamb shanks—you might identify them as the lambs' ankles—are a really great buy. They're relatively cheap and very tasty when properly prepared.

No question about it, lamb shanks are an underrated cut of meat, and they unfortunately are rarely cooked to their true potential. Braising seems to bring out shanks' best through the infusion of flavors and the slow, steady tenderizing method. The braising ingredients in this menu include orange rind and juices. This citrus spark—so subtle it is almost indistinguishable—enhances the meat remarkably.

While allowing one one-pound shank per person may seem a bit excessive, it really isn't, for a lot of that weight is bone. Besides, considering the shape of the lamb shanks, just think how tricky it would be to carve them! Occasionally shanks come larger than one pound, but anything bigger than a pound is really too much for one person unless, of course, you have a football player with a gargantuan appetite at the table.

The French frequently serve lovely dried beans called *flageolets* with lamb. While they are available in some American markets, they're not always easy to find. I experimented by substituting some dried lima beans; I think you will find them a pleasant, economical, and novel accompaniment to the shanks, different from the usual potatoes or rice.

For dessert, I'm suggesting what some of you may call a glorified gelatin. Not so! Orange Jelly is a gelatin-based dessert, I will admit, but there all resemblance ends. Prepared with fresh orange juice (and do not substitute frozen or reconstitued, please), it takes only a few more minutes to make than its brilliantly hued counterpart and tastes just about as much like it as a fast-food burger tastes like the real thing!

BRAISED LAMB SHANKS

(MAY BE PARTIALLY PREPARED UP TO 8 HOURS IN ADVANCE)

½ cup Worcestershire sauce
1 cup flour
½ teaspoon salt
Freshly ground black pepper
4 lamb shanks (about 1 pound each)
4 tablespoons vegetable oil
4 tablespoons unsalted butter
1 cup finely chopped onions
1 teaspoon minced garlic
1 red pepper, finely chopped
1 cup minced carrots (2 large)
1 tablespoon grated orange rind
2 teaspoons dried rosemary, crushed
1½ cups strained fresh orange juice

Pour the Worcestershire sauce into a shallow bowl. Spread out the flour, salt, and pepper on a piece of paper toweling and mix with your fingers until well combined. First dip each lamb shank in the sauce on all sides. Then roll the lamb shanks in the seasoned flour and shake off any excess.

Heat the oil in a large skillet, preferably one with high sides, over moderately high heat. When it is smoking, brown the lamb shanks in it, turning them every few minutes. (You may have to brown the shanks in two batches so that they are not crowded in the pan). When they are done, transfer them to an ovenproof casserole equipped with a tight-fitting lid.

Rinse and dry the skillet. Return it to low heat and add the butter. When it has melted, sauté the onions, garlic, red pepper, and carrots, stirring frequently, until they are soft, about 10 minutes. Thoroughly mix in the orange rind, rosemary, and orange juice. Pour the mixture over the lamb shanks in the casserole. Cover the lamb shanks with the casserole lid and refrigerate them until 1 hour before final preparation.

TIME ALLOWANCE FOR FINAL PREPARATION: 1¼ TO 1½ HOURS

Preheat the oven to 350 degrees.

Place the covered casserole on a rack in the center of the oven and bake for 60 to 75 minutes, or until the shanks are tender when pierced with the tip of a knife.

Transfer the shanks to a heated serving platter or individual plates. Scrape the remaining contents of the casserole into an electric blender or food processor fitted with a steel blade and whirl until the vegetables are pureed. Pour the sauce over the shanks and serve immediately.

SERVES 4

DRIED BEANS, FRENCH STYLE

(MAY BE PARTIALLY PREPARED UP TO 24 HOURS IN ADVANCE)

1 cup dried large lima beans
2 small onions, peeled and cut in half
2 cups water
3 tablespoons unsalted butter
1 teaspoon minced garlic
½ teaspoon salt
Freshly ground black pepper
4 tablespoons minced fresh parsley

Fill a 4- to 5-quart kettle two-thirds full with water. Bring the water to a boil. Drop the beans into the water and stir briefly. Bring the water to a boil again, and then boil the beans for 2 minutes. Remove the kettle from the heat and set it aside, with the beans still in it, for 1 hour.

Drain the beans. Rub off their tough outer skins with your fingers. Place the beans and the onion halves in a saucepan and pour in 2 cups of water. Bring the water to a boil, lower the heat, and simmer, covered, for 30 minutes or until the beans are soft. Remove and discard the onion pieces, then drain the beans in a sieve.

Melt the butter over low heat in the same saucepan and sauté the garlic in it for 2 to 3 minutes, stirring occasionally. Add the beans, salt, and pepper. Stir well.

If you are preparing the beans more than 6 hours in advance, cover the pan of beans and refrigerate until 1 hour before final preparation. Otherwise, simply set the pan aside in a cool corner of the kitchen.

TIME ALLOWANCE FOR FINAL PREPARATION: 15 MINUTES

Reheat the beans by placing the saucepan, covered, over very low heat. Stir the beans every few minutes so that they do not scorch. When they are heated through, add the parsley and stir to mix.

SERVES 4

ASPARAGUS PARMESAN

(MAY BE PARTIALLY PREPARED UP TO 6 HOURS IN ADVANCE)

1½ to 2 pounds fresh asparagus
¼ cup unsalted butter, melted
2 tablespoons strained fresh lemon juice
¼ teaspoon salt
Freshly ground black pepper
3 tablespoons freshly grated Parmesan cheese

Trim off the tough white root-end of the asparagus stalks and discard. Fill a large stainless steel or enamel-covered skillet two-thirds full with (unsalted) water and bring to a boil. Carefully place the asparagus in the skillet and bring the water to a boil again. Immediately reduce the heat and simmer the asparagus, partially covered, until they are just tender when pierced with the tip of a knife and still bright green. (This will take between 3 to 7 minutes, depending upon the thickness of the stalks.)

Immediately drain the asparagus and refresh them under cold water to stop their cooking. Pat them dry with paper toweling.

Brush a shallow ovenproof baking dish with some of the melted butter. Arrange the asparagus in the dish, positioning all the stalks in the same direction. Drizzle the remaining butter and the lemon juice over them. Sprinkle with the salt and pepper to taste, and then with the cheese. Cover the baking dish with plastic wrap and hold in a cool section of the kitchen until final preparation.

TIME ALLOWANCE FOR FINAL PREPARATION: 20 MINUTES

Preheat the oven to 400 degrees.

Bake the asparagus for 10 minutes. If the cheese has not melted completely or has become flecked with brown, briefly place the asparagus under a preheated broiler. Serve immediately.

SERVES 4

ORANGE JELLY

(MAY BE PREPARED UP TO 24 HOURS IN ADVANCE;
MUST BE PREPARED AT LEAST 3 HOURS IN ADVANCE)

3 cups freshly squeezed orange juice
¼ to ½ cup sugar, depending on tartness of juice
5 teaspoons unsweetened gelatin (1½ envelopes)
½ teaspoon vanilla
Pinch of salt
3 teaspoons grated orange rind
16 large strawberries, washed and hulled (optional)
½ cup heavy cream, whipped

Strain the orange juice through a fine sieve into a stainless steel or enamel-covered saucepan. Add the sugar, a tablespoon at a time, until the desired sweetness is achieved. Sprinkle the gelatin on the surface of the juice. When the gelatin has been absorbed and softened, place the saucepan over low heat and stir the juice until the sugar and gelatin have dissolved. Remove the pan from the heat and cool. Stir in the vanilla and salt.

Refrigerate the jelly, still in its saucepan, until it has thickened to the consistency of mayonnaise. Add the grated orange rind and stir to distribute it evenly. (If you add the rind before the jelly thickens, it will float to the surface and not look as attractive.)

Divide the Orange Jelly among four individual dessert bowls, or transfer it to a large serving bowl. Cover with plastic wrap and refrigerate until ready to serve or until the jelly has solidified, at least 2 hours. Garnish, if you like, with the strawberries, and serve accompanied by whipped cream.

SERVES 4

ENTERTAINING
SIX

I think a group of six makes for an almost perfect gathering. (I say "almost" because there are always exceptions to every blanket statement.) Six is a very cohesive number; six people do not tend to split off into small conversational groups as larger numbers do, leaving the others speculating paranoically on what they are missing. The meal is unified.

For these reasons, I like to do all I can to make the event as interesting and provocative as I can. I select my guests with care, making certain they are compatible. (At larger gatherings a guest can always find a friendly face if he's not too happy with his neighbor and can splinter off from the mainstream if need be. Not so with smaller numbers. We're all stuck with each other, so good fusion is very vital.) It does not matter if one or two people that I've invited are shy and less loquacious because, given the nature of the intimate setting, they will soon blossom and become just as full of conversation as all the rest.

I like the setting for six to be as cozy as I can manage. If the weather's cool, I love having a fire blazing on the hearth, or even a coal stove glowing in the corner. Before the meal, I like to gather my guests in a close setting, perhaps a den or a corner of the living room, to start the conversational spark going. I use a profusion of candles on the dining room table (and sometimes in the living room, too) to give a soft warm light. I like to decorate the table with an arrangement of fruit, nuts, or vegetables, on which the diners can nibble if they want (another kind of informality to contribute to the occasion).

I serve the courses slowly, never rushing people, never interrupting conversation. The effect of really leisurely dining is luxurious—a pleasure few of us have time for very often—and it generates a marvelous sense of well-being and relaxation. At first, to my amusement, I find my guests are often puzzled that plates and glasses don't rapidly appear and disappear. But then they begin to understand, and they wind down, switching gears, allowing their metabolisms to slow.

And all of this never affects the wit or the laughter, the conversation or the repartee. They just seem to improve as the evening progresses.

SHELLFISH DINNER
FOR SIX

Scallops and Shrimp with Leeks

Baked Brown Rice with Toasted Almonds

Mushroom and Spinach Salad with Vinaigrette

Velvet Crème Caramel

Years ago, before I started writing about food, I conducted cooking classes built around the theme "Cooking for Company," obviously the forerunner of *Do-Ahead Entertaining.* The goal was identical: preparation of food sufficiently in advance so that the hostess could be with her company, not away from the fun. My students prepared complete menus and then we ate and evaluated the results.

Scallops and Shrimp with Leeks was one of my most popular do-aheads. My students loved the contrast in taste and texture between the sweet and subtle leeks, soft and delicate scallops, and rather assertive shrimp. Surprisingly, the leeks are not in the least overpowered by the shellfish. The ingredients, in fact, enhance one another. Leeks are a wonderful alternative to onions in many dishes, and it is a delight to find them so readily available in markets these days. At one time, back in the dark ages of meat-and-potatoes cooking, they could be purchased only in specialty markets, and not all of them at that.

Given the shellfish's creamy sauce, which calls out for something to absorb it, a rice dish is almost a necessity. I particularly like brown rice, not just for its nutritional value, but because, very simply, it tastes better. It is crunchier than white rice, and I like to heighten that quality further by adding toasted almonds. If you should ever see brown "basmati" rice in a specialty store, buy it without thinking twice. Basmati is a superb, flavorful Indian rice; its brown variety, which is unhulled, has to be one of the best rices available. It's not widely distributed, so grab it if you can!

There are cream caramels (English), crème caramels (French), and flans (Spanish), and all of them provide a lovely ending to a meal. My recipe for crème caramel is a little richer than most because it calls for all cream and an extra egg yolk. But that's its velvety secret; that's what makes it so smooth.

SCALLOPS AND SHRIMP WITH LEEKS

(MAY BE PARTIALLY PREPARED UP TO 8 HOURS IN ADVANCE)

6 medium-size leeks (about 3 pounds)
1 pound sea scallops
1 pound large shrimp, peeled and deveined
1 tablespoon strained fresh lemon juice
½ teaspoon salt
Freshly ground black pepper
3 tablespoons minced fresh dillweed
1 cup heavy cream
½ cup sour cream

Cut the roots and the green portion of the leaves off the leeks. This will leave a white stalk about 4 inches long. Wash the leeks thoroughly, and remove and discard one layer of the tough outer skin.

Fill a 3- to 4-quart saucepan two-thirds full with salted water. Bring it to a boil and drop in the leeks. When the water returns to a boil, lower the heat and simmer the leeks for 5 minutes, or until barely tender.

Drain the leeks, then refresh them in cold water to prevent further cooking. Transfer them to paper toweling and pat dry. When the leeks are completely cool, cut them crosswise into ½-inch slices with a sharp knife.

Generously butter an ovenproof baking dish that is about 8 by 10 inches in size. Spread the leek slices over the bottom of the dish. Cut the scallops into a uniform size if they vary greatly in shape. Layer the scallops and shrimp over the leeks. Sprinkle with lemon juice, salt, pepper, and 2 tablespoons of the dillweed. Cover with plastic wrap and refrigerate. Remove the dish from the refrigerator 1 hour before final preparation.

TIME ALLOWANCE FOR FINAL PREPARATION: 25 MINUTES

Preheat the oven to 400 degrees.

Combine the cream and sour cream in a small bowl. Blend well, then spoon evenly over the shellfish. Place the baking dish in the oven and bake for 15 to 20 minutes, or until the cream is bubbling and the shrimp and scallops have become opaque. Be careful not to overcook or the shellfish will toughen.

Sprinkle the remaining tablespoon of dillweed over the cream and serve.

SERVES 4

BAKED BROWN RICE WITH TOASTED ALMONDS

(MAY BE PARTIALLY PREPARED UP TO 2 DAYS IN ADVANCE)

2 tablespoons unsalted butter
3 tablespoons finely chopped onions
¾ cup brown rice, washed
½ teaspoon salt
1½ cups chicken stock (or substitute water)
¼ cup sliced almonds

Preheat the oven to 325 degrees.

In a 2- to 3-quart flameproof casserole with a tight-fitting lid, melt 1 tablespoon of butter over low heat. Add the onions and, stirring occasionally, cook until wilted, about 5 minutes. Add the rice and salt and stir until all the rice kernels are well coated with butter. Pour in the chicken stock, stir the rice again, raise the heat, and bring the stock to a boil. Immediately cover the casserole and transfer it to the oven. Bake the rice for 1 hour, or until all the liquid has been absorbed.

Remove the rice from the oven and let it cool. If you are preparing the rice more than 6 hours in advance, cover the casserole and refrigerate it until 1 hour before final preparation. Otherwise, cover the casserole and set it aside in a cool corner of the kitchen.

TIME ALLOWANCE FOR FINAL PREPARATION: 35 MINUTES

Preheat the oven to 300 degrees.

Place the covered casserole in the oven and heat the rice for 20 minutes, or until it is steaming hot.

While the rice is heating, melt the remaining tablespoon of butter in a small skillet over moderately low heat. Add the almonds and toast them until they are golden, about 5 minutes, stirring frequently.

Add the almonds to the rice and stir to mix. Serve immediately.

SERVES 6

NOTE: If you cannot reheat the rice in the oven, place the casserole in a large skillet. Fill the skillet with water and bring it to a boil over moderate heat. Reheat the rice in this improvised double boiler, stirring it occasionally, for about 20 minutes, or until it is steaming hot.

MUSHROOM AND SPINACH SALAD WITH VINAIGRETTE

(SALAD MAY BE PARTIALLY PREPARED UP TO 6 HOURS IN ADVANCE;
VINAIGRETTE MAY BE PREPARED UP TO 3 DAYS IN ADVANCE)

1 pound spinach, washed, tough stems cut off and discarded
½ cup thinly sliced red onion
6 ounces mushrooms, trimmed and thinly sliced
2 recipes Vinaigrette (see page 24)

Line a salad bowl with paper toweling. Place the spinach leaves and onions in the bowl, and toss with your hands to mix. Cover the salad with a dampened linen towel and refrigerate until time for final preparation.

TIME ALLOWANCE FOR FINAL PREPARATION: 5 MINUTES

Remove the paper and linen toweling from the salad. Add the sliced mushrooms. Toss the spinach and mushrooms with your hands or a salad fork and spoon.

Vigorously shake the bottle of vinaigrette. Pour the dressing over the salad. Toss the spinach and mushrooms until they are completely coated with the dressing.

SERVES 6

VELVET CRÈME CARAMEL

(MAY BE PARTIALLY PREPARED UP TO 24 HOURS IN ADVANCE)

1 cup sugar
2 tablespoons water
2 eggs
1 egg yolk
½ teaspoon vanilla
2 cups light cream, scalded

Preheat the oven to 325 degrees. Bring a kettle full of water to a boil.

Combine ½ cup of sugar with the 2 tablespoons of water in a small skillet over high heat. Stir only until the sugar is dissolved. Continue to boil the syrup until it starts to turn golden brown. Immediately remove the skillet from the heat, as the syrup will continue to darken. Pour the syrup into a 4-cup ring mold, swirling it around the bottom of the mold to distribute it evenly. Work quickly, as the syrup will harden as it cools.

In a mixing bowl, beat the eggs and egg yolk with the remaining ½ cup sugar and the vanilla until they are well combined. Beat in the scalded cream. Pour the mixture into the caramelized mold and set the mold into a larger baking dish. Add boiling water until the water comes halfway up the sides of the mold. Place the baking dish in the oven and bake the custard for 40 minutes.

Remove the mold from the water bath and allow the custard to cool. If you are making the custard more than 4 hours in advance, refrigerate the mold, covering with plastic wrap, until 1 hour before final preparation. Otherwise, set the mold, covered, in a cool corner of the kitchen.

TIME ALLOWANCE FOR FINAL PREPARATION: 5 MINUTES

Run a knife around the edges of the mold to loosen the custard. Set the mold in a bath of hot water for 1 or 2 minutes to melt the caramel. Remove the mold from the hot water and place a serving platter with a rim upside down on top of the mold. Turn the mold and platter over and give a hard shake. The custard should slip out easily with the caramel sauce dribbling down its sides.

(The custard may be unmolded up to 2 hours before serving, if desired, and stored in a cool corner of the kitchen. Its flavor is enhanced if it is served at room temperature.)

SERVES 6

AN ACTOR'S PIE
FOR SIX

*Alfred Lunt's Russian
Hamburger "Pie"*

*Sautéed Mushrooms and Cherry
Tomatoes*

Hot Herbed Bread

*Mixed Green Salad with
Vinaigrette**

Chocolate-Sauced Cake

Recipe sources are often as intriguing as the recipes themselves. The late Alfred Lunt, for example, was better known first as an actor and then as husband to the ethereally beautiful Lynn Fontanne than he ever was as a cook. Yet his recipe for Russian Hamburger "Pie" should certainly add to his reputation. It came to my attention via the friends-of-friends route. Obviously it isn't a pie in any traditional sense, unless a meat crust with a cabbage filling qualifies. Even its Russian heritage is dubious, although some of the filling's chief ingredients—cabbage, onion, dill, and sour cream—are staples in Russian cuisine. Nevertheless, it makes for good and unusual fare, and certainly fulfills this book's do-ahead obligations.

Since Lunt's "pie" is so hearty, try a simple but cheery sauté of mushrooms and tomatoes as a side dish. Nothing else is really necessary—but who could resist a salad and a slice of hot, aromatic, herbed bread? Or, for that matter, a smashing dessert from caloric heaven: chocolate cake, steaming hot from the oven, with a built-in chocolate sauce coursing through its center?

* Prepare 1½ the recipe on page 24, omitting the cherry tomatoes.

ALFRED LUNT'S RUSSIAN HAMBURGER "PIE"

(MAY BE PARTIALLY PREPARED UP TO 12 HOURS IN ADVANCE)

2 pounds lean ground round
1 teaspoon salt
Freshly ground black pepper
3 tablespoons unsalted butter
1 cup coarsely chopped onions
4 cups coarsely chopped green cabbage (about half a small cabbage)
1 cup cooked rice
¼ cup plus 2 tablespoons minced fresh dillweed
1 cup sour cream

Press about 1½ pounds of the ground round into a 10-inch pie plate that is 1½ inches deep, shaping the meat to form a "pie crust" about ¾ inch thick. Sprinkle the meat with ¼ teaspoon salt and some freshly ground black pepper.

Melt the butter in a large skillet over low heat. Add the onions and sauté them, stirring occasionally, until they are soft, about 5 minutes. Add the chopped cabbage, increase the heat to medium, and sauté for an additional 5 minutes, tossing the vegetables frequently. Remove the skillet from the heat and add the rice, ½ teaspoon salt, a generous grinding of pepper, and ¼ cup dillweed. Stir to blend the ingredients thoroughly. When the cabbage has cooled, pile it as the "filling" in the ground beef shell.

On a piece of wax paper, pat the remaining ½ pound of beef into a disk about 8 inches in diameter and ½ inch thick. Place the disk, with the wax paper still intact to act as a stabilizer, upside down on top of the "filling" and carefully peel off the wax paper. Patch any broken sections and secure the bottom edge of the "pie" to the top. Sprinkle the surface of the "pie" with the remaining ¼ teaspoon of salt and a few more grindings of pepper. Cover tightly with plastic wrap (so that the meat does not discolor). Refrigerate until 2 hours before final preparation.

TIME ALLOWANCE FOR FINAL PREPARATION: 50 MINUTES

Preheat the oven to 325 degrees.

Spread the surface of the "pie" with a generous layer of sour cream. Place the "pie" in the oven and bake for 45 minutes. Sprinkle the remaining 2 tablespoons of dillweed over the top crust before serving. Cut the pie in wedges and serve.

SERVES 6

SAUTÉED MUSHROOMS AND CHERRY TOMATOES

(MAY BE PARTIALLY PREPARED UP TO 8 HOURS IN ADVANCE)

4 tablespoons unsalted butter
1 pound mushrooms, stems trimmed
¼ cup strained fresh lemon juice
1 pound cherry tomatoes, washed and hulled
¼ cup minced fresh parsley

In a 12- to 14-inch skillet, melt the butter over low heat. Add the whole mushrooms and, stirring frequently, cook them until they just exude their juices, about 15 minutes. Add the lemon juice, toss once more, and remove the skillet from the heat. Cover the skillet and set it aside in a cool corner of the kitchen until final preparation.

TIME ALLOWANCE FOR FINAL PREPARATION: 10 MINUTES

Uncover the skillet and return it to moderately high heat. Toss the mushrooms with a large spoon as they warm. When they are hot, increase the heat to high and add the cherry tomatoes. Sauté the mixture for 2 minutes, stirring frequently, or until the tomatoes are just cooked but are not bursting their skins (which overcooking will do). Taste for seasoning and adjust if necessary.

Transfer the mushrooms and tomatoes to a heated serving bowl and sprinkle with the parsley. Serve immediately.

SERVES 6

CHOCOLATE-SAUCED CAKE

(MAY BE PARTIALLY PREPARED UP TO 8 HOURS IN ADVANCE)

2 tablespoons unsalted butter
1 ounce (1 square) unsweetened chocolate
1½ cups cake flour
1¼ cups sugar
1½ teaspoons baking powder
¼ teaspoon salt
½ cup milk

1 egg, beaten
1 teaspoon vanilla
½ cup semisweet chocolate bits
2 tablespoons unsweetened cocoa
½ cup firmly packed dark brown sugar
1 cup water, boiling
1 cup heavy cream, whipped or plain

Melt the butter and chocolate in the top of a double boiler over barely simmering water.

Meanwhile, combine the cake flour, ¾ cup sugar, the baking powder, and salt, and sift them into a mixing bowl. In a separate bowl, combine the milk, egg, and vanilla, and beat thoroughly. When the butter and chocolate have melted, scrape them into the milk mixture and stir well. Pour the milk-and-chocolate mixture into the dry ingredients, mixing until they are well blended. Finally, fold in the chocolate bits. Pour the batter into a generously buttered 1½-quart souffle or baking dish.

Combine the cocoa, brown sugar, and remaining ½ cup of white sugar in a sieve placed over a mixing bowl. Push the mixture through the sieve with the back of a spoon. Transfer it to the top of the cake batter, distributing it as evenly as possible. Cover the baking dish with plastic wrap and hold in a cool corner of the kitchen until final preparation.

TIME ALLOWANCE FOR FINAL PREPARATION: 55 MINUTES

Shortly before sitting down to dinner, preheat the oven to 350 degrees.

Pour the boiling water over the topping on the cake. Place the baking dish in the oven and bake 45 minutes. The water and the topping will form a chocolate syrup that will penetrate the cake.

Serve the cake hot or at room temperature, with plain or whipped cream.

SERVES 6

STUFFED FLOUNDER FILLETS FOR SIX

Celeriac Salad

Spinach-Stuffed Flounder Fillets

Buttered Peas with Mint

Julia's Rhubarb

Chicken breasts, veal scallops, and flounder (or sole) fillets seem to be the most versatile basic ingredients for entrees. While each can maintain a strong self-image, the introduction of an herb, a sauce, an accompanying vegetable, or a novel method of cooking can produce a totally different result in which the base can absorb the best of its surroundings.

I once mentioned this theory to my family, but they would have none of it. "Chicken always tastes like chicken," my son emphatically retorted. "And fish is fish." (He doesn't care for it much.)

I was challenged, of course. For one week I fed them chicken breasts in different guises. I served sautéed chicken breasts, breaded chicken breasts, minced chicken breasts—I can't even remember all the variations on the theme. But I recall emphatically that there were no "What? Chicken again?" groans. On the seventh and final night, when I pointed out how they'd been my chicken-eating guinea pigs, they graciously reversed their stands.

I haven't tried the experiment with seven consecutive nights of sole fillets, but I may someday, just to make my point again. I'll have Sole Meunière, Fillets of Sole with Dill Cream (see page 65), and certainly this menu's Spinach-Stuffed Flounder Fillets, a party dish if ever there was one. These neat little rolls stuffed with a spinach-mushroom blend may be served with or without hollandaise sauce.

For a first course, make a salad from a vegetable common in Europe: celeriac, also called celery knob or celery root. This root is found increasingly in American markets, but many consumers confront it with puzzlement. It looks like a wart-covered potato, but it tastes like the sweetest of celery hearts. It is good either raw or cooked. Serve it as an appetizer—*celeri remoulade*, as it's known in France—or with the entree, if you prefer.

I think you'll love the dessert, Julia's Rhubarb, a recipe given to me by a friend. It's really a variation on the New England "crisp" theme, but I never before encountered a version with rhubarb. Every spring, when the first stalks of rhubarb are poking their way through the rain-soaked ground, it turns up on our dinner table—sometimes more than once a week.

CELERIAC SALAD

(MAY BE PARTIALLY PREPARED UP TO 4 HOURS IN ADVANCE)

3/4 cup mayonnaise
1 1/2 teaspoons dry mustard
2 teaspoons Worcestershire sauce
3 tablespoons strained fresh lemon juice
Freshly ground black pepper
2 medium-size celeriacs (celery knobs), about 3/4 pound each, peeled, roots
*   trimmed*
1/2 cup minced fresh parsley
12 lettuce leaves, washed and dried
12 sprigs watercress, tough stems removed

In a shallow mixing bowl, combine the mayonnaise, mustard, Worcestershire sauce, lemon juice, and pepper. Mix this dressing until well blended. Taste, and adjust the seasonings.

Cut the celeriacs in half from the leaf to the root ends. Cut each half into julienne strips about 1½ inches long and ¼ inch square. Place the strips of celeriac in the dressing and toss to completely coat each piece. Cover with plastic wrap and refrigerate until 30 minutes before final preparation.

TIME ALLOWANCE FOR FINAL PREPARATION: 10 MINUTES

Add the minced parsley to the mayonnaise-coated celeriac strips. Toss well. Divide the lettuce leaves among six salad plates and spoon equal portions of the celeriac on top of them. Garnish with the watercress sprigs.

SERVES 6

SPINACH-STUFFED FLOUNDER FILLETS

(MAY BE PARTIALLY PREPARED UP TO 12 HOURS IN ADVANCE)

3 tablespoons unsalted butter
¼ cup minced shallots
6 ounces coarsely chopped mushrooms
1 (10-ounce package) spinach, tough stems removed
Salt and freshly ground black pepper
¼ teaspoon freshly grated nutmeg
6 fillets of flounder, about ½ pound each
½ cup white wine
Springs of watercress
6 lemon wedges

In a large skillet, melt 2 tablespoons of the butter over moderately low heat. Add the shallots and mushrooms, and sauté them, stirring frequently, until the mushrooms have exuded their juices, about 10 minutes.

Meanwhile, chop the spinach very fine, using either a food processor fitted with a steel blade or a sharp knife. Add it to the shallots and mushrooms, and cook, stirring frequently, until the spinach starts to wilt, about 2 minutes. Season with salt, pepper, and nutmeg, and cook another 2 minutes, or until it is barely done. Do not overcook. Transfer the mixture to a strainer and drain, pressing down hard on the vegetables to release all liquid.

Cut the fillets in half lengthwise along the line of their backbone. Spread each half with a heaping tablespoon of the spinach mixture. Starting at one narrow end, roll each half up tightly. Secure each roll with a toothpick and place, seam side down, in a buttered baking dish large enough to contain all the fillets compactly. Dot the tops of the rolls with the remaining tablespoon of butter. Drizzle the white wine over the fish, cover the baking dish tightly with aluminum foil, and refrigerate. Remove the dish from the refrigerator 1 hour before final preparation.

TIME ALLOWANCE FOR FINAL PREPARATION: 50 MINUTES

Preheat the oven to 350 degrees.

Bake the fillets, still covered with foil, for 30 minutes. Remove the foil and cook another 15 minutes. Transfer the rolls to a heated serving platter, discarding any liquid left in the baking dish. Garnish with sprigs of watercress and lemon wedges.

Serve plain or with hollandaise sauce.

SERVES 6

HOLLANDAISE SAUCE
¼ cup strained fresh lemon juice
2 tablespoons water
3 egg yolks
1 cup unsalted butter, melted and cooled
¼ teaspoon salt
Freshly ground black pepper

Combine the lemon juice and water in a stainless steel saucepan. Place the pan over moderate heat and, stirring occasionally, reduce the mixture until only 2 tablespoons of liquid remain. Remove the pan from the heat and cool. Return the pan to very low heat and add the egg yolks. Whisk the yolks until they have thickened, always watching the heat and lifting the pan off the heat if the bottom becomes too hot to touch with a bare hand. Add the melted butter, drop by drop, until it is completely incorporated, removing the saucepan from the heat briefly if necessary. Season to taste with the salt and pepper.

The sauce should thicken to the consistency of mayonnaise. If it separates from too much heat, immediately remove it from the heat and add 2 ice cubes. Beat vigorously. The sauce will be slightly thinner but will come together again.

YIELD: APPROXIMATELY 1 CUP

JULIA'S RHUBARB

(MAY BE PARTIALLY PREPARED UP TO 6 HOURS IN ADVANCE)

2 pounds rhubarb, leaves trimmed and discarded, cut into ½-inch slices (about 4 cups)
¾ cup dark brown sugar
¾ cup flour
½ cup white sugar
¼ teaspoon salt
6 tablespoons unsalted butter, softened
1 cup heavy cream, whipped

Generously butter a deep, 2-quart ovenproof casserole or baking dish. Combine the rhubarb pieces with the brown sugar in the dish and toss well to mix. Cover with plastic wrap and hold in a cool corner of the kitchen until final preparation.

In a mixing bowl, combine the flour, white sugar, and salt, and stir briefly to mix. Add the softened butter in pieces and rub them into the flour with your fingers until the mixture resembles coarse meal. Cover the mixture with plastic wrap and hold in a cool corner of the kitchen until final preparation.

TIME ALLOWANCE FOR FINAL PREPARATION: 50 MINUTES

Preheat the oven to 350 degrees.

Spoon the topping evenly over the surface of the rhubarb.

Bake the rhubarb, uncovered, for 45 minutes, or until the topping is crisp and light brown. Serve hot or at room temperature with dollops of whipped cream.

SERVES 6

A COOL-WEATHER PICNIC FOR SIX

Mushroom and Barley Soup

Tomato Quiche

Cold Cuts and Country Pâté

French Bread

Apple Turnovers

Picnics should not be limited to hot weather. They do not require lazy days or nights by sea or lake, bodies slathered with suntan lotion or insect repellent, soggy sandwiches or charred hamburgers and hot dogs.

There's such a thing as cool-weather picnics. These are tailgate picnics, before football or ice-hockey games; or midwinter-thaw picnics, when the cold abates for a few days; or spring is-just-around-the-corner picnics, when the ground is once again soft underfoot. Such picnics, however, are not spread-out-the-blanket-and-sit-on-the-ground affairs. These are stand-up, feet-stomping (to keep the toes warm) picnics requiring what my husband called "finger food."

This menu is intended for a tailgate picnic, because I like to focus on some sort of event, but it could easily serve for any of the aforementioned. So consider the fall setting of red and yellow leaves, roadside stands overloaded with baskets of apples and mounds of pumpkins, and a gathering of automobiles outside a stadium. What more enjoyable way to start a rousing afternoon than with a few friends and a picnic basket well stocked with finger food?

To ward off the potential chill, bring a supply of hot Mushroom and Barley Soup. (This recipe makes more than enough for six, but you'll probably want seconds during intermissions.) Buy an assortment of cold cuts, spreads, perhaps a country pâté, and a couple of loaves of good French bread. Offer your guests a pretty quiche with tomatoes festooned across its surface, made at home ahead of time, but appetizing even unheated.

For dessert, apples, of course—but, for a party effect, wrapped in pastry and presented as portable turnover treats.

MUSHROOM AND BARLEY SOUP

(MAY BE PARTIALLY PREPARED UP TO 3 DAYS IN ADVANCE)

2 tablespoons unsalted butter
½ pound mushrooms, coarsely chopped
1 cup chopped onions
¼ cup chopped carrots (1 medium)
1 (16-ounce) can whole tomatoes, drained and coarsely chopped
½ cup medium-grain barley
2 quarts chicken stock
Salt and freshly ground pepper to taste
½ pound mushrooms, thinly sliced
1 (10-ounce) package frozen corn, thawed
1 (10-ounce) package frozen peas, thawed
¼ cup minced fresh parsley

Melt the butter in a 4- to 6-quart kettle. Over medium heat, sauté the chopped mushrooms, the onions, and the carrots in the butter for 5 minutes, stirring frequently. Add the tomatoes, barley, and chicken stock. Bring to a boil over high heat, then reduce the heat to moderately low and simmer for 1 hour, partially covered. Taste, and adjust seasoning. Add the sliced mushrooms and simmer 15 minutes. Finally, add the corn and peas and cook for 5 minutes longer. If you are not serving the soup immediately, cool, cover, and refrigerate.

TIME ALLOWANCE FOR FINAL PREPARATION: 20 MINUTES

Over moderately high heat, bring the soup to a boil, stirring occasionally. Let the soup simmer 5 minutes, then garnish with the minced parsley and serve.

(If you are transferring the soup to Thermoses, preheat the Thermoses by filling them with boiling water and allowing them to stand for 2 minutes. Drain the Thermoses before transferring the hot soup.)

SERVES 6 TO 8

TOMATO QUICHE

(MAY BE PREPARED UP TO 12 HOURS IN ADVANCE)

1 9-inch unbaked pie shell
1 cup coarsely grated imported Swiss-style cheese, such as Gruyère or Jarlsberg
3 eggs
¾ cup light cream
½ teaspoon salt
1½ teaspoons dried oregano
1 large tomato (about ½ pound)
2 tablespoons freshly grated Parmesan cheese

Preheat the oven to 400 degrees.

Line the pie shell with aluminum foil and weight it down with uncooked rice or beans. Bake it for 10 minutes, then remove the foil and weights, reduce the heat to 350, and bake 10 minutes longer. Remove the pie shell from the oven and cool it on a rack.

Keep the oven set at 350 degrees.

When the pie shell is cool to the touch, evenly distribute the grated Swiss-style cheese in it.

With a whisk or rotary beater, beat the eggs in a small bowl until they are light and frothy. Add the cream, salt, and 1 teaspoon of oregano, and beat until well combined. Pour the mixture over the cheese. Place the quiche in the oven and bake it for 30 minutes, or until the filling seems set but not too firm.

With a serrated knife, cut the tomato into thin slices. Arrange the slices, overlapping, in concentric circles on top of the pie filling. Sprinkle the tomatoes with the Parmesan cheese and the remaining ½ teaspoon of oregano. Return the quiche to the oven and bake it 10 minutes. Then place it under a preheated broiler for 5 minutes to brown the top.

If you are not eating the quiche immediately, allow it to cool. Then wrap it in plastic wrap and refrigerate it until 2 hours before serving. The quiche may be briefly reheated (at 325 degrees for 15 minutes) or served at room temperature.

SERVES 6

APPLE TURNOVERS

(SHOULD BE PREPARED NO MORE THAN 3 HOURS BEFORE SERVING)

4 Golden Delicious apples (about 1½ pounds), peeled, cored, and sliced
½ cup plus 1 tablespoon sugar
½ teaspoon ground cinnamon
1 tablespoon strained fresh lemon juice
Pinch of salt
2 sheets frozen puff pastry (17½ ounces), thawed
1 egg

Preheat the oven to 425 degrees.

In a medium-size mixing bowl, combine the apple slices, ½ cup sugar, ¼ teaspoon cinnamon, lemon juice, and salt. Toss to mix well. Set aside.

Carefully unfold the rolled sheets of puff pastry, following the manufacturer's directions. Lay each one out on a floured board and roll each one into a 10-inch square using a floured rolling pin. Divide each sheet into four equal 5-inch squares by cutting lengthwise and crosswise through their centers.

Place 5 or 6 slices of sugared apples in the center of the diagonal half of each pastry square, leaving a ½-inch border. Lightly moisten the edges with water. Bring the empty half of the square over on top of the apples and secure it to the bottom edge by pressing the two together with the tines of a fork. (The turnover should end up in the shape of a triangle.) Repeat until all the squares have been filled, folded, and sealed.

In a small mixing bowl, beat the egg until frothy. Add 1 tablespoon sugar and the remaining ¼ teaspoon cinnamon. Brush the pastry turnovers lightly with the egg wash. Transfer them to a buttered baking sheet and bake for 15 minutes. Reduce the heat to 350 degrees and bake 10 to 15 minutes longer, or until the tops are nicely puffed and golden.

Serve the turnovers warm or at room temperature.

YIELD: 8 TURNOVERS

SUPER-SIMPLE CHICKEN DINNER FOR SIX

Orange Chicken

Oven-Fried Potatoes

Creamed Spinach and Mushrooms

Grapefruit and Banana Fruit Salad

Bittersweet Chocolate Pecan Clusters

Occasionally everyone faces the horrible predicament of a commitment to entertaining during a frenetically busy period. At a point like this, it matters little whether the guests number six or sixty. (In fact, sometimes it's easier if it's the latter. Then you can throw in the towel and call a caterer.) You curse yourself for such bad planning; you vow never to entertain again if you can possible help it.

Don't give up just yet. This menu for six is child's play for the busy cook. Orange Chicken is simple and refreshing. Oven-Fried Potatoes—not really fried, but baked in butter and oil—give the pleasant hot crunchiness of deep-fried potatoes without the fuss and grease. Creamed Spinach with Mushrooms, cooked to green perfection, offers wonderful taste and visual contrast.

For dessert, cut up some fruit and serve it with cookies; try homemade Bittersweet Chocolate Pecan Clusters, or purchase cookies from the bakery if you're really pressed for time. This is a dinner you can prepare and still feel relaxed.

ORANGE CHICKEN

(MAY BE PARTIALLY PREPARED UP TO 8 HOURS IN ADVANCE)

2 (3-pound) chickens, quartered
1 tablespoon minced gingerroot
1 teaspoon minced garlic
1 tablespoon grated orange rind
3 tablespoons soy sauce
1 cup strained fresh orange juice

Place the chicken quarters skin side up in a baking pan large enough to contain them compactly. Sprinkle the ginger, garlic, and orange rind over the pieces. Drizzle the soy sauce and orange juice over the top. Cover the baking pan with plastic wrap and, if you are not baking the chicken immediately, refrigerate it until 1 hour before final preparation. (If you have the opportunity, baste the chicken pieces with the juice occasionally during the waiting period, but it is not strictly necessary.)

TIME ALLOWANCE FOR FINAL PREPARATION: 45 MINUTES

Preheat the oven to 400 degrees.

Baste the chicken with the juices in the bottom of the pan. Place the pan in the oven and bake for 35 minutes, basting every 10 minutes. If the skin is not as brown and crisp as you would like it at the end of the cooking period, briefly place the chicken under the broiler.

Transfer the chicken pieces to a heated platter. Pour the pan juices into a small saucepan and reduce them by one-third over high heat. Serve the orange reduction as an accompaniment to the chicken.

SERVES 6

OVEN-FRIED POTATOES

◆

(MAY BE PARTIALLY PREPARED UP TO 12 HOURS IN ADVANCE)

¼ cup unsalted butter
¼ cup oil
½ teaspoon minced garlic
¼ teaspoon salt
Freshly ground black pepper
½ teaspoon dried thyme
3 pounds boiling potatoes, peeled and cut into ¼-inch-thick slices
2 tablespoons minced fresh parsley

In a shallow baking dish about 9 by 12 inches in size, melt the butter with the oil over low heat. Remove the dish from the heat. Add the garlic, salt, pepper, and thyme and mix well. Add the sliced potatoes and toss until they are completely coated with the butter mixture. Cover the dish with plastic wrap. If you are holding the potatoes longer than 3 hours, refrigerate them until 1 hour before final preparation. Otherwise, merely store the dish in a cool corner of the kitchen.

TIME ALLOWANCE FOR FINAL PREPARATION: 1 HOUR

Preheat the oven to 375 degrees.

Toss the potatoes to recoat them with the butter and oil. Place the baking dish, uncovered, in the oven and bake the potatoes 45 to 50 minutes, turning them frequently, until they are tender when pierced with the tip of a knife.

Place the potatoes under the broiler for 5 minutes, or until they are nicely browned. Sprinkle with the parsley and serve immediately.

SERVES 6

CREAMED SPINACH AND MUSHROOMS

(MAY BE PARTIALLY PREPARED UP TO 6 HOURS IN ADVANCE)

2 tablespoons unsalted butter
½ pound mushrooms, coarsely chopped
¾ cup water
2 (10-ounce) packages spinach, tough stems discarded, coarsely chopped
1 cup heavy cream
½ teaspoon salt
Freshly ground black pepper
Freshly grated nutmeg

Melt the butter in a large skillet over low heat. Add the mushrooms and sauté them, stirring occasionally, until the juices they exude have evaporated, about 10 to 15 minutes. Remove the skillet from the heat and reserve.

Pour the water into a 2- to 3-quart stainless steel or enamel saucepan, and pile the spinach on top of it. Cover the pan and bring the water to a boil over high heat. Steam the spinach, stirring it once or twice, for 3 minutes, or until it is just wilted but still bright green. (Do not overcook it.) Remove the pan from the heat. Drain the spinach in a strainer, pressing hard with the back of a spoon to squeeze out all the moisture. Return the drained spinach to the same saucepan, add the mushrooms, and toss to mix. Cover tightly. Reserve in a cool corner of the kitchen until final preparation.

TIME ALLOWANCE FOR FINAL PREPARATION: 5 MINUTES

Pour the cream over the spinach and mushrooms and mix thoroughly. Sprinkle with salt, pepper, and a few gratings of nutmeg. Stir well. Place the saucepan, covered, over moderate heat, and heat the spinach and mushrooms for 3 to 5 minutes, stirring occasionally, until steaming hot. Serve immediately.

SERVES 6

BITTERSWEET CHOCOLATE PECAN CLUSTERS

(MAY BE PREPARED UP TO 24 HOURS IN ADVANCE)

3 ounces semisweet chocolate
1 ounce unsweetened chocolate
1 tablespoon unsalted butter
½ cup firmly packed light brown sugar
1 tablespoon water
1 teaspoon vanilla
1 egg, beaten
2 tablespoons flour
⅛ teaspoon baking powder
Pinch of ground cinnamon
Pinch of salt
½ cup coarsely chopped pecans
1 cup semisweet chocolate bits

In the top of a double boiler set over simmering water, melt the semisweet and unsweetened chocolates and the butter, stirring occasionally. When the chocolate has melted, remove the top of the double boiler from the water below, and allow it to cool slightly. Stir in the sugar and mix until blended. Add the water, vanilla, and egg and beat well. Place the flour, baking powder, cinnamon, and salt in a sifter or sieve and sift them into the chocolate. Blend thoroughly. Finally stir in the pecans and chocolate bits. Let the batter rest for 10 minutes to become firm.

While the batter is resting, preheat the oven to 350 degrees.

Generously grease two cookie sheets.

Drop the batter by the heaping teaspoonful onto the prepared cookie sheets, leaving about 2 inches between each spoonful. If the nuts and chocolate chips do not seem to be adhering to the batter, simply press them into a more cohesive mass with a spoon or your fingers. (It is a strange-looking batter with the nuts and chips barely contained, but the results are very satisfying.)

Bake the clusters for approximately 15 minutes, or until they seem firm. (The chips, of course, will still be soft but will harden upon cooling.) Let the clusters cool on the cookie sheet for 2 minutes before transferring them to a rack to cool completely.

YIELD: ABOUT 30 CLUSTERS

A MELLOW RAGOUT
FOR SIX

Veal Ragout

Buttered Noodles

*Watercress and Endive Salad
with Martha McCarthy's
Curry-Basil Dressing*

*Chocolate Almond Meringue
"Pie" with Bittersweet Chocolate
Sauce*

Veal has a reputation as one of the more expensive items in the butcher's case, but stewing veal is not so very hard on the pocketbook. Given an hour or so of slow cooking, complementary vegetables and herbs, and a gentle hand with the cream-enriched sauce, stewing veal can become an aromatic and tender ragout (French for any meat and vegetable stew). Most of the work can be done a couple of days in advance; in fact, like all stews, veal ragout benefits from cooking ahead, which allows the flavors to mellow and blend.

Simple buttered noodles are the perfect foil for the veal's sauce, and a wonderful soaker-upper. A salad rounds off the meal beautifully. The Watercress and Endive Salad has a very special dressing flavored with curry and basil, given to me by my sister-in-law, Martha McCarthy. For a very different effect, try it, slightly sweetened, over a fruit salad.

The dessert is a chocolate and almond meringue "pie," filled with the ice cream of your choice and bathed in a bittersweet chocolate sauce. This superlative combination of fluff and crunch is not so rich, however, that your guests will be forced to refuse second helpings.

VEAL RAGOUT

(MAY BE PREPARED THE DAY IT IS TO BE SERVED,
BUT IS BETTER PREPARED 2 OR 3 DAYS IN ADVANCE AND REHEATED)

3 pounds stewing veal, cut into small pieces (about ¾-inch cubes)
1 medium onion, peeled and stuck with 3 whole cloves
2 bay leaves
4 sprigs parsley
1 carrot, broken in thirds
1 celery stalk, broken in thirds
1 pound small white onions, unpeeled
12 ounces whole mushrooms, stems trimmed
3 tablespoons unsalted butter
1 teaspoon imported Hungarian paprika
3 tablespoons flour
1 teaspoon salt
¼ teaspoon freshly ground black pepper
½ cup heavy cream
½ cup sour cream
2 egg yolks
3 tablespoons minced fresh parsley

Place the veal pieces in a 4- to 6-quart kettle and add enough water to just cover them. Bring the water to a boil and spoon off any scum that rises to the surface. Add the onion and cloves, bay leaves, parsley sprigs, carrot, and celery; simmer 1 hour.

Meanwhile, fill a 2-quart saucepan two-thirds full with water, and drop the small white onions into it. Let them boil 5 minutes, then remove them with a slotted spoon. When they are cool enough to handle, slice off their root ends. Squeeze the onion skins so that they slip off. Return the onions to the water and cook them until tender, about 15 to 25 minutes, depending upon their size. Add the mushrooms and simmer 5 more minutes. With a slotted spoon, transfer the mushrooms and onions to a bowl, reserving the cooking liquid.

When the veal has cooked 1 hour and is tender when pierced with the tip of a knife, remove and discard the onion and the carrot and celery pieces. With a slotted spoon, transfer the veal to a 4-quart flameproof casserole equipped with a lid, alternating layers of veal with the mushrooms and onions. Strain the broth in which the veal has been cooking into the reserved mushroom cooking liquid. Set the casserole aside.

In a 2-quart saucepan, melt the butter over moderately low heat. Add the paprika, flour, salt, and pepper. Stir constantly until the mixture is well blended and has thickened. Cook, stirring, 1 minute. Slowly beat in 3 cups of the reserved veal and mushroom liquid. Cook until the sauce comes to a boil and has thickened. Pour the sauce over the contents of the casserole, and allow to cool. Cover the casserole with its lid, and refrigerate until 1 hour before final preparation.

TIME ALLOWANCE FOR FINAL PREPARATION: 30 MINUTES

Place the casserole, covered, over low heat. The sauce will have jelled, so stir occasionally as it warms so that it liquefies evenly. Simmer 20 minutes, or until the meat is heated through.

In a small bowl, combine the cream and sour cream and, mix well with a whisk. Add the egg yolks and blend thoroughly. Spoon ½ cup of the veal sauce into the cream mixture; mix well. Then stir this mixture into the casserole. Slowly bring the sauce to just under a boil (watch carefully, for it can curdle), and then remove the casserole from the heat. Sprinkle the minced parsley over the ragout's surface and serve immediately.

SERVES 6

WATERCRESS AND ENDIVE SALAD
WITH
MARTHA MCCARTHY'S CURRY-BASIL DRESSING

(SALAD MAY BE PARTIALLY PREPARED UP TO 6 HOURS IN ADVANCE;
DRESSING MAY BE PREPARED UP TO 3 DAYS IN ADVANCE)

WATERCRESS AND ENDIVE SALAD
1 bunch watercress, washed and dried, stalks trimmed
3 heads Belgian endive, ends trimmed, cut crosswise into ½-inch pieces, leaves
  separated
¼ pound thinly sliced mushrooms
2 tablespoons minced red onion
1 ripe avocado, peeled and sliced, pit discarded

To make the salad: Line the bottom of a salad bowl with paper toweling. Place the watercress, endive, mushrooms, and red onion on top of it, and toss the greens with your hands or a salad fork and spoon to distribute the ingredients.

Lay another paper towel lightly on top of the salad. Refrigerate the salad until final preparation.

MARTHA MCCARTHY'S CURRY-BASIL DRESSING

2 tablespoons red wine vinegar
¼ teaspoon salt
½ teaspoon dried sweet basil
¼ teaspoon dry mustard
Freshly ground black pepper
1 teaspoon brown sugar
¼ teaspoon curry powder
6 tablespoons vegetable oil

To make the dressing: In a jar with a tight-fitting lid, combine the vinegar, salt, basil, mustard, pepper, sugar, and curry powder. Stir until the dry ingredients are completely dissolved. Add the oil, cover the jar with its lid, and shake vigorously. Store the dressing in a cool corner of the kitchen until ready to use.

YIELD: ½ CUP DRESSING

TIME ALLOWANCE FOR FINAL PREPARATION: 5 MINUTES

Remove the paper toweling from the salad. Add the sliced avocado. Shake the dressing vigorously and pour it over the greens. Toss the salad until the greens are completely coated with the dressing.

SERVES 6

CHOCOLATE ALMOND MERINGUE "PIE" WITH BITTERSWEET CHOCOLATE SAUCE

(THE "PIE" MAY BE PREPARED 24 HOURS IN ADVANCE; THE SAUCE 2 DAYS IN ADVANCE. THE ENTIRE "PIE" SHOULD BE ASSEMBLED JUST BEFORE SERVING)

CHOCOLATE ALMOND MERINGUE PIE

½ cup slivered almonds
4 egg whites
Pinch of salt
¼ teaspoon cream of tartar
1 cup sugar

1 teaspoon vanilla
2 tablespoons unsweetened cocoa
1 tablespoon cornstarch
1 quart ice cream, softened

To make the meringue: Preheat the oven to 300 degrees.

Place the almonds on a pie plate and toast them in the oven, stirring occasionally, until they are golden brown, about 10 minutes. Cool. In a blender or a food processor fitted with a steel blade, whirl the almonds to a fine powder. (Do not overprocess or the nuts will become oily.)

Lower the oven temperature to 275 degrees.

In a large mixing bowl, combine the egg whites with the salt and cream of tartar. Beat until frothy. Gradually add the sugar while continuing to beat briskly. When the egg whites are stiff and glossy, beat in the vanilla. Combine the cocoa and powdered almonds in a sieve and push them with the back of a spoon onto the whites. Carefully fold them into the whites, mixing only until no trace of white is visible.

Butter a 10-inch pie plate and dust it with the cornstarch, shaking off any excess. Pile the meringue into the prepared plate and swirl the mixture up the sides of the plate with a rubber spatula, flattening down the center, to form a pie-shaped meringue shell. (Do not worry if the "pie" is not perfectly formed; it will be filled with ice cream and no one will notice.)

Place the meringue in the oven and bake it, undisturbed, for 2 hours. Turn off the heat and allow the meringue to remain in the oven an additional ½ hour to dry out and cool.

Loosely cover the "pie" with wax paper and store it in a cool, dry spot until ready to fill.

BITTERSWEET CHOCOLATE SAUCE

4 ounces bittersweet chocolate, cut into chunks
¼ cup very strong coffee
¼ cup strained fresh orange juice
¼ cup sugar
Pinch of salt

To make the sauce: In the top of a double boiler, over simmering water, combine the chocolate, coffee, orange juice, sugar, and salt. Cook, stirring occasionally, until the chocolate has melted. Mix the ingredients until they are well blended.

If you are preparing the sauce well in advance, store it in a jar with a tight-fitting lid and refrigerate it until ready to reheat. If you are preparing it within 4 hours of serving, simply leave it in the top of the double boiler, off the heat and covered, until ready to reheat.

YIELD: 1 CUP SAUCE

TIME ALLOWANCE FOR FINAL PREPARATION: 15 MINUTES

Reheat the sauce over boiling water until very hot, about 10 minutes. Transfer the sauce to a sauceboat.

Mound the softened ice cream into the meringue "pie" shell, swirling it attractively.

Serve the "pie" cut in wedges, accompanied by the chocolate sauce.

SERVES 6

FLEX YOUR MUSSELS OVER PASTA FOR SIX

Linguine with Mussel Sauce

Greek Salad with Lemon Vinaigrette

Hot French Bread

Trifle à la Milano

Mussels are at long last getting the attention they deserve, which took a long time in the United States. As a young girl summering on Cape Cod, I used to watch many of the French-Canadian visitors to Massachusetts gathering mussels by the bucketful. I remember thinking how very odd these people were to want to eat the blue-black, barnacle-encrusted creatures so abundant in Nauset harbor.

In recent summers, though, not a day has passed when I have not seen professional pickers in the same harbor, hauling loads away to market, or watched engrossed families walking out beyond the low-tide mark to scoop up clumps of mussels for dinner. (If you want to gather your own, please do remember the cardinal rule: Never take mussels that have been exposed to air; always take them from water beyond the low-tide line.)

The main dish in this menu is a variation on an old favorite: linguine or spaghetti with clam sauce. It evolved from my favorite recipe simply because one day I was too lazy to go clam-gathering and substituted mussels, which are much easier to gather. Since no vegetable is really needed, I suggest a fairly substantial salad, full of little dividends such as olives, radishes, peppers, and feta cheese. (Hence the name "Greek.") Don't forget to include hot French or Italian bread with the dinner; you'll really want it to soak up the juices.

For dessert, try a medley of berries, briefly simmered, then layered between subtly flavored almond macaroons and spoonfuls of whipped cream. (At one time this dessert could only be made in summer, when the berries were in season, but nowadays they seem to be available year-round, and pretty good quality berries at that.) Like the mussels, this dessert is another variation on a theme, the English trifle, but, unlike the traditional sponge cake, the macaroons give it much more bite and pizzazz.

LINGUINE WITH MUSSEL SAUCE

(MAY BE PARTIALLY PREPARED UP TO 8 HOURS IN ADVANCE)

4 pounds mussels
1 cup dry white wine
1 to 2 cups water
1 medium onion, peeled and halved
1 carrot, broken in thirds
1 bay leaf
1/2 cup fruity, imported olive oil
1 tablespoon minced garlic
3 tablespoons finely chopped fresh basil leaves (or 1 tablespoon dried basil)
1/2 cup minced fresh parsley
1 pound linguine
Salt and freshly ground black pepper to taste

Thoroughly clean the mussels: Pull off their whiskery "beards," scrape off any barnacles clinging to their shells, and wash them thoroughly.

Pour the wine and enough water into a 6-quart kettle to bring the liquid level to 1 inch. Add the onion, carrot, bay leaf, and mussels. Cover the kettle and set it over high heat. When your hear the liquid boiling, reduce the heat to moderate so that the broth will not boil over; do not uncover the kettle. Steam the mussels

5 to 10 minutes, or until their shells are open, stirring to redistribute them once or twice. (The timing depends on size.) With a slotted spoon, remove them from the broth to cool. (The sink is a good place for this.) Discard any mussels whose shells have not opened. Strain the mussel broth through a sieve lined with a double thickness of dampened cheesecloth. Reserve 1 cup of the strained broth.

When the mussels are cool enough to handle, remove them from their shells. Cut them crosswise into ½-inch pieces, or leave them whole if they are small. Put the mussel meat in a bowl, cover it with plastic wrap, and refrigerate. Remove the bowl from the refrigerator 1 hour before final preparation.

Pour the olive oil into a 1- to 2-quart saucepan. Add the garlic and cook it over moderate heat for 3 minutes, or until soft. Reduce the heat to moderately low, add the basil and parsley, and simmer 2 minutes. Add the reserved cup of mussel broth. Remove the pan from the heat, cover, and set in a cool corner of the kitchen until final preparation.

TIME ALLOWANCE FOR FINAL PREPARATION: 15 MINUTES

Cook the linguine according to package directions. (Unless it is fresh, it generally takes about 10 minutes.)

While the linguine is cooking, reheat the parsley-infused oil. When it is hot, add the reserved mussels and cook them until they are heated through, not more than 3 minutes. Do not overcook, or they will toughen. Taste, and add salt and pepper as needed.

Drain the linguine. Divide it among six shallow bowls and ladle the mussel sauce over it. Serve immediately.

SERVES 6

GREEK SALAD WITH LEMON VINAIGRETTE

(SALAD MAY BE PARTIALLY PREPARED UP TO 6 HOURS IN ADVANCE; VINAIGRETTE MAY BE PREPARED UP TO 3 DAYS IN ADVANCE)

GREEK SALAD
1 medium head Boston lettuce, washed, dried, and broken into 2-inch pieces
1 bunch watercress, washed, dried, and stems trimmed
¼ cup thinly sliced scallions, including 1 inch of green leaves
¼ cup minced fresh parsley
½ cup thinly sliced radishes
1 green pepper, cored, seeded, and cut in ½-inch dice

1 medium cucumber, washed but not peeled, thinly sliced
1 cup cherry tomatoes, hulled
12 black Greek olives
¼ pound feta cheese, crumbled
Salt and freshly ground black pepper to taste

To make the salad: Line the bottom of a large salad bowl with paper toweling. Combine the lettuce, watercress, scallions, parsley, radishes, peppers, cucumbers, tomatoes, and olives. Toss with a salad fork and spoon or your hands. Lay another piece of toweling over the top and refrigerate until final preparation.

LEMON VINAIGRETTE
¼ cup strained fresh lemon juice
1 teaspoon dried oregano
½ teaspoon salt
Freshly ground black pepper
¾ cup fruity, imported olive oil
1 clove garlic, peeled and halved lengthwise

To make the dressing: In a jar with a tight-fitting lid, combine the lemon juice, oregano, salt, and pepper, and stir until the salt dissolves. Add the olive oil and garlic. Cover the jar tightly and shake the dressing vigorously. Store the dressing in a cool corner of the kitchen until ready to use. (Remove the garlic pieces before dressing the salad.)

YIELD: 1 CUP DRESSING

TIME ALLOWANCE FOR FINAL PREPARATION: 5 MINUTES

Remove the paper toweling. Shake the dressing vigorously. Sprinkle the feta cheese over the salad greens. Pour the vinaigrette over the salad. Using a salad fork and spoon, toss well to coat all the leaves with the dressing. Taste for seasoning and adjust. (The feta cheese is rather salty; you may not want to add any more salt.)

SERVES 6

TRIFLE À LA MILANO

◆

(MAY BE PREPARED UP TO 6 HOURS IN ADVANCE;
SHOULD BE PREPARED AT LEAST 2 HOURS IN ADVANCE)

½ cup water
¾ cup sugar
¾ cup strawberries, hulled and washed
1 cup blueberries, picked over, stems discarded, washed
1 cup raspberries, picked over, washed
Pinch of salt
12 to 14 Amaretti di Saronno dry macaroons (available in specialty food markets), halved
1 cup heavy cream, whipped

Combine the water and sugar in a 2-quart saucepan, and bring to a boil over moderately high heat, stirring until the sugar has dissolved. When the syrup is boiling, add the strawberries. Allow them to cook 1 minute. (The syrup will not continue to boil.) Next add the blueberries and cook them 1 minute before adding the raspberries. Let the raspberries cook 1 minute. Add the salt, stir briefly, and remove the pan from the heat. Let the berries cool to room temperature.

Place a layer of halved macaroons in the bottom of a 2- to 3-quart baking dish. Ladle half the berry and syrup mixture over them, covering the entire surface. Spread half the whipped cream over the berries, covering them completely. Add another layer of halved macaroons and then the remaining berries and syrup. Top with the remaining whipped cream.

Refrigerate the trifle at least 2 hours before serving to allow the juices to permeate the biscuits. Cover the dish with plastic wrap if you are holding it longer than 2 hours. Serve the trifle chilled.

SERVES 6

RUSSIAN PATTIES FOR SIX

Bitochki with Stroganoff Sauce

Baked Brown Rice*

Brussels Sprouts with Walnuts

Lime Souffle Pie

Bitochki—or patties of ground chicken and veal, to be more prosaic—demonstrate magnificently my thesis concerning the versatility of chicken and veal. These delicate and fragrant, moist and tender patties take on a unique identity as a result of the marriage of the two meats and the addition of cream and dillweed. With the exception of grinding the meats, which can be a bore and a nuisance (but perhaps you can sweet-talk your butcher into doing it for you), they are even simpler to make than meat loaf, and their final preparation is as fast as that of hamburgers.

The Stroganoff Sauce is meant to gild the lily. It complements the patties sublimely, but, I must confess, it is not strictly necessary. The patties can stand alone on their own merit.

Brown rice is an appropriate starch for the meal, but if you should follow my recipe on page 77, I suggest you omit the almonds. The Brussels sprouts in this menu are enhanced with walnuts.

The Lime Souffle Pie is one of those happy kitchen accidents. One evening I was preparing a lime meringue pie. My mind was a million miles away and instead of saving the meringue as a topping, I inadvertantly folded it in with the lime custard. A rather fruitful error, if I say so myself.

* See the recipe on page 77.

BITOCHKI WITH STROGANOFF SAUCE

◆

(BITOCHKI MAY BE PARTIALLY PREPARED UP TO 6 HOURS IN ADVANCE;
THEY MUST BE PREPARED AT LEAST 2 HOURS IN ADVANCE.
SAUCE MAY BE PARTIALLY PREPARED UP TO 2 HOURS IN ADVANCE)

4 tablespoons unsalted butter
½ cup finely chopped onions
¼ cup minced fresh parsley
¼ cup minced fresh dillweed
2 pounds boned and skinned chicken breasts, cut in pieces
1 pound veal, trimmed of fat and membranes, cut in pieces
1 egg, beaten
½ cup heavy cream
1 teaspoon salt
¼ teaspoon freshly ground black pepper
¼ teaspoon freshly grated nutmeg
1 cup lightly toasted bread crumbs
1 tablespoon oil
Sprigs of dillweed

In a medium skillet, over moderate heat, melt 1 tablespoon of the butter. Add the onions and sauté, stirring occasionally, until wilted, about 5 minutes. Add the parsley and dill, mix briefly, remove the skillet from the heat, and reserve.

Force the chicken and veal pieces through the medium-size holes of a meat grinder. Gather the ground meat together, compress it, and grind it a second time. Place the ground meat in a large mixing bowl. Using a rubber spatula, scrape in the onion mixture. Add the egg, cream, salt, pepper, and nutmeg. Beat the mixture briskly with a wooden spoon until it is completely blended.

Spread out the toasted bread crumbs on paper toweling next to the bowl of meat. The meat mixture will be slightly sticky. To facilitate shaping the patties, dip your hands first into a bowl of ice water. Divide the meat into six equal portions. Shape each portion into an oval patty approximately 5 inches in length and 1 inch thick. Coat the patties on all sides in the bread crumbs. Transfer them to a platter and cover loosely with plastic wrap.

Refrigerate the patties for at least 2 hours or as long as 6 hours. Remove them from the refrigerator 1 hour before final preparation.

TIME ALLOWANCE FOR FINAL PREPARATION: 15 MINUTES

Melt the remaining 3 tablespoons of butter and the oil in a skillet large enough to hold all the patties without crowding. (Or cook the patties in two skillets.) Fry the patties over moderately high heat until golden brown, about 5 minutes on each side. Garnish with sprigs of dillweed and serve accompanied by Stroganoff Sauce.

SERVES 6

STROGANOFF SAUCE
3 tablespoons unsalted butter
1/2 pound thinly sliced mushrooms
1/4 cup minced fresh dillweed
1 tablespoon flour
1 1/2 cups sour cream
1/2 teaspoon salt
1/4 teaspoon freshly ground black pepper

Melt the butter in a large skillet over moderate heat. When it is hot, add the mushrooms. After they have exuded their juices, add the dill and toss briefly. Sprinkle the flour over the mushrooms, stirring to mix well. Cook 2 minutes. Add the sour cream, blending thoroughly. Season with the salt and pepper. Stirring occasionally, cook the sauce until it thickens, about 7 minutes. Cover and reserve in a cool corner of the kitchen.

TIME ALLOWANCE FOR FINAL PREPARATION: 5 MINUTES

Return the skillet to moderately low heat. Warm the sauce, stirring frequently, for approximately 5 minutes or until thoroughly hot. Serve immediately with the Bitochki.

YIELD: ABOUT 2 CUPS SAUCE

BRUSSELS SPROUTS WITH WALNUTS

(MAY BE PARTIALLY PREPARED UP TO 12 HOURS IN ADVANCE)

1 1/2 pounds Brussels sprouts
1/2 cup unsalted butter
2 tablespoons strained fresh lemon juice
1/2 teaspoon minced garlic
1/4 cup finely chopped walnuts
Salt and freshly ground pepper to taste

Trim the Brussels sprouts, discarding any discolored leaves. With the tip of a sharp paring knife, cut a shallow "x" in the base of each stem.

Drop the sprouts into a saucepan of salted water and cook until they are just barely tender and still bright green. (You may also steam them, if you prefer.) This will take anywhere from 3 to 7 minutes, depending on the size of the sprouts. Do not overcook them or they will have a bitter aftertaste.

Immediately refresh the sprouts under cold water. Drain them thoroughly, patting them dry with paper towels. Transfer them to a bowl, cover loosely with plastic wrap, and set aside in a cool corner of the kitchen until final preparation.

TIME ALLOWANCE FOR FINAL PREPARATION: 10 MINUTES

In a stainless steel or enamel skillet equipped with a lid, melt the butter over moderate heat. Add the lemon juice, garlic, and walnuts and sauté gently, stirring occasionally, for 2 minutes. Lower the heat and add the sprouts, tossing to coat them with the butter and nuts. Cover the skillet and heat the sprouts, shaking the pan occasionally, for 3 to 4 minutes, or until they are steaming hot but still green. (They will lose their color if cooked too long.) Serve immediately.

SERVES 6

LIME SOUFFLE PIE

(MAY BE PARTIALLY PREPARED UP TO 24 HOURS IN ADVANCE)

2 teaspoons grated lime rind
½ cup strained fresh lime juice
1½ to 2 cups sugar
½ cup unsalted butter
4 egg yolks, slightly beaten
4 egg whites, at room temperature
Pinch of salt
1 prebaked 9-inch pie shell

In a small saucepan, combine the lime rind and juice, between 1 and 1½ cups sugar (the amount you use depends upon the tartness of the limes and your personal preference), and the butter. Over moderately low heat, stir until the butter and sugar melt. Add the egg yolks and, whisking constantly, slowly bring the mixture to just below a boil. Be careful not to let the lime custard scorch.

Remove the custard from the heat. The custards should be slightly thick and should coat the back of a spoon. It will thicken more as it cools. Lay a sheet of plastic wrap directly on top of the custard to prevent a "skin" from forming. Transfer the custard to the refrigerator and hold it there until 1 hour before final preparation.

TIME ALLOWANCE FOR FINAL PREPARATION: 45 MINUTES

Preheat the oven to 375 degrees.

With an electric mixer, or by hand, beat the egg whites with a pinch of salt until they are frothy. Slowly add ½ cup sugar and continue beating until the whites are stiff but still very glossy. Spoon one-third of the whites into the lime custard. Mix thoroughly to lighten the custard. Then fold the lime mixture into the remaining egg whites very gently, mixing only until no trace of white remains.

Spoon the mixture into the prebaked pie shell, mounding it toward the center. Bake the pie for 30 minutes, or until the top is golden brown and the "souffle" firm to the touch. Do not overcook it; the filling's interior should be somewhat moist.

YIELD: 1 9-INCH PIE

NOTE: This pie is delicious served hot from the oven, but it is equally good served at room temperature. It "holds" for at least 4 hours after baking.

MIDDLE EASTERN LAMB
FOR SIX

Roast Leg of Lamb Istanbul

Sesame Rice

Zucchini Provençal

Strawberries with Mango Cream

One Easter I was getting ready to prepare the traditional roast leg of lamb for some friends who were coming for the holiday dinner with my husband and me. I found myself rather bored by the idea of yet another roasted, garlic-infused leg of lamb with all the usual fixings—mint sauce, roasted potatoes, baby asparagus. Dull.

"After all," I thought, "Christianity was born in the Middle East." So I hit the spice shelf and made a Middle Eastern dinner.

The recipes in this menu are the direct result. The entire meal is Mediterranean style, with spices, herbs, and yogurt common to the cultures of those sun-baked lands and azure sea. So well received was the dinner, I might add, that in our family it is no longer relegated to Easter.

The meal is not so exotic as it might seem. The spices are not overpowering but just potent enough to remind us that familiar foods can be treated in new ways that distract and please the palate.

(When the directions for the lamb tell you to trim away all the fat, please do so. Whack away until the flesh is exposed. The butcher's preparation is never thorough enough for this dish, in which the meat must be totally exposed to allow the ginger, yogurt, and spices to penetrate.)

One word about the dessert: simple strawberries topped with mango cream. The cream is a smooth blend of ripe mango and yogurt, pureed to a mayonnaise-like consistency—a superb embellishment for any fruit. Curiously, it does not taste like either mango or yogurt. See if your guests can recognize the sauce's components. If they can't, don't tell them. Let's keep it our secret.

ROAST LEG OF LAMB ISTANBUL

(MAY BE PARTIALLY PREPARED UP TO 12 HOURS IN ADVANCE;
MUST BE PARTIALLY PREPARED AT LEAST 3 HOURS IN ADVANCE)

3 tablespoons grated gingerroot
1 teaspoon minced garlic
2 tablespoons strained fresh lime juice
1/2 cup plain yogurt
1 teaspoon salt
1/4 teaspoon freshly ground black pepper
1 (6- to 7-pound) leg of lamb
1 tablespoon ground coriander
1/2 teaspoon ground cloves
1/2 teaspoon ground cinnamon
1/2 teaspoon ground cardamom

In a small bowl, combine the ginger, garlic, lime juice, yogurt, salt, and pepper, and blend well.

With a sharp knife, trim the lamb of as much fat as possible, including the thin "fell" or membrane. Next, score cross-hatches 1/4 inch deep across all the surfaces of the meat as if preparing a ham for glazing. Place the lamb on a platter and brush the yogurt marinade generously on its underside. Turn it over and brush the remaining marinade over the rest of the meat. The lamb must marinate at least 3 hours, or as long as 12 hours, to allow the spices to permeate the flesh. Refrigerate it only if you are preparing it more than 3 hours in advance, in which case cover it loosely with plastic wrap and remove it from the refrigerator 2 hours before final preparation.

In a small skillet, preferably one with a nonstick surface, combine the coriander, cloves, cinnamon, and cardamom. Toast over moderately low heat, stirring frequently, until the spices start to darken, about 3 to 4 minutes. Set aside and reserve.

TIME ALLOWANCE FOR FINAL PREPARATION: 1¾ HOURS

Preheat oven to 350 degrees.

Transfer the lamb to a roasting pan and discard any juices that may have accumulated on the platter. (Do not disturb the marinade left clinging to the meat.) Using a teaspoon, sprinkle the toasted spices over the lamb's surface.

Calculate the lamb's roasting time based on its store-bought weight, before all the fat was trimmed off, as follows: 11 minutes per pound for rare; 14 minutes per pound for medium to well-done. (The times may seem short, but the lamb will be overcooked if you follow traditional roasting times.)

Roast the lamb undisturbed for the calculated time. When it is done, transfer it to a heated platter and let it rest for 15 minutes before carving it.

Meanwhile, pour the roasting pan juices into a saucepan. Stirring constantly, boil the juices over high heat untl they have reduced by one-third. Serve in a gravy boat as a sauce for the lamb.

SERVES 6

SESAME RICE

(MAY BE PARTIALLY PREPARED UP TO 12 HOURS IN ADVANCE)

3½ cups chicken stock (or substitute water)
4 tablespoons unsalted butter
½ teaspoon salt
1½ cups long-grain rice
¾ cup sesame seeds (1½ 2⅜-ounce packages)

Pour the chicken stock into the top of a large double boiler. Add 2 tablespoons of the butter and place the top of the double boiler directly over the heat. Bring the stock to a boil. Add the salt and rice, and stir to separate the kernels. Bring to a boil over high heat, stir the rice again, then reduce the heat and simmer the rice, covered, for 20 minutes. Remove from the heat and cool. Do not worry if all the liquid has not been absorbed.

Meanwhile, place the sesame seeds in a large frying pan, preferably one with a nonstick surface. Stirring constantly, toast them over medium heat until they turn golden brown, about 5 minutes. Do not let them burn. Remove the skillet from the heat and let it cool.

Stir the seeds into the cooled rice, mixing until they are well distributed. Dot the rice's surface with the remaining 2 tablespoons of butter. Cover and reserve in a cool corner of the kitchen until final preparation.

TIME ALLOWANCE FOR FINAL PREPARATION: 25 MINUTES

Place the rice-filled top of the double boiler over boiling water. Reduce the heat and steam the rice, covered, for 15 minutes, turning occasionally, or until it is thoroughly reheated. Transfer the rice to a heated serving dish and serve immediately.

SERVES 6

ZUCCHINI PROVENÇAL

(MAY BE PARTIALLY PREPARED UP TO 8 HOURS IN ADVANCE)

3 tablespoons unsalted butter
1 large red pepper, cored, seeded, and cut in 1-inch pieces
½ pound whole mushrooms, ends trimmed
1 pound white onions, peeled
1 pound small zucchini, ends trimmed, cut in 1-inch slices
1 (28-ounce) can Italian peeled tomatoes, ¼ cup juice reserved
2 teaspoons dried oregano
1 teaspoon dried sweet basil
½ teaspoon salt
¼ teaspoon freshly ground black pepper

In a large skillet, melt 2 tablespoons of the butter over low heat. Add the peppers and mushrooms and sauté over low heat just until soft, stirring occasionally. With a slotted spoon, transfer them to a 2- to 3-quart ovenproof casserole equipped with a lid. Add the remaining tablespoon of butter to the skillet, increase the heat to moderately high, and add the onions. Sauté the onions, tossing and stirring them frequently, until they brown slightly and become glazed on all sides, about 8 minutes. With the slotted spoon, transfer the onions to the casserole. Add the zucchini pieces, tomatoes, reserved tomato juice, oregano, basil, salt, and pepper to the casserole, and toss to mix well. Cover and refrigerate until 1 hour before final preparation.

TIME ALLOWANCE FOR FINAL PREPARATION: 1 HOUR

Preheat the oven to 350 degrees
Place the casserole, covered, in the oven and bake for 45 to 60 minutes, or until the onions and zucchini are tender when pierced with the tip of a knife.

SERVES 6

STRAWBERRIES WITH MANGO CREAM

(CREAM MAY BE PREPARED UP TO 8 HOURS IN ADVANCE)

1 large, very ripe mango, peeled, pitted, and cut in pieces
1 (8-ounce) container plain yogurt
2 tablespoons minced fresh mint leaves
1 teaspoon strained fresh lime juice
1 quart strawberries, washed and hulled
Whole mint leaves

Place the mango pieces in the bowl of a food processor fitted with a steel blade, and whirl until they are partially pureed. Add the yogurt, minced mint leaves, and lime juice, and whirl until smooth.

Transfer the Mango Cream to a glass bowl or jar, cover it tightly, and refrigerate until 1 hour before serving.

TIME ALLOWANCE FOR FINAL PREPARATION: 5 MINUTES

Divide the strawberries among six dessert plates, mounding them prettily. Spoon generous portions of the Mango Cream over the tops of the berries. Garnish with whole mint leaves.

SERVES 6

SHORT-ORDER CHICKEN FOR SIX

Leek and Asparagus Soup

Super-Swift Roast Chicken

Wild Rice

Carrot Salad with Dill

Upside-Down Pear Pie

Food people—that is, those in the business of producing or writing about food—quite naturally love to talk food. In fact, sometimes I think that's all they talk about. And if they're in the restaurant business—as is my dear friend Sally Darr, owner and chef of New York's well-known La Tulipe—they also love simple food when they have a night off to cook for themselves.

During a culinary gossip session a few years ago, Sally told me she had started roasting chicken a new way, at a considerably higher temperature and for a shorter time than is customary. "It's simply sensational," Sally reported with her contagious enthusiasm. "The skin is crisp and the meat is juicy."

For my very next meal, I roasted a small chicken in Sally's manner. As promised, the results were "sensational." I then tested the method on a range of sizes, even on an 8-pound capon. They all worked beautifully. The version given in this menu is basically Sally Darr's, fancied up a bit with tarragon butter.

I suggest you start the meal with Leek and Asparagus Soup, refreshing either hot or cold. Asparagus seem to be available year-round these days, and some Mexican imports are almost the equal in quality—despite their long trip—of local asparagus at the height of their season. With the chicken, serve toothsome wild rice, a special treat and a nice foil to what some regard as a prosaic entree (although, after they taste the chicken, your guests will agree it's anything but ordinary). Wild rice expands more in cooking than white rice does, so a little goes a long way. A tangy, colorful carrot salad perked up with dill also fits the bill.

Finish your dinner with Upside-Down Pear Pie. It's a muted, subtle version of the popular Tart Tatin (or Upside-Down Apple Pie), and it's every bit as good, if not better.

LEEK AND ASPARAGUS SOUP

(MAY BE PARTIALLY PREPARED UP TO 24 HOURS IN ADVANCE)

1 pound fresh asparagus, tough ends trimmed and discarded
1 large leek, roots and green leaves trimmed and discarded, thoroughly cleaned,
*   cut into 1/4-inch slices crosswise*
4 cups chicken stock
1 tablespoon unsalted butter
1/2 teaspoon salt
Freshly ground black pepper
1 cup heavy cream

Cut off the tender asparagus tips and reserve. Cut the stalks into 1-inch lengths. Place the asparagus pieces (not the tips) and leek slices in a 2- to 3-quart saucepan. Cover them with the chicken stock and bring it to a boil. Lower the heat, partially cover, and simmer the vegetables for 20 minutes, or until the asparagus is tender when pierced with the tip of a knife.

Meanwhile, cut the reserved asparagus tips in half lengthwise. In a skillet equipped with a tight-fitting lid, melt the butter over low heat. Add the asparagus tips and toss to coat all the pieces with butter. Cover the skillet and steam the tips for 5 minutes, or until they are still bright green and slightly crunchy in texture. If you are preparing the soup within 6 hours of serving it, reserve the asparagus tips, covered, in a cool corner of the kitchen. If not, refrigerate them until final preparation.

When the asparagus pieces simmering in the stock are tender, remove the saucepan from the heat and to let it cool slightly. When it is cool enough to handle, ladle one-third of its contents into the container of a blender, and whirl until the vegetables are as smooth as fibrous vegetables can become. Set a strainer over a large bowl and pour the puree into it. Repeat until the asparagus pieces and leeks have been pureed. Push as much of the mixture through the strainer as you can, using a wooden spoon. Discard the pulp. Add the salt, pepper, and cream. Mix thoroughly.

Cover and refrigerate the soup. If you are serving it cold, refrigerate for at least 3 hours. If you plan to serve it hot, refrigerate until the final preparation.

TIME ALLOWANCE FOR FINAL PREPARATION: 5 TO 15 MINUTES

If you are serving the soup cold, ladle it into individual soup bowls and divide the asparagus tips evenly among them.

If you are serving the soup hot, transfer the soup to a saucepan and heat slowly over moderately low heat, stirring occasionally, for 10 minutes. If the asparagus tips have been refrigerated, warm them briefly over low heat until they have come to room temperature. Ladle the hot soup into six heated soup bowls and divide the asparagus tips among them.

SERVES 6

SUPER-SWIFT ROAST CHICKEN

◆

(MAY BE PARTIALLY PREPARED UP TO 2 HOURS IN ADVANCE)

1 (5- to 6-pound) roasting chicken
2 tablespoons unsalted butter
2 teaspoons dried tarragon
¼ teaspoon freshly ground black pepper
Watercress sprigs

Remove any clumps of fat from the inside of the chicken. Place them in a small frying pan, preferably one with a nonstick surface. Slowly render the fat over very low heat. When all the fat is rendered, remove the pan from the heat and set it aside.

Wash the chicken thoroughly. Stuff the cavity with paper towels to absorb all remaining moisture.

In a small bowl, mix the butter with 1 teaspoon of the tarragon and stir until well combined.

Gently ease your forefinger under the skin of the chicken from the vent end of the bird and make a 2-inch-wide pocket on either side of the breastbone as far toward the neck end as you can reach without actually reaching all the way through. (You want to form pockets, not tunnels.) Press equal amounts of the tarragon butter into each pocket, pushing them up toward the neck by gently massaging the bird's skin on the outside. Sprinkle the skin with the pepper and the remaining teaspoon of tarragon. You do not have to truss the bird; the skin will crisp better over all the surfaces if you leave the legs askew, but if you prefer a neat, compact-looking roast, truss it. Cover the chicken loosely with plastic wrap and set it in a cool corner of the kitchen until final preparation.

TIME ALLOWANCE FOR FINAL PREPARATION: 1½ HOURS

Preheat the oven to 425 degrees. Calculate the chicken's cooking time, figuring 15 minutes per pound.

Remove the paper towels from the chicken's cavity.

Warm the rendered fat. Place the chicken on a rack in a roasting pan and brush its skin with some of the rendered fat. Roast the chicken for the prescribed time, basting it two or three times with the remaining rendered fat. Do not lower the oven temperature while the chicken cooks. (To test for doneness, pierce the thigh with the tines of a fork. The juices should run clear: if they don't, roast the bird 10 minutes longer.)

When the chicken is done, transfer it to a heated serving platter and garnish it with watercress sprigs.

SERVES 6

CARROT SALAD WITH DILL

(MAY BE PARTIALLY PREPARED UP TO 6 HOURS IN ADVANCE;
MUST BE PREPARED AT LEAST 30 MINUTES IN ADVANCE)

2 recipes Vinaigrette (see page 24)
2 teaspoons sugar
3 tablespoons grated orange rind
1½ pounds carrots, peeled, ends trimmed
½ cup minced fresh dillweed
12 to 18 large Boston lettuce leaves, washed and dried

Place the vinaigrette in a bowl and add the sugar and orange rind. Whisk briefly. Let the orange macerate in the vinaigrette for at least 30 minutes before dressing the carrots.

TIME ALLOWANCE FOR FINAL PREPARATION: 15 MINUTES

Grate the carrots. Transfer them to a salad bowl. Add the dillweed and toss to mix until the dill is evenly distributed throughout the carrots.

Whisk the vinaigrette briskly. Pour it over the carrots and toss until the dressing has coated all the carrots.

Arrange 2 or 3 lettuce leaves on 6 salad plates. Mound equal portions of the carrot salad on top of them.

SERVES 6

UPSIDE-DOWN PEAR PIE

(MAY BE PARTIALLY PREPARED UP TO 6 HOURS IN ADVANCE)

1½ cups sugar
⅓ cup water
2 tablespoons unsalted butter
8 ripe pears (about 3 pounds), peeled, cored, and cut in eighths
½ teaspoon ground cinnamon
1 sheet frozen puff pastry (about ½ pound), thawed
1 cup heavy cream, whipped

Generously butter the bottom and sides of a 2-inch deep, 9½-inch round pie plate.

Place 1 cup of the sugar and the water in a small skillet over moderately high heat. Stir only until the sugar dissolves. Bring the syrup to a boil (but do not stir anymore or it may crystallize) and cook until it starts to turn golden brown. Immediately remove the pan from the heat and pour the caramelizing syrup into the prepared pie plate, swirling it around to coat the bottom and sides as evenly as possible.

Melt the butter in a large skillet. Add the pear slices. Sprinkle the pears with the remaining ½ cup of sugar and the cinnamon. Cook the pears over moderate heat until they begin to soften, about 8 to 12 minutes, depending on their ripeness. Toss the pears occasionally as they cook. Remove the pan from the heat and cool.

When the pears are cool enough to handle, select the most uniform slices and arrange them in concentric circles on top of the now-hardened caramel. Pile the remaining slices on top. (The arrangement of the top slices does not matter, as they will not be visible.) Cover the pie plate with plastic wrap and set it aside in a cool corner of the kitchen.

Cut a round of cardboard 9½ inches in diameter. Place it on top of the puff pastry and use it as a guide to cut out a circle of pastry. Do not cut the pastry with a sawing motion, but instead cut straight down with the tip of a sharp knife. (It is important that the edges of the pastry are not sealed, or it will not rise properly.) Place the pastry on the cardboard in the freezer section of your refrigerator until final preparation.

TIME ALLOWANCE FOR FINAL PREPARATION: 35 MINUTES

Preheat the oven to 400 degrees.

Remove the puff pastry circle from the freezer and allow it to thaw for 10 minutes. Cut three slashes in the center for vents.

Gently lay the puff pastry on top of the pears. Bake the pie for 20 to 25 minutes, or until the crust is nicely puffed and golden. Using oven mitts, invert a serving platter over the pie and turn it upside down. The pie should slip onto the serving platter very easily. Serve it steaming hot, accompanied by the whipped cream.

SERVES 6

SAVORY SWORDFISH FOR SIX

Fresh Cream of Tomato Soup

Grilled Swordfish Braciole

Cheese-Crusted Eggplant Sticks

Buttered Beet Tops

Apple Tart

Summer brings many culinary blessings: local tomatoes, an abundance of fresh fish and shellfish, a plethora of berries, and wonderful tree-ripened fruit. This menu ideally should be produced in summer because the principal ingredients must be at their prime.

Take Fresh Cream of Tomato Soup, served hot or cold. To make it excel, use local tomatoes, "hot" off the vine. Canned tomatoes or pallid imports from Florida and California just won't give you the same results. (The soup won't ever be bad, mind you, but it will be so much better with vine-ripened tomatoes.) Besides the good tomatoes, the soup's secret is the orange juice, which adds something very special.

Along the same line, consider swordfish, without a doubt one of the most popular fish in the United States. Fortunately, swordfish freezes very well, so it is available throughout the United States year-round. (If you are fortunate enough to live near the sea, you know what a great delicacy fresh swordfish is.)

Swordfish is caught by two methods: harpooning and deep-lining. Harpooning is done only in summer; deep-lining is done year-round. When the fish is harpooned, it dies quickly of exposure to air, and is brought to market almost immediately. When a swordfish is caught on deep lines, it dies by drowning, which produces a slightly mushy texture when the fish is cooked. Most frozen swordfish is deep-lined. If you ever have the opportunity to buy fresh harpooned swordfish, grab it. You're in for a treat.

Swordfish Braciole may present something of a challenge in obtaining the thin slices required. All I can advise is that you go to your most favorite and friendliest local fishmonger WHEN HE ISN'T BUSY and plead with him to humor your request. With his wonderfully sharp knives, he wil be able to slice the fish as you want it. It will require a little extra effort because he won't be able to just reach into his display case, pull out a swordfish steak, wrap it up, and hand it to you. So smile your best smile and wheedle it out of him!

Eggplants, of course, are available all year, although they are better when locally grown. Cut into sticks, rolled in cheese-flavored bread crumbs, and baked, they make a different and very appetizing vegetable no matter what the season. The recipe is all the more attractive because it requires no last-minute hoopla.

Although autumn is the season for apples—and what fun it is to go to orchards to pick them yourself!—storage is so sophisticated these days that apples are good any time. The Apple Tart is easy to make and tasty. What more can you ask? It's pretty, too.

FRESH CREAM OF TOMATO SOUP

(MAY BE PARTIALLY PREPARED UP TO 24 HOURS IN ADVANCE)

1 tablespoon unsalted butter
1 cup coarsely chopped onions
2 tablespoons minced shallots
3 pounds tomatoes, peeled, seeded, and coarsely chopped
1 cup strained fresh orange juice
2 tablespoons minced fresh tarragon (or 2 teaspoons dried tarragon)
1 teaspoon sugar
1/2 teaspoon salt
1/4 teaspoon freshly ground black pepper
1/2 cup sour cream
1 cup heavy cream
1 tablespoon minced fresh chives

In a large nonreactive skillet, melt the butter over low heat. Add the onions and shallots and sauté them, stirring occasionally, until soft but not brown, about

5 minutes. Add the tomatoes, orange juice, tarragon, sugar, salt, and pepper, and blend well. Bring the mixture to a boil, then simmer it, covered, over moderately low heat for 30 minutes. Remove from the heat and cool.

Ladle the mixture into the bowl of a food processor fitted with a steel blade. Puree until smooth. Add the sour cream and whirl until blended. Transfer the mixture to a large pitcher or plastic container and stir in the heavy cream. Taste, and adjust the seasoning to your taste.

Cover and refrigerate the soup. If you are serving it cold, allow at least 3 hours for it to become chilled. If you are serving it hot, keep it refrigerated until final preparation.

TIME ALLOWANCE FOR FINAL PREPARATION: 5 TO 15 MINUTES

If you are serving the soup cold, divide it among 6 soup bowls. Sprinkle the chives on top.

If you are serving the soup hot, transfer it to a saucepan and heat slowly over moderately low heat, stirring occasionally, for about 10 minutes. Do not let it come to a boil.

Ladle the hot soup into six heated soup bowls and garnish with the chives.

SERVES 6

GRILLED SWORDFISH BRACIOLE

♦

(MAY BE PARTIALLY PREPARED UP TO 12 HOURS IN ADVANCE)

3 pounds swordfish, sliced ¼ inch thick
1½ cups olive oil
1 teaspoon minced garlic
¾ cup finely chopped onions
1½ cup bread crumbs
1 teaspoon grated lemon rind
1 tablespoon dried sweet basil
5 tablespoons minced fresh parsley
½ teaspoon salt
Freshly ground black pepper
4 tablespoons unsalted butter, melted
6 lemon wedges

Swordfish varies enormously in size. You should have approximately 3 pounds to feed six people, but more important for this recipe is the thinness of the slices. When you get the steaks home, cut off the skin and the so-called tails (save them for the cat, or some such use). Place each steak between two pieces of wax paper and whack the fish with a cleaver, mallet, or rolling pin until it is even thinner! If the steaks are from a large fish, you should be able to cut two 3- by 10-inch strips from each steak. If the steaks are small, you will have only one strip 3 to 4 inches wide and perhaps 8 inches long. The precise size doesn't matter. The thinness does!

Prepare all your strips. Cut some kitchen cord into 8-inch lengths and set them aside while you make the stuffing.

Pour 1 cup of the olive oil in a skillet and sauté the garlic and onion over moderate heat until wilted, about 5 minutes.

Place the bread crumbs in a shallow bowl. Scrape the contents of the skillet over the bread crumbs. Add the lemon rind, basil, 3 tablespoons of the parsley, salt, and pepper, and toss to mix well. Divide the mixture evenly among the prepared swordfish strips and spread the stuffing with a spatula or flat knife to within ½ inch of the strips' edges. Starting at one end, roll each strip to make a 3-inch-long cylinder. Do not worry if the fish is torn in places; it adheres to itself quite well. Secure the rolls with the cut lengths of kitchen cord. Transfer the rolls to a plate or platter, cover with plastic wrap, and refrigerate until 1 hour before final preparation.

TIME ALLOWANCE FOR FINAL PREPARATION: 20 MINUTES FOR GRILLING THE SWORDFISH
PLUS TIME TO PREPARE COALS

Prepare a charcoal grill. When the coals are red-hot but not flaming you can begin cooking the fish.

Brush the swordfish rolls with the remaining ½ cup of olive oil. Place the fish on a greased rack about 5 inches above the coals. Do not allow the rolls to touch. If the grill has a cover, use it but keep the vents open. If the grill has no cover, watch the coals carefully and try to prevent flaming by sprinkling them with water if flames rise up. Turn the rolls every 5 minutes. In 15 minutes the fish should be nicely cooked. To make sure, cut off the end of one roll and taste. If the fish is not cooked through, cook 5 minutes longer.

Transfer the swordfish rolls to a heated platter and carefully cut off the strings with sharp scissors. (The cooked fish is delicate and tears easily.) Drizzle the melted butter over the rolls and sprinkle with the remaining 2 tablespoons of parsley. Serve with the lemon wedges.

SERVES 6

CHEESE-CRUSTED EGGPLANT STICKS

(MAY BE PARTIALLY PREPARED UP TO 4 HOURS IN ADVANCE)

1½ pounds eggplant (2 small or 1 large)
¼ cup plus 1 teaspoon salt
1 cup bread crumbs, preferably homemade
1 cup freshly grated Parmesan cheese
2 teaspoons dried oregano
¼ teaspoon freshly ground black pepper
2 eggs, lightly beaten
1 cup flour

Cut off both ends of the eggplant. Peel the eggplant, then cut it into sticks approximately 2 inches long by ½ inch square. (The size will depend on the size of the eggplant. A length up to 3 inches is fine.) Place the eggplant sticks in a colander. Sprinkle with ¼ cup salt. Toss to coat all sides of each stick. Weight the sticks down with canned goods or a heavy frying pan. Allow them to drain for 1 hour. Place them on paper toweling and pat dry with extra toweling. Do not be concerned if the eggplant discolors.

While the eggplant is draining, combine the bread crumbs, cheese, oregano, remaining 1 teaspoon salt, and pepper in a shallow bowl and mix well with your fingers. Place the eggs in another shallow bowl, and the flour in a third bowl. Grease two cookie sheets generously with butter (or use nonstick sheets, ungreased). Arrange the bowls from left to right as follows: flour, eggs, bread crumbs. Place the cookie sheets on the far right.

When the eggplant sticks have finished draining and are completely dried, dredge them lightly in the flour, shaking off any excess. Immerse them completely in the beaten egg. Roll them on all sides in the crumb mixture. Set the breaded sticks in rows side by side but not touching each other on the cookie sheets. Cover loosely with plastic wrap and hold for final preparation.

TIME ALLOWANCE FOR FINAL PREPARATION: 35 MINUTES

Preheat the oven to 400 degrees.
Bake the sticks, uncovered, for 25 minutes, turning once. Serve immediately, piping hot.

SERVES 6

APPLE TART

◆

1 sheet frozen puff pastry (about ½ pound), thawed
6 Golden Delicious apples, peeled and halved
½ cup sugar
4 tablespoons unsalted butter, cut into bits
3 tablespoons apricot preserves
1 cup heavy cream, whipped (optional)

Preheat the oven to 400 degrees.

On a lightly floured surface, roll out the puff pastry into a 14-inch square or round. Transfer it to a 12-inch tart pan with a removable bottom, gently pressing it into the pan and trimming off any excess.

Core the halved apples with a melon-baller. Place them cut side down, then cut them into ¼-inch-thick slices. Lay the slices along the outer edge of the tart by fanning them slightly to one side so that they overlap and still retain their half-apple shape. Repeat until the outer edge is filled. Then arrange the slices decoratively in the center area of the tart. Sprinkle the entire surface of the apple tart with the sugar, then dot with the butter pieces.

Bake the tart 20 minutes, then check to see that one side of the tart is not browning more rapidly than the other. If it is, turn the tart a half-circle. Bake 25 minutes longer. Carefully remove the tart from the oven and place on a rack to cool.

Melt the apricot preserves in a small saucepan over low heat, stirring constantly. Strain the preserves and discard the pulp. Using a pastry brush, gently brush the apricot glaze over the apples. Carefully remove the sides from the tart pan, letting the tart continue to rest on the metal bottom of the pan, and place the tart on a platter. Serve at room temperature, with or without whipped cream.

SERVES 6

A DOUBLE TASTE
OF THE ORIENT
FOR SIX

Teriyaki Flank Steak

Oriental Noodles with Chinese Cabbage

Snow Peas Tossed in Butter

Chocolate Feather Pie with Coconut Crust

Flank steaks used to be way down on the list of desirable beef steak cuts. They were tough and stringy and had to be cut on the diagonal to achieve any semblance of tenderness. But they had one redeeming virtue: they were cheap. So my impoverished friends and I, struggling on our minuscule postgraduate salaries, occasionally bought one when our craving for "red" meat needed to be satisfied.

To spark up the meat as best we could, we embarked on a series of experiments in preparation and presentation that ran the gamut from stuffing to marinating to dousing the meat in hideous ketchup sauces. When one particularly talented friend borrowed from her knowledge of Japanese cuisine, Teriyaki Flank Steak was born, to the delight of the rest of us. Unlike many recipes, it did not die with time. I used it when my children were young and had to be coddled into accepting "foreign" food. And, while flank steaks still need to be cut on the diagonal for the sake of tenderness, I often prepare them teriyaki style when I want a slightly different but very easy meat dish. Flank steaks no longer can be called cheap, but that's the way of all things.

I suggest serving Oriental Noodles with Chinese Cabbage with the flank steak. Even though the steak shows a Japanese influence and the noodles a Chinese influence, they go well together. In fact, the noodle dish was served to me by friends in Hawaii, and everybody knows that state's cuisine is a real mishmash of heritages.

For dessert, I offer a figure-defying chocolate pie with an unusual coconut crust. The pie should feed as many as eight but then, it is so delectable that few can resist seconds. I wouldn't count on having any leftovers.

TERIYAKI FLANK STEAK

◆

(MAY BE PARTIALLY PREPARED UP TO 6 HOURS IN ADVANCE;
MUST BE PARTIALLY PREPARED AT LEAST 4 HOURS IN ADVANCE)

1 (2- to 2½-pound) flank steak, trimmed
1 teaspoon minced garlic
¼ cup soy sauce (preferably light)
¼ cup sake (rice wine) or dry sherry
1 tablespoon brown sugar
2 teaspoons ground ginger

In a platter or shallow baking dish large enough to contain the flank steak comfortably, combine the garlic, soy sauce, sake, sugar, and ginger. Mix until the sugar and ginger have dissolved. Add the flank steak, turning it once or twice to coat it well with the marinade. Cover it loosely with plastic wrap and marinate it in the refrigerator for 4 to 6 hours. Turn it occasionally to recoat it with the marinade. Remove it from the refrigerator at least 1 hour before final preparation.

TIME ALLOWANCE FOR FINAL PREPARATION: 15 MINUTES

Preheat the broiler.

Remove the streak from the marinade and pat it dry with paper toweling. Discard the marinade. Place the steak on a flat rack in a roasting pan and set it about 3 inches below the broiler element. Broil it for 3 to 4 minutes on each side for rare meat. (Timing depends on the intensity of heat.) Flank steak should be served rare; it tends to toughen the longer it cooks. However, if you prefer medium or well-done meat, broil it 1 minute longer on each side for medium, or 2 minutes for well-done. Test for doneness by making a small incision in a thick section of the meat. If it is to your liking, transfer it to a heated platter and let it rest 5 minutes. Carve it in very thin slices on the diagonal to increase its tenderness.

SERVES 6

NOTE: Sometimes it is difficult to find large flank steaks. Feel free to substitute two small steaks for the one large one. You will have enough marinade for two steaks, but reduce the cooking time slightly.

ORIENTAL NOODLES WITH CHINESE CABBAGE

(MAY BE PARTIALLY PREPARED UP TO 3 HOURS IN ADVANCE)

½ red pepper, cored and seeded
5 scallions, roots trimmed
1 (1-pound) Chinese cabbage, outer leaves removed
1 (14-ounce package) Chinese-style soft noodles
2 tablespoons oil
1 tablespoon imported sesame oil
¼ cup light soy sauce
¼ cup sake (rice wine) or dry white wine

This noodle dish is prepared essentially by the stir-fry method. A certain amount of preparation may be done ahead of time to facilitate the last-minute cooking.

Cut the red pepper into ¼-inch dice. Place it in a cup, cover with plastic wrap, and reserve for final preparation.

Slice the scallions, including the green leaves, very thin. Collect the white slices and green slices separately in small bowls, cover them with plastic wrap, and reserve.

Slice the cabbage crosswise into ⅓-inch-thick slices. (You should have about 3 cups.) Reserve it, well wrapped, in another bowl.

TIME ALLOWANCE FOR FINAL PREPARATION: 15 MINUTES

Fill a 3- to 4-quart kettle with water to within 2 inches of the rim. Bring it to a boil. When it is boiling, add the noodles, stir to separate them, and cook for exactly 1 minute after the water starts to boil again. Immediately drain the noodles and refresh them in cold water. Set them aside in a colander to drain.

Pour the oil and sesame oil in a wok or large skillet placed over moderately high heat. When the oils are hot, add the red pepper and white scallions and cook, stirring constantly, for 1 minute. Add the Chinese cabbage, stir briefly, cover, and steam 1 minute. Add the noodles, soy sauce, and wine, and stir until heated through, about 1 to 2 minutes. Transfer the noodle mixture to a heated serving dish, sprinkle with the green scallions, and serve immediately.

SERVES 6

CHOCOLATE FEATHER PIE WITH COCONUT CRUST

(MAY BE PREPARED UP TO 8 HOURS IN ADVANCE;
MUST BE PREPARED AT LEAST 3 HOURS IN ADVANCE)

CRUST

3 tablespoons unsalted butter, melted
1¼ cups shredded sweetened coconut (about 5 ounces)

To make the crust: Preheat the oven to 325 degrees.

Generously butter the bottom and sides of a 9-inch pie plate.

In a mixing bowl, sprinkle the melted butter over the shredded coconut. Toss until all the coconut is moistened with the butter. Firmly press the mixture into the pie plate, building it up on the sides. Place the pie shell in the oven and bake for 20 to 30 minutes, or until the coconut has turned a delicate brown. Remove it from the oven and cool.

FILLING

1 cup unsalted butter, softened
1½ cups sugar
3 ounces unsweetened chocolate, melted and cooled
4 eggs
2 teaspoons vanilla
2 tablespoons coarsely grated semisweet chocolate

To make the filling: In the bowl of an electric mixer, whip the butter until light. Add the sugar very gradually, periodically scraping down the sides of the bowl. When the sugar is thoroughly combined with the butter, beat in the melted chocolate. Add the eggs, one at a time, beating for 5 minutes after each addition. (This is necessary to obtain the right consistency.) Finally beat in the vanilla. Scrape the mixture into the prepared coconut pie shell and refrigerate for at least 2 hours to chill before serving.

Just before serving, sprinkle the chocolate curls over the surface of the pie.

SERVES 6

ENTERTAINING
EIGHT

Entertaining a group of eight borders on The Big Time. It is still manageable, however. It rarely requires adding leaves to the dining room table or bringing out some small tables for the greater-than-usual number of guests. It generally doesn't necessitate borrowing or renting more equipment. Furthermore, feeding and serving eight is not so demanding a number that it means hiring extra help. It can all be managed relatively easily by one or two hosts who, if they are quick on their feet and unobtrusive, can bring on the food, remove used plates, keep the wine glasses filled, and spark an occasional conversational lag—all without disturbing their guests or, even more important, making them feel guilty.

Looking at it positively, eight is actually a relatively small number. But, unlike entertaining for six—where everyone seems to partake of one conversational topic at a time—eight guests will subdivide into a couple of groupings, regroup and subdivide again into different units several times during the course of an evening. Discussions are generally animated, and the sound of many voices rising and falling in intense conversation contributes mightily to the success of the event.

Because of this size factor, the evening is a bit more restrained than smaller dinners. Although some hosts may like to have their guests help themselves informally to the food (which can be presented very attractively on a sideboard or an abutting smaller table), others may prefer to serve it to their guests from the head of the table.

I have a sturdy hot-table on wheels to which I am devoted. It not only serves to keep the food warm, it also leaves me more space on the dining table for candles, special floral decorations, or my budding collection of individual salt and pepper shakers. I position the hot-table close by my side and am able to serve very easily from it. If I am presenting a roast, which I often serve when entertaining eight, I always carve it in the kitchen. Much as I love to show it off at the table, I refrain. It's not half as dramatic that way, I will agree, but it's considerably more efficient. Furthermore, how many of us are skilled carvers, with a surgeon's grace? We deserve the privacy of our kitchens and not fourteen alarmed or sympathetic eyes watching us as we hack away.

I like hosting a party of eight. It's big enough so that I don't worry about my guests' overall compatibility or faltering conversations. And it's small enough so that I can manage it all by myself.

A ROYAL FEAST
FOR EIGHT

Crown Roast of Lamb

Wild Rice Pilaf with Currants

Baked Stuff Tomatoes

*Mixed Green Salad with
Vinaigrette**

Lemon Mousse Crêpes

Every now and then, for one reason or another, you have to pull out the stops and come up with a perfectly splendid, albeit expensive, dinner. It may be for an important relative, for the boss and his wife, or for a very special occasion, such as a twenty-first birthday. At these times, price is no object. It's the dinner that counts.

Crown roast of lamb is truly fit for royalty—and for a royal purse. Since it's going to cost a bundle anyway, don't make small economies and buy from a cut-rate butcher. Seek out the best, and get the best. (In the end, the difference will only be a few dollars.) You want good-tasting meat expertly assembled.

There are many ways *not* to cook a crown roast; I suggest you follow this menu's recipe to achieve juicy, succulent results. If your butcher presents you with a mass of ground lamb in the center of the crown, thank him, but reserve it for another meal such as Lamb Patties, Indian Style, on page 50. (A lamb-stuffed crown requires much longer roasting, which will render the delicate chops gray and tasteless.) Instead, stuff the crown after it has finished roasting with a delectable wild rice pilaf, studded with currants. Wild rice also is expensive, but you need only 1½ cups because it triples in volume, which shouldn't break the bank.

Lemon Mousse Crêpes are the ideal dessert for this luxurious dinner. I first tasted them at a celebrated restaurant in Hong Kong, and they so impressed me that I tried re-creating them when I got home. They're light and lemony, and look so appealing—a very festive ending to an extraordinarily festive meal.

* Double the recipe on page 24.

CROWN ROAST OF LAMB

(MAY BE PARTIALLY PREPARED 12 HOURS IN ADVANCE)

1 crown roast of lamb, consisting of 4 racks tied together (about 4 pounds)
½ teaspoon salt
Freshly ground black pepper
1 clove garlic, peeled and cut in slivers (optional)
¼ cup unsalted butter, melted
1 recipe Wild Rice Pilaf with Currants (see page 137)
Sprigs of fresh mint

Ask your butcher to prepare a crown of lamb by tying together 4 racks into a crown shape, trimming off all excess fat, and scraping the ends of the rib bones clean.

Sprinkle the meat all over with the salt and pepper; rub the salt and pepper well into the chops. If you like garlic, make small slits in the meat with the tip of a sharp paring knife and insert garlic slivers. Wad a large piece of aluminum foil into a ball, and place it in the center of the crown so that the crown will hold its shape during the roasting period. Cover the rib ends of the crown with foil to prevent them from charring. Refrigerate the crown, covered, until 2 hours before final preparation.

TIME ALLOWANCE FOR FINAL PREPARATION: 45 MINUTES

Preheat oven to 425 degrees.

Stand the lamb crown upright in a roasting pan and brush it with some of the melted butter. Roast it for 30 minutes for rare meat, 35 minutes for pink. At 10-minute intervals, brush the crown again with melted butter. Remove the lamb from the oven after the prescribed roasting time and let it rest for 5 minutes. Discard the aluminum foil from the crown's center and rib bones.

Transfer the lamb to a heated serving platter. Fill its center with the hot Wild Rice Pilaf. Cover the rib bones with paper frills, garnish the roast with mint sprigs, and serve immediately, allowing about 3 ribs per person.

SERVES 8

WILD RICE PILAF WITH CURRANTS

◆

(MAY BE PARTIALLY PREPARED UP TO 24 HOURS IN ADVANCE)

½ cup pine nuts (pignoli)
1½ cups wild rice, rinsed
½ cup dried currants
3 tablespoons unsalted butter
¾ cup finely chopped onions
Salt and freshly ground black pepper to taste
2 tablespoons chopped fresh mint

Place the pine nuts in a small nonstick skillet and toast them to a golden brown over moderate heat, stirring occasionally. Remove the pan from the heat and reserve the nuts.

Fill a 2- to 3-quart saucepan two-thirds full of salted water. Bring the water to a boil. Add the wild rice and bring the water to a second boil, stirring constantly. Lower the heat, partially cover the rice, and simmer 30 minutes. Stir the rice once, add the currants, partially cover, and simmer 15 to 30 minutes longer, or until the rice has fully expanded and is just tender but not mushy. Immediately drain the rice and currants and transfer them to the top of a large double boiler.

While the rice is simmering, melt the butter over low heat in a medium skillet. Add the onions and sauté them, stirring frequently, until soft, about 5 minutes. Set the onions aside until the rice and currants have been transferred to the double boiler.

Scrape the onions over the rice. Add the reserved toasted pine nuts. Toss the rice until all the ingredients are well mixed. Taste, and add salt and pepper as desired. Cover and set aside in a cool corner of the kitchen until final preparation.

TIME ALLOWANCE FOR FINAL PREPARATION: 25 MINUTES

Place the top of the double boiler over boiling water. Reduce the heat, cover the rice, and steam it for 15 to 20 minutes, turning it occasionally, or until it is very hot. Mound the rice in the center of the crown roast and sprinkle the chopped mint on top.

SERVES 8

BAKED STUFFED TOMATOES

◆

(MAY BE PARTIALLY PREPARED UP TO 24 HOURS IN ADVANCE)

8 slightly underripe tomatoes (about ½ pound each), halved crosswise
4 tablespoons unsalted butter
⅓ cup minced shallots
2 cups finely chopped mushrooms
2 teaspoons crushed dried rosemary
½ teaspoon salt
Freshly ground black pepper
4 teaspoons toasted bread crumbs, preferably homemade

With a melon-baller, scoop the pulp out of the tomatoes, being careful not to break the skins, which will serve as shells. Place the shells upside down on a rack to drain. Coarsely chop the pulp and place in a strainer to drain. Reserve shells and pulp.

Melt 2 tablespoons of the butter in a 1- to 2-quart nonreactive saucepan. Add the shallots and mushrooms. Sauté them over low heat, stirring occasionally, until the juices evaporate, about 10 minutes. Mix in the rosemary, salt, and pepper. Remove the saucepan from the heat, and cool. Add the chopped tomato pulp and mix well.

Spoon the tomato and mushroom mixture into the reserved tomato shells. Sprinkle each stuffed tomato with ½ teaspoon of bread crumbs and dot with the remaining 2 tablespoons of butter. Place the stuffed tomatoes in a shallow baking dish large enough to contain them compactly, cover the dish with plastic wrap, and refrigerate until 1 hour before final preparation. (If you are preparing the tomatoes within 6 hours of final preparation, merely set them aside, covered, in a cool corner of the kitchen.)

TIME ALLOWANCE FOR FINAL PREPARATION: 45 MINUTES

Preheat the oven to 350 degrees.
Bake the tomatoes, uncovered, for 40 minutes, or until the tops are lightly browned. Serve immediately.

SERVES 8

LEMON MOUSSE CRÊPES

◆

(THE CRÊPES MAY BE PREPARED UP TO 3 DAYS IN ADVANCE;
THE FILLING MAY BE PARTIALLY PREPARED UP TO 6 HOURS IN ADVANCE;
THE FILLED CRÊPES MUST BE ASSEMBLED JUST BEFORE BAKING)

CRÊPES
1 cup milk
1 egg
2 egg yolks
3 tablespoons sugar
1 tablespoon unsalted butter, melted
¾ cup flour
1 tablespoon unsalted butter

To make the crêpes: In a blender or the bowl of a food processor fitted with a steel blade, combine the milk, egg, egg yolks, sugar, and melted butter, and whirl for 10 seconds. Add the flour through the feed tube and whirl until smooth. Let the batter stand for 1 hour.

In a crêpe pan or medium-size nonstick skillet set over moderate heat, melt the tablespoon of butter to grease the pan. Pour a small amount of batter into the skillet; it should form about a 3-inch circle. Lift the pan and, with a circular motion, swirl the batter so that it spreads out into a round about 5 inches in diameter. (The crêpes should be as thin as possible.) Cook the crêpe until small bubbles form and its surface is nearly dry. Carefully lift the crêpe with a spatula and turn it over, being careful not to tear it. Cook the other side for just a few seconds. It will not tan as nicely as the first side. Transfer the crêpe to a plate, good side up. Top it with a small square of wax paper.

(Sometimes the first two crêpes do not turn out well. The skillet may not have attained the right heat. Be prepared to discard them. You will have enough batter.)

Repeat the procedure until all the batter has been used, which should produce between 18 and 22 crêpes, even allowing for a few discards. Separate each crêpe from the next with wax paper. It should not be necessary to grease the pan between crêpes after the first few have been made.

Cover the stack of crêpes well with plastic wrap. Refrigerate until 1 hour before final preparation.

LEMON MOUSSE FILLING

4 tablespoons unsalted butter
½ cup flour
1 cup half-and-half
¾ cup strained fresh lemon juice
4 tablespoons grated lemon rind
3 egg yolks
1½ cups sugar
Pinch of salt
5 egg whites
Confectioners' sugar

To make the filling: Melt the butter over low heat in a small saucepan. Add the flour and cook it for 1 or 2 minutes, stirring constantly. Slowly add the half-and-half, beating continuously so that no lumps form. Beat in the lemon juice and rind. Off the heat, add the egg yolks, one at a time, beating after each addition. Return the mixture to the heat and slowly stir in 1 cup of the sugar and a pinch of salt. Stir until the sugar has dissolved, then cook, stirring occasionally, until the custard thickens. Remove the pan from the heat. Transfer the mixture to a bowl, cover it with plastic wrap, and refrigerate until 1 hour before final preparation.

TIME ALLOWANCE FOR FINAL PREPARATION: 25 MINUTES

Preheat the oven to 400 degrees.

In a large mixing bowl, with an electric mixer, beat the egg whites with a pinch of salt until frothy. Slowly beat in the remaining ½ cup sugar. Beat the whites until they stand in peaks. Stir one-quarter of the whites into the reserved lemon mixture to lighten it, then gently fold the mixture into the remaining whites.

Spread about 2 heaping tablespoons of the lemon mixture over the less-pretty side of each crêpe. Fold each crêpe in half, then in half again to form quarters. (The browned side of the crêpe should be on the outside.) Place the crêpes side by side on buttered cookie sheets or jelly-roll pans and bake for about 8 to 10 minutes, or until they are puffed. The filling should be light and fluffy but still somewhat moist.

Serve hot, sprinkled with confectioners' sugar, allowing two crêpes per person.

SERVES 8

A LIGHT BUT SATISFYING LUNCHEON FOR EIGHT

Shrimp and Avocado Ring with Dill Sauce

Crustless Spinach Tart

Red Pepper and Fennel Salad with Basil Vinaigrette

Hot Rolls with Sweet Butter

Fruit Salad

Coconut Upside-Down Cake

Luncheons are difficult to plan because people have such different appetites. Some barely nibble; others consume enough for ten people or so it seems to me, and I'm no slouch when it comes to food.

My solution is to serve light food, but enough of it to keep everyone happy. I like to offer several choices so that my guests can help themselves to one or more dishes and take large helpings or small. The point is, everyone must leave my table satisfied.

This menu fits the bill. The Shrimp and Avocado Ring with Dill Sauce is a spicy, tomato-based aspic. The Crustless Spinach Tart, chock-full of cheese, is filling and nutritious. The salad of Red Peppers and Fennel is pretty and an unusual taste combination. All these dishes can be made well in advance because they can be served at room temperature—even the tart, although I prefer it warm.

For dessert I like to offer a choice. At a luncheon, there are always guests who prefer fruit to a sweet. But I can't disappoint the many who relish a homemade cake or pie. Coconut Upside-Down Cake, with its freshly grated coconut, should satisfy even the fussiest guest, being moist and dense, sweet and rich, all at the same time.

SHRIMP AND AVOCADO RING WITH DILL SAUCE

(MAY BE PARTIALLY PREPARED UP TO 2 DAYS IN ADVANCE;
MUST BE PREPARED AT LEAST 5 HOURS IN ADVANCE.
SAUCE MAY BE PREPARED UP TO 2 DAYS IN ADVANCE)

3 envelopes unflavored gelatin
1 cup cold water
4 cups tomato juice
1 cup tomato ketchup
1 cup chopped celery
1/2 cup finely chopped onions
1/2 pound cooked, shelled, and deveined large shrimp, cut in half lengthwise
1 green pepper, cored, seeded, and finely chopped
1/4 cup strained fresh lemon juice
1 tablespoon prepared horseradish, drained
1/4 teaspoon salt
1 ripe avocado, peeled and thinly sliced
Sprigs of watercress

Sprinkle the gelatin over the cold water in a large mixing bowl. Let it soften for 5 minutes. Bring 2 cups of tomato juice to a boil in a small nonreactive saucepan. Pour it directly over the gelatin. Stir until the gelatin has dissolved. Add the remaining 2 cups tomato juice, the ketchup, celery, onions, shrimp, green pepper, lemon juice, horseradish, and salt. Stir well to blend.

Refrigerate the mixture for 1 to 2 hours, until the aspic has thickened to the consistency of raw egg whites. Do not allow it to solidify. (If it does, hold it at room temperature until it softens. Stir occasionally.)

Rinse a 2-quart ring mold with cold water, then drain it but do not dry it. Arrange the avocado slices attractively along the bottom of the mold. Spoon the gelatin mixture over the avocado, taking care not to disturb the arrangement. Cover the mold tightly with plastic wrap and refrigerate it until the aspic has firmed, about 2 hours, or until you are ready to serve it.

TIME ALLOWANCE FOR FINAL PREPARATION: 5 MINUTES

To unmold the aspic, immerse the mold up to its rim in a bath of hot water. Hold it there for 1 minute. Remove it from the bath and place a large, round serving platter over the mold. Turn over the mold and platter and give them a shake. The aspic should slide out easily. If it doesn't, repeat the process.

CRUSTLESS SPINACH TART

◆

(MAY BE PARTIALLY PREPARED UP TO 6 HOURS IN ADVANCE)

1 (10-ounce) package spinach, tough stems removed
1 pound ricotta cheese, at room temperature
1 cup freshly grated Parmesan cheese
3 eggs, beaten
2 tablespoons vegetable oil
1 teaspoon minced garlic
1 teaspoon salt
¼ pound mushrooms, thinly sliced
1 small zucchini (about ½ pound), ends trimmed, thinly sliced
½ green pepper, cored, seeded, and chopped

In a 2- to 3-quart nonreactive saucepan, bring 1 inch of water to a boil. Add the spinach, cover, and steam it 3 to 4 minutes over high heat, tossing occasionally, until it is *just* tender and still bright green. Drain the spinach thoroughly, squeezing out any excess water. Chop the spinach coarsely and set it aside.

In a large mixing bowl, combine the ricotta and Parmesan cheeses, eggs, oil, garlic, and salt, and beat until thoroughly blended. Add the mushrooms, zucchini, green peppers, and reserved spinach. Toss gently until mixed. Generously grease a 10-inch springform pan. Transfer the spinach mixture to the pan, using a rubber spatula. Cover tightly with plastic wrap and refrigerate until 1 hour before final preparation.

TIME ALLOWANCE FOR FINAL PREPARATION: 45 MINUTES

Preheat the oven to 350 degrees.

Bake the spinach tart for 40 minutes, or until it is firm to the touch. Remove the pan from the oven and allow it to cool slightly.

When the pan is cool enough to handle, run a knife around the edge of the pan, unlock the springform, and release the sides. Place the tart, still on the bottom of the springform, on a platter, cut it in wedges, and serve it hot or at room temperature.

SERVES 8

Garnish the aspic with watercress sprigs and serve it with Dill Sauce.

SERVES 8

NOTE: Make certain that the horseradish you are using is from a new bottle. Horseradish loses its tang within a day or two of being opened.

DILL SAUCE
1½ cups sour cream
½ cup mayonnaise
¼ cup minced fresh dillweed
Salt and freshly ground black pepper to taste

In a small mixing bowl, combine the sour cream, mayonnaise, and dill. Stir briskly until smooth and well blended. Taste and add salt and pepper as needed. Cover and refrigerate until ready to use. Transfer to a sauceboat for serving.

YIELD: ABOUT 2 CUPS SAUCE

RED PEPPER AND FENNEL SALAD WITH BASIL VINAIGRETTE

(MAY BE PARTIALLY PREPARED UP TO 3 HOURS IN ADVANCE)

4 large fennel bulbs (about 1 pound each), stalks trimmed, cut in ½-inch dice
½ pound radishes, trimmed and sliced paper-thin
3 red peppers, cored, seeded, and cut in ½-inch dice
¼ cup minced red onion
2 recipes Basil Vinaigrette (see page 37)

Line a salad bowl with paper towels. Add the fennel, radishes, peppers, and onions, and toss to mix with your fingers or a salad fork and spoon. Cover with paper toweling and refrigerate until time for final preparation.

TIME ALLOWANCE FOR FINAL PREPARATION: 5 MINUTES

Remove the toweling from the salad bowl. Shake the Basil Vinaigrette vigorously and pour three-fourths of it over the salad. Toss the salad until all the ingredients are well coated with the dressing, adding more dressing if you wish.

SERVES 8

COCONUT UPSIDE-DOWN CAKE

(MAY BE PREPARED UP TO 24 HOURS IN ADVANCE)

6 tablespoons unsalted butter
1/2 cup firmly packed light brown sugar
1 1/2 cups grated fresh coconut (see instructions below)
2 tablespoons vegetable shortening
1/2 cup white sugar
2 eggs
1 cup sifted cake flour
1 1/2 teaspoons baking powder
Pinch of salt
1/4 cup milk
1/2 teaspoon vanilla
1 cup heavy cream, whipped

Preheat the oven to 350 degrees.

Place 4 tablespoons of the butter and the brown sugar in an 8-inch-square baking dish. When the oven is warm, put the dish in the oven and leave it there until the butter melts and the sugar partially dissolves. Remove the dish from the oven and stir until the sugar completely dissolves and is well combined with the butter. Sprinkle 1 cup of the grated coconut evenly over the mixture. Set the dish aside. Keep the oven set at 350 degrees.

In a medium-size mixing bowl, combine the remaining 2 tablespoons butter and the vegetable shortening. Beat them until fluffy. Slowly add the white sugar, continuing to beat. Add the eggs, one at a time, beating well after each addition. In another bowl, sift the flour, baking powder, and salt together. Stir half the flour mixture into the egg mixture, then stir in half the milk. Stir in the remaining flour, followed by the rest of the milk. Add the vanilla and beat until smooth. Fold in the remaining 1/2 cup of grated coconut.

Pour the batter over the brown sugar and butter topping, distributing it as evenly as possible but being careful not to mix the topping and the batter. Bake the cake 45 minutes, or until a toothpick inserted in the center of the cake (but not down into the topping, which will remain somewhat liquid) comes out clean. Immediately run a knife around the edges of the baking dish to release the cake and invert it onto a serving platter. Scrape out any residue of topping in the dish and replace it on the surface of the cake.

Serve the cake warm or at room temperature, with whipped cream.

YIELD: 1 8-INCH-SQUARE CAKE

NOTE: To make grated fresh coconut, you will need a whole coconut. (When purchasing the coconut, hold it close to your ear and shake it. Buy the one that sounds the most full of liquid when shaken. Older, less flavorful coconuts tend to be dried out.)

Preheat the oven to 425 degrees.

Place the coconut on a towel (to steady it) on a hard surface, such as a floor. With an ice pick or screwdriver and a hammer, punch holes through 2 of its 3 eyes. Drain out the coconut milk. Either discard it or reserve it for another use.

Bake the coconut for 15 minutes, or until its shell has cracked. Allow it to cool slightly. Then place it back on the towel on a hard surface. Whack it with a hammer until the shell splits open. Break it up into medium-sized pieces and pry off and discard the shell. Peel away the dark brown inner skin with a sharp paring knife. Cut the coconut into smaller pieces. Drop them in batches into a food processor fitted with a steel blade and whirl 5 to 10 seconds, or until the coconut meat is finely grated.

A SPANISH CLASSIC FOR EIGHT

Cold Cream of Cucumber Soup

Paella

Mushroom and Spinach Salad*

Caramel Crème Brûlée

Many of us have enjoyed Paella (saffron rice with a medley of chicken and shellfish) at one time or another, whether in its native Spain or in Spanish restaurants in the United States. But how many of us have thought of making it at home? Paella comes in many versions, all with different varieties and proportions of meats and shellfish. Some of them include rings of squid. All depend on local custom, the availability of fresh seafood, and the inclinations of the cook.

Paella is a dream dish for do-ahead entertaining. It can be assembled well in advance and requires only minimal last-minute attention. Furthermore, despite some of its high-priced ingredients (such as lobster and shrimp), it really is quite inexpensive when made for a group because it only needs small amounts of the more costly items.

For the first course, serve a soothing cold Cream of Cucumber Soup. Its lightness and delicacy play counterpoint to the hearty Paella. A spinach salad also complements the entree. Follow the recipe given on page 78; it was planned for six, but smaller salad portions are more than adequate for this dinner for eight. The Caramel *Crème Brûlée* (or Burnt Caramel Cream), one of my favorite desserts, is rich yet ethereal, soft as a cloud—something your guests will never forget.

* See the recipe on page 78.

COLD CREAM OF CUCUMBER SOUP

(MAY BE PARTIALLY PREPARED UP TO 2 DAYS IN ADVANCE;
MUST BE PARTIALLY PREPARED AT LEAST 2 HOURS IN ADVANCE)

4 large cucumbers
2 tablespoons unsalted butter
½ cup minced scallions (white parts only)
2 tablespoons flour
2 cups chicken broth
1 teaspoon salt
Freshly ground black pepper
2 cups light cream
2 tablespoons minced fresh dillweed

Cut one of the cucumbers in half. Tightly wrap one half in plastic wrap and reserve it in the refrigerator.

Peel the remaining 3½ cucumbers, split them in half lengthwise, and scrape out all their seeds with a teaspoon. Cut them crosswise into 1-inch pieces.

Melt the butter in a large skillet equipped with a tight-fitting lid. When it has melted, add the scallions and sauté them over low heat until they are soft, about 5 minutes. Sprinkle the flour over the scallions and cook for 2 minutes, stirring constantly. Add the cucumber pieces, increase the heat to moderately high, and cook them until they turn slightly green and transparent, about 5 minutes. Stir frequently so that they do not burn. Add the chicken broth, salt, and pepper, and bring the broth to a boil. Reduce the heat to low, cover the skillet, and cook the cucumbers for 15 minutes, or until they are very tender when pierced with the tip of a knife. Remove the pan from the heat and allow the cucumbers to cool slightly.

Transfer the cucumbers and broth in batches to a blender or food processor fitted with a steel blade, and puree until smooth. Pour the cucumber base into a large plastic container or glass jar, tightly cover and refrigerate for at least 2 hours to chill properly, or until time for final preparation.

TIME ALLOWANCE FOR FINAL PREPARATION: 10 MINUTES

Pour the cream into the cucumber base and blend well.

Remove the reserved cucumber half from the refrigerator and, without peeling it, cut it into 16 paper-thin slices.

Ladle the soup into individual soup bowls. Garnish each serving with 2 cucumber slices and a sprinkling of dillweed. Serve the soup chilled.

SERVES 8

PAELLA

(MAY BE PARTIALLY PREPARED UP TO 24 HOURS IN ADVANCE)

1½ pounds chorizo or linguica sausage(s)
2½ to 3 pounds assorted chicken pieces (thighs, legs, and breasts)
¼ cup vegetable oil
½ cup olive oil
2 (1½-pound) live lobsters, cut into approximately 8 pieces each, chest section
  discarded
½ cup finely chopped onions
1 teaspoon minced garlic
1 green pepper, cored, seeded, and cut into thin strips
2 large tomatoes (about ½ pound each), peeled and coarsely chopped
1 teaspoon salt
3 cups long-grain rice
¼ teaspoon ground saffron
6 cups boiling water
12 cherrystone clams (about 1 pound)
¾ pound mussels, well scrubbed, "beards" torn off
½ pound medium shrimp, peeled and deveined
1 cup fresh peas (or frozen peas, thawed)

Place the sausage(s) in a small skillet and cover with water. Bring to a boil over high heat. Prick the sausage(s) in several places with the tip of a knife or the tines of a fork. Reduce the heat and simmer for 5 minutes. Drain on paper towels and slice ¼ inch thick.

If you are using chicken breasts, cut each half breast in half crosswise. Chicken thighs and legs may remain whole. Pour the vegetable oil and ¼ cup of the olive oil into a very large skillet, preferably one with high sides. Heat the oil over high heat. When it is smoking, add the chicken pieces; turn them frequently to brown them on all sides. (Do not crowd the chicken pieces. Cook them in batches, if necessary.) When they have browned, transfer them to a plate and reserve. Add the lobster pieces to the skillet and cook them over high heat for 3 to 4 minutes, or until the shells start to turn pink. Turn the pieces frequently as they cook. Transfer them to another plate and reserve. Add the sausage slices to the pan and brown them rapidly. Spread them on paper towels to drain.

Pour the remaining ¼ cup of olive oil into a 14-inch paella pan or a flameproof casserole at least 14 inches in diameter and 4 inches deep. Over moderate heat, sauté the onions, garlic, peppers, and tomato until the tomato is soft and all the exuded juices have evaporated. Add the salt and rice; stir to blend.

Bring 1 cup of the water to a boil in a small saucepan. Add the saffron and mix well. Pour the saffron-water over the rice mixture and stir until well blended. Remove the casserole from the heat.

Arrange the chicken, lobster, sausage, clams, mussels, and shrimp on top of the rice. Cover tightly with plastic wrap or the casserole's lid, and refrigerate until 1 hour before final preparation.

TIME ALLOWANCE FOR FINAL PREPARATION: 45 MINUTES

Preheat the oven to 400 degrees.

Bring the remaining 5 cups of water to a boil. Pour it into the paella pan or casserole, stirring only to distribute it among the kernels of rice in the bottom of the dish. Place the pan or casserole over high heat and bring the liquid to a boil once more. Transfer the pan, uncovered, to the lowest rack in the oven and bake for 20 minutes. Add the peas, toss to mix well, and return the pan to the oven for another 5 to 10 minutes, or until all the liquid has been absorbed. Serve directly from the pan or casserole, steaming hot.

SERVES 8

CARAMEL CRÈME BRÛLÉE

(MAY BE PREPARED UP TO 24 HOURS IN ADVANCE;
MUST BE PREPARED AT LEAST 6 HOURS IN ADVANCE)

8 egg yolks
¾ cup firmly packed dark brown sugar
4 cups heavy cream, scalded
1 tablespoon vanilla

Preheat the oven to 350 degrees.

Bring a kettle full of water to a boil.

With a beater, beat the egg yolks until pale yellow in color. Add ½ cup of the brown sugar, a heaping spoonful at a time, and continue beating until the mixture is thick and dark yellow. Beating constantly, add the scalded cream in a slow, steady stream. Add the vanilla and mix well. Strain the custard into a 1½- to 2-quart baking or souffle dish. Place the dish in a large shallow pan, place them in the middle of the oven, and pour in enough boiling water to come halfway up the sides of the dish.

Bake the custard for 1 to 1¼ hours, or until the custard seems set. (It will be very soft, but it will solidify as it cools. Make sure the center seems as set as the area around the edges.) Remove the dish from the hot water and allow it to cool.

Cover with plastic wrap and refrigerate until the custard is thoroughly chilled (about 2 hours).

The burnt topping should be executed at least 2 hours, or up to 4 hours, before serving the Caramel Crème Brûlée.

Preheat the broiler.

Sprinkle the top of the custard as evenly as possible with the remaining ¼ cup brown sugar, pushing the sugar through a strainer or using a teaspoon and gently tapping the sugar onto the surface.

Place the dish about 3 inches away from the broiler element and, watching it carefully, broil for 2 to 4 minutes, or until the sugar melts and forms a caramelized crust. Do not let it burn or become too hot.

Remove the custard from the broiler and allow it to cool before returning it to the refrigerator. Chill the custard for another 2 hours, or up to 4 hours, before serving it direct from the refrigerator.

SERVES 8

A GRILLED LEG OF LAMB FOR EIGHT

Mustard-Coated Grilled Lamb

Mint "Sauce" Jelly

Sautéed Summer Squash

Red Potatoes with Chive Butter

Cottage Pudding with Praline Sauce

I devote as much of the warm-weather months as possible to grilling. The food seems to taste better—or perhaps it's just that it tastes differently—and the aromas from a grill generate an informality I particularly like when I entertain.

The trick, of course, is to find novel foods to grill. Lamb fits those requirements nicely, even though I frequently use it with vegetables in kebabs. But a leg, boned and butter-flied and maybe marinated, certainly makes a pleasant change. (This menu's mustard-encrusted version was inspired by a favorite roast of mine from *Mastering the Art of French Cooking, Vol. I,* by Simone Beck, Louisette Bertholle, and Julia Child.)

One other thought for unusual grilling, for which there really aren't any hard and fast recipes: grilling fresh, unblemished vegetables. Not only are they a delicious corollary to the meat, they're a visual embellishment as well. A food stylist friend of mine introduced me to this delight. Depending on what he has on hand, and what colors complement his main course, he may halve some peppers (coring or seeding them first), quarter some onions, slice an unpeeled eggplant, or split some baby zucchini lengthwise. He then brushes them on all sides with olive oil and lays them on the grill beside whatever meat he's cooking. With a few turns, they're done, the flesh still a little hard, the skin pleasantly cross-hatched with the charring from the grill.

With lamb, grilled or roasted, my family prefers mint sauce, instead of the kelly-green jelly so widely served. One fall day a few years back, when my daughter and I were collecting mint from our patch on Cape Cod to make such a sauce, we reflected that the frosts would soon be upon us and the mint would go. Why, we wondered, couldn't we conceive a mint-sauce jelly that would have the tart, acidic taste of a vinegared mint sauce yet, by dint of the jelly's preservative qualities, be enjoyable in mint-barren winter? This menu's recipe is the result: not as pretty as traditional mint jelly but much tastier.

To accompany the lamb, I like serving sautéed yellow summer squash highlighted with slices of bright red pepper. (Take care not to overcook them, for the crunchy texture as well as the vivid hues will diminish.)

The dessert on this menu is an old favorite: Cottage Pudding, enhanced with a buttery praline sauce. I think it should be served warm, but it isn't half bad at room temperature if you heat up the sauce.

MUSTARD-COATED GRILLED LAMB

(MAY BE PARTIALLY PREPARED UP TO 8 HOURS IN ADVANCE;
SHOULD BE PARTIALLY PREPARED AT LEAST 2 HOURS IN ADVANCE)

¼ cup vegetable oil
1 tablespoon strained fresh lemon juice
2 tablespoons light soy sauce
¼ cup whole-grain or country-style Dijon mustard
2 teaspoons minced garlic
1 tablespoon ground ginger
1 tablespoon minced fresh rosemary leaves (or 1 teaspoon dried rosemary, crushed)
1 (8- to 9-pound) leg of lamb, excess fat trimmed, boned, and butterflied.

Prepare a marinade by combining the oil, lemon juice, soy sauce, mustard, garlic, ginger, and rosemary in a small bowl and blending them well. Using a pastry brush, coat the leg of lamb on both sides with the marinade. Place the lamb on a platter and refrigerate it for at least 2 hours, or up to 8 hours. Remove it from the refrigerator at least 1 hour before final preparation.

TIME ALLOWANCE FOR FINAL PREPARATION: 30 TO 45 MINUTES
PLUS TIME FOR PREPARING COALS IF GRILLING THE LAMB

The lamb may be cooked either over charcoal or under a preheated broiler. Because the thickness of the meat varies so greatly, the final product will have either rare and medium portions (cook the lamb 10 to 12 minutes per side) or medium and well-done portions (cook the lamb 12 to 15 minutes per side).

Do not remove the marinade from the lamb.

To grill:

Prepare the coals. They should be red-hot but not flaming when you begin to grill the meat.

Place the lamb on a greased rack about 5 inches above the coals, fat side down. If you have a grill with a cover, cover the lamb. If not, watch the coals carefully. Try to prevent flaming by sprinkling the coals with water if flames should rise up. Turn the lamb after the prescribed time and cook it the same length of time on its other side. Check for doneness by cutting into one of the thick sections; if it is too rare, cook it 2 or 3 minutes longer.

Transfer the lamb to a heated platter and let it rest 5 minutes before carving.

To broil:

Preheat the broiler.

Place the lamb on a rack about 3 inches below the broiler element, fat side up. Cook it the prescribed length of time, then turn and cook it the same length of time on its other side. Check for doneness by cutting into one of its thick sections.

Transfer the lamb to a heated platter and let it rest 5 minutes before carving.

SERVES 8

MINT "SAUCE" JELLY

(CAN HOLD IN STERILIZED JARS 1 YEAR)

2 cups packed mint leaves, stems discarded, plus ½ cup minced mint leaves
1½ cups distilled white vinegar
½ cup water
1 tablespoon strained fresh lemon juice
3½ cups sugar
1 3-ounce packet of pectin (Certo recommended)

Place the 2 cups of packed mint leaves, vinegar, and water in a blender or in the bowl of a food processor fitted with a steel blade. Whirl until the mint is finely minced. Transfer the mixture to a 1- to 2-quart saucepan and bring to a boil over high heat. Immediately remove the pan from the heat, cover, and let rest 10 minutes.

Strain the mixture into a mixing bowl, pressing down on the solids to extract all remaining juice. Discard the mint leaves. Measure the liquid. Pour 1¾ cups of liquid back into the saucepan. (Discard any extra.) Add the lemon juice and sugar. Bring to a boil, stirring to dissolve the sugar. Add the pectin, bring to a boil again (watch carefully to prevent boiling over), and boil exactly 1 minute, stirring constantly.

Remove the saucepan from the heat. Add the remaining ½ cup of minced mint leaves and mix well. Pour into 4 8-ounce sterilized jelly jars (or the equivalent). As the jelly cools and thickens, stir each jar with a sterilized spoon to keep the mint leaves evenly distributed.

Cover the jars with melted paraffin. Store in a cool spot.

YIELD: 4 8-OUNCE JARS

SAUTÉED SUMMER SQUASH

(MAY BE PARTIALLY PREPARED UP TO 2 HOURS IN ADVANCE)

4 tablespoons unsalted butter
1 medium onion (about ½ pound), peeled and thinly sliced
3 small yellow summer squash (about ½ pound each), ends trimmed, thinly sliced
1 tablespoon minced garlic
1 red pepper, cored, seeded, and cut into thin strips
Salt and pepper to taste

Melt the butter in a large skillet over low heat. Add the sliced onions and sauté them briefly, stirring frequently, until they just begin to wilt. Remove the skillet from the heat. Pile the squash slices on top of the onions, sprinkle with the minced garlic, and scatter the pepper strips over the top. Cover with a lid or plastic wrap, and reserve in a cool spot in the kitchen until time for final preparation.

TIME ALLOWANCE FOR FINAL PREPARATION: 5–8 MINUTES

Place the skillet over moderately high heat. Sauté the vegetables without stirring for 1 minute. Then stir-fry, tossing and cooking the vegetables until they are crisp-tender, about 3 to 4 more minutes. Do not overcook.

Remove from the heat and season to taste. Serve immediately.

SERVES 8

COTTAGE PUDDING WITH PRALINE SAUCE

("PUDDING" MAY BE PARTIALLY PREPARED UP TO 6 HOURS IN ADVANCE;
SAUCE MAY BE PREPARED UP TO 24 HOURS IN ADVANCE)

COTTAGE PUDDING

6 tablespoons unsalted butter, softened
¾ cup firmly packed light brown sugar
1 large egg
1¾ cups flour
2 teaspoons baking powder
½ teaspoon salt
¾ cup milk
1 teaspoon vanilla

To make the "pudding": Preheat the oven to 350 degrees.

With an electric mixer or a wooden spoon, beat the butter with the brown sugar until light and fluffy. Beat in the egg, blending well.

Sift the flour, baking powder, and salt into a mixing bowl. In three parts, add the flour alternately with the milk to the butter mixture. Stir in the vanilla.

Generously butter an 8- or 9-inch-square baking dish. With a rubber spatula, scrape the batter into the dish, spreading it out to the edges and corners of the dish. (The batter will be fairly stiff.) Bake the "pudding" (which is more like a cake) for 30 to 35 minutes, or until a straw inserted in the center comes out clean.

Remove the "pudding" from the oven and leave it in its baking dish. Cover it loosely with aluminum foil and set aside until final preparation.

PRALINE SAUCE

1 cup light cream
2 tablespoons unsalted butter
¾ cup firmly packed light brown sugar
1 tablespoon light corn syrup
1 teaspoon strained fresh lemon juice
Pinch of salt
½ cup whole pecans, toasted

To make the sauce: Combine the light cream, butter, brown sugar, and corn syrup in a heavy 1-quart saucepan, and bring to a boil over moderately low heat, stirring constantly. Continue cooking over low heat until the sauce thickens slightly, about 7 to 10 minutes. Stir in the lemon juice and salt and remove from heat. Blend in the pecans.

Cool the sauce, cover the saucepan, and set aside until final preparation.

YIELD: ABOUT 1½ CUPS

TIME ALLOWANCE FOR FINAL PREPARATION: 20 MINUTES

FINAL ASSEMBLY

1 cup heavy cream, whipped
½ cup pecans, toasted and coarsely chopped

Preheat the oven to 300 degrees.

Return the "pudding" to the oven and let it warm for 15 minutes. Remove it from the oven and, working quickly, cut it into 3-inch-square serving pieces.

While the "pudding" is warming, heat the sauce over moderately low heat, stirring occasionally, until it is very hot.

Center a square of warm "pudding" on each dessert plate. Immediately ladle three or four *spoonfuls* of the hot Praline Sauce over the "pudding," then top with a dollop of whipped cream. Garnish with a sprinkling of chopped pecans. Serve immediately.

SERVES 8

GRILLED FISH STEAKS FOR EIGHT

Barbecued Swordfish Laurel

Julienned Beets

Fresh Corn Pudding

Chocolate Almond Torte with Bittersweet Mocha Sauce

In cooking with herbs, there are traditional marriages we all use or at least take for granted. Rosemary enhances lamb, tarragon seems perfect for chicken, and dill seems to bring out the best in fish.

These are the obvious, familiar combinations. But consider the lowly bay leaf, whose authoritative presence can perk up a feeble soup or stew. Also known as laurel, it is the same leaf that was woven into the wreaths with which the Romans crowned their heroes and leaders. (According to Waverly Root in *Food*, Julius Caesar wore his all the time, not for self-aggrandizement, but to hide his baldness!)

In the Mediterranean countries, laurel trees proliferate, and bay leaves appear in cooking much more often than here. I first encountered the combination of fish and bay leaves in a Turkish restaurant (now out of business) in New York City, where chunks of swordfish were skewered alternately with bay leaves. Swordfish Laurel produces a similar harmony of flavors.

(Some varieties of laurel are deadly poisonous, so please don't be tempted to gather your own. I did once, in California. Fortunately I picked the right kind, so I am still here to tell the tale.)

Corn and beets go beautifully with swordfish. Although I know few will ever relinquish eating corn on the cob when it is in season, a change is nice every now and then.

For dessert, I offer one of my favorite recent re-creations, a heavenly dense Chocolate Almond Torte made entirely without flour. A similar torte was served in a hotel in the Bahamas where I vacationed, but the owner-chef wouldn't share her recipe despite my wheedling. What could I do but to try to reproduce it on my own? While I don't profess to have duplicated it, my version is at least a kissin' cousin.

BARBECUED SWORDFISH LAUREL

◆

(MAY BE PARTIALLY PREPARED UP TO 6 HOURS IN ADVANCE)

4 tablespoons unsalted butter
2 cloves garlic, peeled and halved lengthwise
6 bay leaves
1 tablespoon strained fresh lemon juice
2 (2-pound) swordfish steaks, about 1 inch thick
2 tablespoons minced fresh parsley

Melt the butter over very low heat in a small saucepan. Add the garlic halves, bay leaves, and lemon juice. Place the saucepan in a skillet or a larger saucepan filled with an inch of water. Still over very low heat, which will keep the butter liquid but in no danger of burning, allow the garlic and bay leaves to steep for at least 1 hour or up to 2 hours. Remove and discard the garlic and bay leaves. Set the herbed butter aside until you are ready to barbecue the swordfish, allowing a few minutes to remelt it should it solidify in the meantime.

TIME ALLOWANCE FOR FINAL PREPARATION: 30 MINUTES PLUS TIME FOR PREPARING COALS

Prepare a charcoal grill. For swordfish steaks approximately 1 inch thick, allow 8 minutes on the first side and about 5 to 8 minutes on the second, depending on the heat of the coals. Increase or decrease the time based on the thickness of the steaks and the heat of or distance from the coals. When the coals are red-hot but not flaming, brush the swordfish on both sides with the herbed butter. Arrange the rack about 5 inches above the coals. Cook the steaks for the prescribed time on the first side, brushing once with the butter. Brush again with the butter, turn, brush again, and cook until done. Check the fish for doneness during the final cooking by prodding its surface with your finger. It is done when it feels soft but somewhat resistant. (When it becomes hard and firm, unfortunately, it is overdone and dry.)

Cut the steaks into serving portions and serve immediately, sprinkled with the parsley.

SERVES 8

JULIENNED BEETS

(MAY BE PARTIALLY PREPARED UP TO 4 HOURS IN ADVANCE)

3 bunches of beets, leaves trimmed and discarded
⅓ cup unsalted butter
2 cups packed shredded iceberg lettuce
Salt and freshly ground black pepper to taste

Cut the root and leaf ends off the beets. With a swivel-blade peeler, remove the skin. Cut the beets into julienne strips ¼ inch square.

Melt the butter over low heat in a large skillet equipped with a tight-fitting lid. When the butter has melted, remove it from the heat and spread out the beets in the butter on the bottom of the pan. Place the shredded lettuce on top. Cover the skillet with its lid and leave it in a cool spot in the kitchen until time for final preparation.

TIME ALLOWANCE FOR FINAL PREPARATION: 30 MINUTES

Place the covered skillet over moderately low heat. Steam the beets for 30 minutes, or until tender. Stir them occasionally. Just before serving, toss them well to distribute the lettuce throughout. Serve the beets with the lettuce, seasoned with salt and pepper to taste.

SERVES 8

FRESH CORN PUDDING

(MAY BE PARTIALLY PREPARED UP TO 12 HOURS IN ADVANCE)

2 tablespoons unsalted butter
1 red pepper, cored, seeded, and finely chopped
½ cup finely chopped onions
1 tablespoon flour
½ cup heavy cream
½ cup sour cream
3 eggs
2 cups grated or scraped fresh corn (about 5 ears)

2 cups whole kernel fresh corn (about 5 ears)
¾ teaspoon salt
Freshly ground black pepper

In a medium-size skillet, melt the butter over low heat. Add the pepper and onion, and sauté them until wilted, about 5 minutes. Sprinkle the flour over them and stir until most of the butter has been absorbed. Remove the skillet from the heat.

In a small bowl or measuring cup, combine the heavy cream and sour cream and mix until well blended. Pour the cream mixture over the pepper and onion mixture and stir thoroughly to blend.

In a large mixing bowl, beat the eggs until frothy. Blend in the pepper, onion, and cream mixture, then add both the grated and whole kernel corn. Mix well. (Sometimes the batter separates, but this will disappear in the baking process.) Season to taste with salt and pepper. Transfer the mixture to a 2- to 3-quart baking dish, seal tightly with plastic wrap, and refrigerate until 1 hour before final preparation.

TIME ALLOWANCE FOR FINAL PREPARATION: 50 MINUTES

Preheat the oven to 325 degrees. Bring a kettle of water to a boil.

Place the baking dish in a shallow roasting pan. Fill the pan with enough boiling water to come halfway up the sides of the baking dish. Bake the pudding, uncovered, for 40 to 45 minutes or until it is set in the middle. Serve immediately.

SERVES 8

CHOCOLATE ALMOND TORTE WITH BITTERSWEET MOCHA SAUCE

♦

(TORTE AND SAUCE MAY BE PARTIALLY PREPARED UP TO 2 DAYS IN ADVANCE)

CHOCOLATE ALMOND TORTE

6 ounces semisweet chocolate
2/3 cup unsalted butter, softened
1 cup sugar
5 eggs
1½ cups ground almonds (about 7 ounces)
1 teaspoon baking powder
½ teaspoon almond extract
¼ cup toasted sliced almonds

To make the torte: Preheat the oven to 375 degrees.

Butter a 9-inch springform pan, line the bottom with wax paper cut to fit, and butter the wax paper.

Melt the chocolate in the top of a double boiler over simmering water. Remove the double boiler from the heat and reserve.

Meanwhile, cream the butter in the bowl of an electric mixer until fluffy (you may do this by hand or with the electric mixer). Gradually beat in the sugar. Beat in the eggs, one at a time. The mixture will appear to be separated. With a spatula, scrape the melted chocolate over the butter mixture and stir until blended. Add the ground almonds and baking powder, and mix thoroughly. Finally stir in the almond extract.

Scrape the batter into the prepared springform pan and bake for 30 minutes, or until the entire surface of the cake appears firm and dry. (The center of the cake may seem moist when you test the cake for doneness. That is all right.)

Remove the torte from the oven and set the pan on a rack to cool. When it is no longer warm to the touch, run a knife around the sides of the pan to loosen the torte. Release the springform and remove the sides. Invert a serving platter over the torte, and turn over the cake and the platter. Carefully lift off the bottom of the pan and the wax paper. If you are not serving the cake within the next hour, cover it with plastic wrap and refrigerate until ready to serve.

BITTERSWEET MOCHA SAUCE

1 cup semisweet chocolate bits
1 ounce unsweetened chocolate
3 tablespoons strong coffee

½ cup light cream
3 tablespoons light corn syrup
Pinch of salt
¼ teaspoon almond extract

To make the sauce: In the top of a double boiler, over simmering water, melt the semisweet and unsweetened chocolates with the coffee. When they have melted, gradually add the cream and corn syrup. Stir in the salt and almond extract. Mix until well blended and smooth. Pour the sauce into a bowl or jar, cover well, and refrigerate.

YIELD: ABOUT 1½ CUPS SAUCE

TIME ALLOWANCE FOR FINAL PREPARATION: 10 MINUTES

Transfer the sauce to a small saucepan and slowly warm it over low heat, stirring frequently. When it is hot, cut the torte in small wedges. Ladle two or three generous spoonfuls of the sauce over each wedge and garnish with a sprinkling of toasted almonds on top.

SERVES 8

A RELAXING BRUNCH FOR EIGHT

Bloody Marys and Mimosas

Curried Shrimp Quiche

Tabbouleh Salad

Orange-Ginger Coffee Cake

Mulled Apricot "Tea"

Honeydew Melon Wedges and Bakery-Bought Cookies

Brunch seems to be all the rage these days, and, for the life of me, I really don't know what it is. It certainly is not a combination of breakfast and lunch; who waits until noon or early afternoon, skipping breakfast entirely, for "brunch?" Yet every hotel and restaurant in town seems to serve "brunch" on Sundays, and they're all packed with happy customers.

By my definition, brunch is a light luncheon, generally including one or more egg dishes to impart a breakfast flavor. It usually includes alcoholic beverages, to which I'm not averse, but I prefer them to be well infused with a juice (or to be wine or champagne) to keep things light.

I've tried to make this menu as easy on the cook as possible because I, for one, am not an organized early-morning person. All the dishes can be partially, if not entirely, assembled the night before, so that only a few embellishments need to be made in a sleepwalker's trance the morning of the affair.

CURRIED SHRIMP QUICHE

(MAY BE PARTIALLY PREPARED UP TO 24 HOURS IN ADVANCE)

1 recipe for pie dough, sufficient for an 11-inch tart shell
2 tablespoons unsalted butter
2 tablespoons minced scallions (white parts only)
1 teaspoon curry powder
¼ pound thinly sliced mushrooms

¾ pound large shrimp, peeled, deveined, and halved lengthwise
3 eggs
1 cup light cream
Freshly ground black pepper
½ cup grated Gruyère cheese (about ¼ pound)

Preheat the oven to 425 degrees.

On a floured surface, roll out the pie dough to a diameter of 13 inches, taking care not to stretch it. Carefully transfer the dough to an 11-inch tart pan, preferably the type with a removable base. Fit the dough into the tart pan and, with a rolling pin, trim off the excess dough so that it is even with the edge of the tart pan. Prick the dough all over with the tines of a fork. Cut a circle of aluminum foil to fit the interior of the tart, place it on top of the dough, and weight it down with uncooked beans or rice.

Place the tart shell in the oven for 15 minutes, then remove the weighted foil. Reduce the oven temperature to 350 degrees and bake the shell 10 minutes longer. Set the tart shell aside to cool. When it has cooled, cover it loosely with aluminum foil and put it in a cool corner of the kitchen.

While the shell is baking, melt the butter in a large skillet over moderate heat. Add the scallions and curry powder and, stirring frequently, cook until the scallions are soft. Drop in the mushrooms and sauté them for 5 minutes, or until they just begin to exude their juices. Add the shrimp and, stirring frequently, cook them for about 1 minute, or until they just begin to lose their translucent appearance. Immediately transfer the mixture to a bowl to cool. When it is cool, cover with plastic wrap and refrigerate until 30 minutes before final preparation.

TIME ALLOWANCE FOR FINAL PREPARATION: 45 MINUTES

Preheat the oven to 375 degrees.

In a small bowl, beat the eggs until they are frothy and well blended. Beat in the cream and pepper. Transfer the shrimp mixture to the baked tart shell. Sprinkle the cheese over the top of the mixture, then pour in the egg mixture.

Place the tart on a sheet pan or cookie sheet and bake for 30 minutes, or until the filling is set.

Remove the quiche from the tart pan's circular sides, but let it remain on the pan's metal bottom. Cut in wedges and serve hot or at room temperature.

SERVES 8

TABBOULEH SALAD

◆

(MAY BE PREPARED UP TO 24 HOURS IN ADVANCE;
IS BEST WHEN PREPARED 2 OR 3 HOURS IN ADVANCE)

There are many versions of Tabbouleh, often with much more bulgur or parsley. Exact measurements for the vegetables and herbs are not necessary. An extra quarter cup of this or that simply doesn't matter. Don't use so much extra, however, that you don't have enough oil and lemon juice to adequately coat the ingredients.

> ¼ cup bulgur wheat
> 1 cup chopped scallions, including 1 inch of green leaves
> 2 cups minced fresh parsley
> 1 cup minced fresh mint
> 4 large tomatoes (about 2 to 3 pounds), peeled, seeded, and cut into ½-inch
>   dice
> ½ cup fruity, imported olive oil
> ½ teaspoon salt
> ¼ teaspoon freshly ground black pepper
> Pinch of cayenne (optional)
> 2 tablespoons strained fresh lemon juice

Place the bulgur wheat in a small mixing bowl and pour boiling water over it to cover by 1 inch. Let it rest at least 1 hour, preferably 2, during which time the bulgur wheat will absorb much of the water. Drain well.

Toss the scallions, parsley, mint, and tomatoes in a salad bowl. Mix them well. Add the drained bulgur wheat and toss to blend. Add the oil, salt, pepper, cayenne (if desired), and lemon juice. Toss again to thoroughly blend the dressing with the ingredients.

Cover the Tabbouleh with plastic wrap and refrigerate it until 1 hour before serving. Just before bringing it to the table, give the salad another toss or two.

SERVES 8

ORANGE-GINGER COFFEE CAKE

(MAY BE PREPARED UP TO 24 HOURS IN ADVANCE)

3 cups flour
½ teaspoon salt
1 tablespoon ground ginger
1 teaspoon baking soda
7 tablespoons dark brown sugar
4 tablespoons unsalted butter
1 tablespoon grated orange rind
¼ cup orange marmalade
½ cup orange juice

Preheat the oven to 450 degrees.

Generously butter a 9-by-5-inch loaf pan.

In a sieve set over a medium-sized mixing bowl, combine 2 cups of the flour, the salt, ginger, baking soda, and 4 tablespoons of the brown sugar. Stir to sift. Cut 3 tablespoons of the butter into the dry ingredients until the mixture resembles coarse meal. In a small bowl, mix together the orange rind, marmalade, and juice, and stir until blended.

With a rubber spatula, scrape the marmalade mixture into the flour mixture and beat well to combine the ingredients. The dough will be sticky. Turn out the dough onto a surface dusted with ¾ cup flour. Knead the dough lightly until all the flour has been absorbed. Place the dough in the prepared loaf pan, patting it into the corners with your fingers.

In another bowl, combine the remaining ¼ cup flour with the remaining 3 tablespoons brown sugar and mix well. Rub in the remaining tablespoon of butter until the mixture is crumbly. Sprinkle the topping over the dough, distributing it as evenly as possible.

Bake the coffee cake for 25 to 30 minutes, or until a toothpick inserted in the center comes out clean. Remove the pan from the oven, loosen the cake from the pan, and transfer it to a serving plate. Serve it hot or at room temperature, sliced and generously buttered.

YIELD: 1 9-INCH LOAF

MULLED APRICOT "TEA"

◆

(MAY BE PARTIALLY PREPARED UP TO 24 HOURS IN ADVANCE)

2 cups (½ pound) fresh cranberries
1 quart apricot nectar
3 cinnamon sticks
4 whole cloves
1 tablespoon grated orange rind
1 (6-ounce) can frozen orange juice, thawed
3 (6-ounce) cans water
½ to ¾ cup sugar, according to taste
8 small cinnamon sticks or thin orange slices

In a 2- to 3-quart nonreactive saucepan, combine the cranberries, apricot nectar, cinnamon sticks, cloves, and orange rind. Bring the mixture to a boil over moderately high heat, stirring occasionally. Boil until the cranberries pop.

Strain the liquid into a large bowl, discarding the spices and berries. Add the frozen juice, water, and ½ cup of the sugar. Stir until the sugar is dissolved and add up to ¼ cup more if you like a sweeter drink.

Cover the bowl with plastic wrap or transfer it to bottles, and refrigerate until final preparation.

TIME ALLOWANCE FOR FINAL PREPARATION: 10 MINUTES

Pour the "tea" into a large, nonreactive pot or kettle. Over moderately high heat, bring it to just below the boiling point. Pour it into heated mugs and garnish, if you like, with cinnamon sticks or orange slices.

SERVES 8

SCANDINAVIAN STEW FOR EIGHT

Danish Sailors' Stew

Oven-Steamed Carrots with Tarragon

Mixed Green Salad with Vinaigrette*

Frozen Almond Cream

In the bone-chilling cold of late fall, winter, and early spring, nothing seems so satisfying to our bodies as hearty stews. The heady aroma exuded by the ingredients as they slowly cook permeates all the corners of the house and brings eager anticipation to everyone within range.

Danish Sailors' Stew was nostalgically described to me by my Danish stepmother, Annie B, when she first came to this country many years ago. Her directions were vague, and I didn't bother with notes. But the memory lingered, and the unusual combination of ingredients haunted me off and on until I recently started to experiment with the dish.

And what a stew it turned out to be! My gratitude goes out to my stepmother and all Danish sailors. As stews go, it is relatively easy to make. The apples and floured meat thicken the gravy naturally as the stew cooks, so there is none of the bother of draining off the liquid when the cooking is done, and no need to remove the fat or thicken the stew with more flour or cornstarch. For this reason I recommend preparing Danish Sailors' Stew just to the point of its final cooking. Aside from putting the stew in the oven 1½ hours before dinner, there's no more work to be done until you take it out. And, when you lift the pot's lid and see the wonderful natural gravy, you'll know you have a real winner.

If for some reason you must cook the stew ahead of time, or you want to warm up some leftovers, you will need to add some liquid, such as beef broth, before reheating it. The potatoes absorb much of the gravy if the stew rests for any prolonged period after being cooked.

I have always liked carrots with stew. This menu's recipe, in which carrots are steamed in a foil package in their own juices and butter, not only enhances the vegetable but eases the cook's burden. All that needs to be done in the final

* Double the recipe on page 24.

preparation is to place the packet in the oven on a rack beneath the stew 30 minutes after the stew has started cooking. They can cook in tandem.

Frozen Almond Cream is my rendition of that old favorite, Bisquit Tortoni, once served in nearly every restaurant in town. It, too, is simple to make, can be done well ahead of time, and requires no ice cream machine, only a freezer.

DANISH SAILORS' STEW

(MAY BE PARTIALLY PREPARED UP TO 8 HOURS IN ADVANCE)

3 tablespoons vegetable oil
1/2 cup flour
3 teaspoons salt
Freshly ground black pepper
3 pounds stewing beef, cut in 1-inch cubes
3 tablespoons unsalted butter
2 teaspoons minced garlic
2 cups chopped onions
3 pounds potatoes, peeled and cut in 1/8-inch slices
4 large apples (about 2 pounds), peeled, cored, and coarsely grated
1 teaspoon dried thyme
1 12-ounce can beer
1/4 cup minced fresh parsley

Heat the oil in a large frying pan, preferably one with high sides. Place the flour, 1 teaspoon of the salt, and the pepper in a brown paper bag, close the bag, and shake briefly to mix. Put about one-third of the beef cubes into the bag, close it, and shake vigorously so that the beef is well coated with the seasoned flour. Transfer the beef to the hot oil and brown the pieces on all sides. As the beef is done, transfer it with a slotted spoon to a bowl and reserve. Proceed with the remaining meat. Do not overcrowd the pan as you brown the pieces of meat because they will not brown and become crisp if they are packed too closely together. Add more oil if necessary.

When all the meat has browned, rinse out the pan, return it to low heat, and melt the butter in it. Add the garlic and onions and sauté them, stirring occasionally, until wilted, about 5 minutes. Set aside and reserve.

Divide the potatoes into four parts and the meat, onions, and apples into three parts. Layer the ingredients into a 4- to 5-quart ovenproof casserole as follows: Place one-fourth of the potatoes on the bottom, followed by one-third of the meat, sprinkled with ½ teaspoon of the salt, a few grindings of pepper, and ¼ teaspoon of the thyme. Top with one-third of the onions and one-third of the apples. (Do not be concerned if the apples turn brown. They become part of the gravy so it won't show.) Repeat the layering two more times; then add a final layering of potato slices followed by a last ½ teaspoon salt, pepper, and ¼ teaspoon thyme. Pour the beer over the ingredients. Cover the casserole tightly with plastic wrap and its own lid, and refrigerate it until 1 hour before final preparation.

TIME ALLOWANCE FOR FINAL PREPARATION: 1¾ HOURS

Preheat the oven to 350 degrees.

Remove and discard the plastic wrap. Bring the liquid in the casserole to a boil over moderate heat. Re-cover the casserole and transfer it to a rack in the center of the oven. Bake undisturbed for 1½ hours. Sprinkle with the parsley before serving.

SERVES 8

OVEN-STEAMED CARROTS WITH TARRAGON

(MAY BE PARTIALLY PREPARED UP TO 8 HOURS IN ADVANCE)

2 pounds carrots, peeled
5 tablespoons unsalted butter
2 teaspoons dried tarragon
¼ cup minced scallions, including 2 inches of green leaves
1 teaspoon salt
1 teaspoon sugar
¼ cup minced fresh parsley

Cut the carrots on the diagonal into ⅛-inch-thick slices.

Melt the butter in a large skillet. Add the tarragon, scallions, salt, and sugar and stir until the salt and sugar have dissolved. Add the carrots, remove the skillet from the heat, and toss until all the slices are well coated with the tarragon-scallion butter.

Tear off a sheet of extra-heavy aluminum foil about 1 yard long. Transfer the carrots to the foil, then scrape any excess butter from the skillet and drizzle it over them. Arrange the carrots on the foil so that 4 inches is left clear on each long side and about 10 inches remains at each end. Bring the 4-inch strips toward each other so that they meet above the carrots. Fold the top ½ inch of the two sheets over on each other so that they form a seal. Repeat with the 10-inch ends of the sheets, bringing them together and folding them over the carrots as many times as possible to obtain a tight seal. In this manner the carrots are packed, almost airtight, within a foil package. (It doesn't have to look beautiful; the package should just be as well sealed as possible.) Refrigerate until 1 hour before final preparation.

TIME ALLOWANCE FOR FINAL PREPARATION: 1¼ HOURS

Preheat oven to 350 degrees.

Place the foil package of carrots, still well sealed, on a cookie sheet in the oven and bake for 1 hour. Do not disturb.

Transfer the carrots to a heated serving dish and pour any accumulated juices over them. Sprinkle with the parsley and serve immediately.

SERVES 8

FROZEN ALMOND CREAM

(MAY BE PREPARED UP TO 24 HOURS IN ADVANCE;
MUST BE PREPARED AT LEAST 4 HOURS IN ADVANCE)

¼ cup blanched almonds
¾ cup sugar
¼ cup water
3 egg yolks
3 tablespoons medium-dry sherry
1 cup heavy cream

Preheat the oven to 350 degrees.

Spread the almonds on a small pie plate and toast them until they just start to brown, about 3 to 5 minutes. Watch that they don't burn.

Transfer the almonds to the bowl of a food processor fitted with a steel blade. Pulsing on and off, whirl them until they are coarsely ground. Add ¼ cup of the sugar and whirl until the almonds are finely ground. Reserve them in a separate dish. Rinse and dry the bowl.

Combine the remaining ½ cup of sugar with the water and bring them to a boil over moderately high heat, stirring constantly. Stop stirring and allow the syrup to boil 20 seconds longer. Immediately remove it from the heat.

Drop the egg yolks and the sherry into the bowl of the food processor, and whirl them until the mixture is light yellow. While the machine is still running, add the hot syrup in a slow stream. Whirl for an additional 20 seconds.

Whip the cream. Using a rubber spatula, gently fold the egg yolk mixture into the whipped cream, folding only until the cream and the eggs are thoroughly combined. Spoon the mixture into eight 6-ounce paper or china souffle cups. Sprinkle the sugared almonds over each. Set the cups on a tray, cover loosely with foil, and freeze for 3 to 4 hours until firm.

SERVES 8

A SHIMMERING ASPIC FOR EIGHT

Ham and Chicken in Aspic with Mustard Mayonnaise

Tomato Salad with Basil

Soft Rolls

Orange Pound Cake

Ham and Chicken in Aspic is my version of a ham in aspic that I once enjoyed in France. I was visiting American friends who owned a small home in the beautiful cathedral-crowned city of Cluny, north of Lyon, the gastronomical center of France—if not the world. We were served luncheon on their tree-shaded terrace, and I have never forgotten the beauty of the dish: pink ham embedded in crystal-clear aspic speckled with green parsley. It was presented as a first course, but it was filling enough to be offered as a luncheon entree. I have included chicken in my recipe for variety of flavor and greater color contrast, not because the original dish in any manner fell short of perfection. However, you may use either ham or chicken alone; simply double the quantity. Either way, the dish is a visual delight.

Fresh basil is now available year-round in many American markets. If native tomatoes or some of the better-tasting imported variety are available, treat your guests to a salad of tomatoes with fresh basil. Please don't substitute dried basil. The salad won't be half so good or half so pretty. If you can't find any fresh basil, use minced fresh parsley instead.

As for dessert, this menu's Orange Pound Cake is a delicate, orange-enhanced delight with which to finish the meal. I like to serve it with scoops of lemon or orange sherbet, and sometimes even a drizzling of Cointreau, that smooth orange-flavored French liqueur.

HAM AND CHICKEN IN ASPIC
WITH MUSTARD MAYONNAISE

(ASPIC MAY BE PARTIALLY PREPARED UP TO 24 HOURS IN ADVANCE; MAYONNAISE MAY BE PREPARED UP TO 48 HOURS IN ADVANCE)

2 pounds boned and skinned chicken breasts
4 cups homemade chicken stock (or substitute canned broth)
1 scallion, roots trimmed, cut in 4 pieces, including 2 inches of green leaves
2 egg whites, lightly beaten
2 egg shells, crumbled
2 envelopes unflavored gelatin
½ cup water
1½ pound canned ham, fat and gelatinous juices discarded
1 cup minced fresh parsley
4 cornichon pickles, minced (available in specialty stores)
Watercress sprigs
Cherry tomatoes

Place the chicken breasts in a 10- or 12-inch skillet that will contain them compactly. Cover them with the chicken stock. Add the scallion pieces and bring the stock to a boil. Immediately lower the heat, cover the pan, and simmer the breasts for 10 minutes.

Remove the skillet from the heat and let the breasts cool in the stock, still covered, for 10 minutes. With a slotted spoon, transfer them to pieces of aluminum foil and wrap each one in foil. Place them in the freezer until they begin to firm (but do not actually freeze), about 1½ to 2 hours. (This will make it easier to cut them neatly later.)

Meanwhile, skim off any fat on the surface of the chicken stock, and strain the stock into a bowl. Measure; there should still be 4 cups of stock. If not, make up the difference with water.

To clarify the stock, pour it into a 2- or 3-quart saucepan. Add the egg whites and crumbled eggshells. Slowly bring the stock to a boil over medium heat, stirring frequently. When it just starts to boil, lower the heat and simmer for 10 minutes without stirring. Remove the pan from the heat and let the stock cool for 10 minutes.

Soften the gelatin in the water. When the stock has cooled, carefully pour it through a strainer lined with a double thickness of cheesecloth into a mixing bowl. Do not squeeze the cheesecloth or in any way disturb the egg sediments that have accumulated during the clarification process. Discard the cheesecloth and the egg particles. Add the softened gelatin to the stock and stir to mix.

Cover the mixing bowl with plastic wrap and refrigerate the stock until it thickens to the consistency of egg whites. Do not allow it to solidify. (If it should, simply transfer it to a saucepan, heat it slowly until it liquefies again, and place it, as before, in the refrigerator.)

After the chicken has become firm but is not yet frozen through, cut it into ½-inch dice. Dice the ham into ½-inch pieces.

When the stock has thickened to the desired consistency, fold in the minced parsley. Spoon a layer ¾ inch thick into a lightly oiled 9 × 5-inch loaf pan. With the loaf pan's 5-inch side facing you, arrange two rows of diced ham about ½-inch thick along the 9-inch length of each side of the pan, leaving the center empty. Fill the center with diced chicken so that you have a pattern of ham-chicken-ham. Sprinkle the ham and chicken with one-third of the cornichon pickles. Spoon a generous layer of the stock on top of the ham and chicken. Repeat the process, but this time place the chicken on top of the ham and the ham on top of the chicken so that you have a pattern of chicken-ham-chicken. Sprinkle with pickles and cover with another layer of stock. Repeat again, this time reverting to the original design of the first ham-chicken-ham layer. Cover the top with a final sprinkling of cornichons and spoon as much stock over the surface as you can fit into the loaf pan. Cover tightly with plastic wrap or aluminum foil and refrigerate until final preparation.

TIME ALLOWANCE FOR FINAL PREPARATION: 5 MINUTES

To serve, run a knife around the inside of the loaf pan. Dip the pan into warm water for 2 to 3 seconds. Place a chilled serving platter upside down on top of the pan, invert both the platter and the loaf pan, give a brisk shake, and the aspic should slip out of the pan onto the platter.

Garnish the aspic with sprigs of watercress and decorative arrangements of cherry tomatoes.

To serve, cut the aspic into thick slices and accompany them with Mustard Mayonnaise.

SERVES 8

MUSTARD MAYONNAISE

1 cup mayonnaise
½ cup sour cream
1 tablespoon Dijon-style mustard
2 tablespoons minced fresh chives

Measure the mayonnaise into a small mixing bowl. Beat in the sour cream with a wire whisk. Mix until the sour cream is thoroughly assimilated into the mayonnaise. Beat in the mustard and chives. Stir until blended. Cover with plastic wrap or store in an airtight container in the refrigerator until ready to serve. Stir once or twice before serving.

YIELD: ABOUT 1½ CUPS

TOMATO SALAD WITH BASIL

(MAY BE PARTIALLY PREPARED UP TO 4 HOURS IN ADVANCE)

3 pounds ripe tomatoes, peeled
½ cup minced scallions, including 2 inches of green leaves
½ cup finely chopped fresh basil leaves
6 tablespoons fruity, imported olive oil
Salt and freshly ground black pepper to taste
2 tablespoons wine vinegar

With a serrated knife, cut the tomatoes into ⅓-inch slices and arrange them, overlapping, on a serving platter. Sprinkle the scallions and basil leaves over the tomatoes. Cover the platter loosely with plastic wrap and set it aside in a cool corner of the kitchen.

TIME ALLOWANCE FOR FINAL PREPARATION: 5 MINUTES

Dribble the olive oil by the tablespoonful over the tomatoes. Sprinkle with salt and pepper to taste. Then, with the same measuring spoon, dribble the vinegar over the tomatoes, distributing it as evenly as possible.

SERVES 8

ORANGE POUND CAKE

(MAY BE PREPARED UP TO 24 HOURS IN ADVANCE)

1 cup unsalted butter, softened
1 cup sugar
4 eggs
1 tablespoon grated orange rind
1 teaspoon grated lemon rind
1 teaspoon vanilla
2 cups flour
½ teaspoon baking powder
½ teaspoon salt
½ cup strained fresh orange juice
Confectioners' sugar
1 quart orange sherbet (optional)

Preheat the oven to 325 degrees.

Generously butter a 9 × 5-inch loaf pan.

With a wooden spoon or an electric mixer, cream the butter in a large mixing bowl until light and fluffy. Gradually add the sugar, beating continuously. Beat the eggs, one at a time. Add the orange and lemon rinds and the vanilla, and mix until thoroughly blended.

Measure the flour, baking powder, and salt into a sifter or strainer placed over another mixing bowl. Sift twice. In two batches, add the flour alternately with the orange juice to the butter and egg mixture. Mix until well blended. Using a rubber spatula, scrape the batter into the buttered loaf pan.

Bake for 1½ hours, or until a straw inserted in the center comes out clean.

Cool the cake in the loaf pan for 10 minutes before turning it out on a rack to cool completely.

When it is cool, transfer the cake to a platter. Lay a paper doily on top of the cake, and sift confectioners' sugar lightly over the top. Carefully remove the doily without disturbing the pattern left by the sugar.

Serve the Orange Pound Cake accompanied, if you like, by scoops of orange or lemon sherbet.

SERVES 8

INDIAN FLAVORS IN A DINNER FOR EIGHT

Indian Spiced Chicken

*Rice Pilaf**

Rennie's Sprouts

Mango Chutney

Walnut Moss

This chicken dinner for eight has been heavily influenced by my love for Indian food. Indian Spiced Chicken is a distant, mild cousin to Tandoori chicken, which originated in northwest India (now Pakistan) but has so grown in popularity that it can be found in Indian restaurants all over the world.

Tandoori chicken is generally skinned, marinated in a complex blend of spices and yogurt, and roasted in a clay oven called a *tandoor.* I have simplified the method to such a degree that probably no self-respecting Indian would consider such a compromise, but most Americans should find this a tasty dish. It can be cooked in an oven or on an outdoor grill. No skinning of the bird is involved, no yogurt is used; all that is required is the possible addition to your spice shelf of coriander, cumin, and turmeric. (Once you have them, you'll undoubtedly find more uses for them.)

Rennie's Sprouts are named for my daughter, who has been serving the dish to the family for years and who eventually scolded me for not crediting her contributions to my recipes. She has been an unstinting aid and an astute critic, and she does, indeed, deserve credit.

* Double the recipe on page 52.

Walnut Moss, too, has associations both with India and family. A very dear uncle, who lived in Bombay all his life, used to serve wonderful Indian food; he frequently crowned a dinner with this unusual dessert because, he said, it soothed the palate after hot spicy foods. He never would reveal the recipe in detail, and for years I have been trying to duplicate it. This comes close. It definitely is not "it," but I think he would not fault it.

INDIAN SPICED CHICKEN

(MAY BE PARTIALLY PREPARED UP TO 12 HOURS IN ADVANCE;
MUST BE PARTIALLY PREPARED AT LEAST 4 HOURS IN ADVANCE)

7 to 9 pounds assorted chicken parts, broiler or fryer size, cut into pieces
1 clove garlic, peeled
1 tablespoon ground coriander
1 teaspoon ground cumin
1 teaspoon turmeric
1/4 teaspoon mace
1/4 teaspoon ground nutmeg
1/4 teaspoon ground cloves
1/4 teaspoon ground cinnamon
1/2 teaspoon ground ginger
1/4 teaspoon salt
1/4 teaspoon freshly ground black pepper
3 tablespoons strained fresh lemon juice
1/4 cup vegetable oil

Arrange the chicken skin side up in a roasting pan (or pans) large enough to hold the pieces without crowding.

Squeeze the garlic through a garlic press into a small bowl or cup. Add the coriander, cumin, turmeric, mace, nutmeg, cloves, cinnamon, ginger, salt, and pepper, and mix well. Pour in the lemon juice and oil and stir until thoroughly blended.

Using a pastry brush, spread the spice mixture over the chicken. (If you have any remaining mixture after you coat the skin, coat the undersides, but keep the chicken positioned skin side up.) Cover the roasting pan loosely with plastic wrap, and refrigerate until 1 hour before final preparation.

TIME ALLOWANCE FOR FINAL PREPARATION: 1 HOUR

Preheat the oven to 425 degrees

Place the pan, uncovered, on a rack in the top third of the oven. Roast the chicken until the meat feels tender when pierced with the tip of a knife, about 45 minutes. (It does not need to be turned.) The skin should appear crisp and deep brown; if not, run it briefly under a preheated broiler.

Serve with mango chutney.

SERVES 8

RENNIE'S SPROUTS

(MUST BE PREPARED JUST BEFORE SERVING; ALLOW 10 MINUTES)

2 tablespoons unsalted butter
2 pounds fresh bean sprouts
2 teaspoons minced garlic
1 tablespoon grated, peeled gingerroot
¼ cup snow peas, ends trimmed, strings pulled off, cut crosswise in thirds
2 tablespoons light soy sauce

Melt the butter in a wok or 14-inch skillet (preferably with high sides) over moderately high heat. When it is foaming, add the bean sprouts, garlic, and ginger. With two spoons or forks, toss the sprouts vigorously every 10 or 15 seconds. After 1 minute of cooking, add the snow peas and soy sauce. Continue sautéing and tossing for another 1 to 2 minutes, or until the sprouts are steaming hot but still fresh and crisp. Do not allow them to cook to the point of wilting. The peas should be bright green. Serve immediately.

SERVES 8

WALNUT MOSS

(MUST BE PREPARED AT LEAST 6 HOURS IN ADVANCE)

4 cups water
¼ teaspoon salt
½ cup quick-cooking tapioca
2½ cups firmly packed dark brown sugar
1 teaspoon vanilla
1 cup chopped walnuts
1 cup heavy cream

Bring the water and salt to a boil over high heat in a 2- to 3-quart saucepan. Slowly add the tapioca, stirring constantly. Add the sugar and mix until it has dissolved. Lower the heat and gently boil for 15 minutes, stirring occasionally. Remove from the heat and mix in the vanilla and walnuts. Allow to cool to room temperature, then transfer to a serving bowl.

Cover the bowl with plastic wrap and refrigerate until thoroughly chilled. The Walnut Moss should be fairly firm when served and will become so only when it is completely cold. Serve with unsweetened heavy cream, either liquid or whipped.

SERVES 8

STUFFED PORK LOIN
FOR EIGHT

*Fruited Loin of Pork with
Cream Sauce*

*Sautéed Carrots and Celery with
Fennel Seeds*

Whipped Potatoes

Layered Apricot Mousse

Pork has a wonderful ability to adapt to embellishments or marinades. It can be cooked straight or "jazzed" up, and either way it's good. There was a time, many years ago, when it was cheaper than chicken and considered an "inferior" meat. Restaurants with dubious reputations would sneak diced pork into their chicken salads to cut costs! Now, with pork-producers deliberately breeding leaner pigs, it has become increasingly popular.

Fruited Loin of Pork is of Scandinavian origin. A pocket cut the length of the loin and filled with prunes and apples not only complements the flavor of the meat but also enhances its appearance—the dark of the fruit standing out starkly in the center of the white flesh as the roast is carved. The sauce, made from the wine-cream pan juices and currant jelly, is delightfully piquant.

With it, try a pleasant combination of celery, onions, and carrots, made even more interesting by the addition of toasted fennel seeds. The dish is easily prepared ahead of time and only needs to be reheated while the pork's sauce is being reduced.

A fruity dessert is a fitting culmination to this meal of fruited pork. Layered Apricot Mousse is light but satisfying, a happy union of apricots and cream, with a center of almonds to add texture, and a brief bath of pureed strawberries for contrast. This recipe calls for frozen berries, but substitute fresh berries sweetened to taste if they are available and look flavorful and ripe.

FRUITED LOIN OF PORK WITH CREAM SAUCE

(MAY BE PARTIALLY PREPARED UP TO 12 HOURS IN ADVANCE)

1 (4- to 5-pound) boneless, center-cut loin of pork (about 8 pounds before boning)
15 pitted prunes
1 large Golden Delicious apple, peeled, cored, and cut in ¾-inch dice
1 tablespoon strained fresh lemon juice
Salt
Freshly ground black pepper
3 tablespoons unsalted butter
3 tablespoons vegetable oil
1 cup dry white wine
1 cup heavy cream
2 tablespoons currant jelly

When you buy the boned loin of pork, have the butcher cut a pocket the length of the loin, but not through the other side or the ends. Or do it yourself by making a deep incision along the length of the loin, in the middle, going to within 1 inch of both ends and the far side.

Place the prunes in a small saucepan and cover them with water. Bring them to a boil, remove from the heat, and let rest 30 minutes. Drain and dry with paper toweling. Drizzle the apple pieces with lemon juice to prevent darkening.

Sprinkle the pocket of the pork loin with salt and pepper to taste; then pack it alternately with the prunes and apple pieces. Sew the opening closed and tie the pork at 3-inch intervals with kitchen cord to help it retain its shape.

Select a flameproof casserole equipped with a tight-fitting lid that is large enough to contain the pork comfortably. (A fish poacher without its rack is the ideal implement.) If you don't have a casserole, use a roasting pan and an aluminum foil cover.

In the casserole or roasting pan, melt the butter with the vegetable oil over moderate heat. When it is foaming, add the pork and brown it on all sides. Drain off all the fat remaining in the pan. Cover the pan with a lid or aluminum foil, and refrigerate the loin until 2 hours before final preparation.

TIME ALLOWANCE FOR FINAL PREPARATION: 2 HOURS

Preheat the oven to 350 degrees.
In a small bowl, combine the white wine and cream.

Pour the mixture over the pork and bring it to a simmer on top of the stove, basting the meat occasionally. Cover the pan with a lid or a double thickness of aluminum foil and bake in the oven for 1½ hours, or until the meat feels tender when pierced with a knife.

Transfer the meat to a heated serving platter. Bring the liquid remaining in the pan to a rapid boil over high heat on top of the stove. Stirring constantly, reduce the liquid to about 1 cup. Add the currant jelly, lower the heat, and simmer until the jelly has melted and the sauce has thickened slightly. Transfer the sauce to a sauceboat.

Carve the loin into ½-inch-thick slices and serve the sauce separately.

SERVES 8

SAUTÉED CARROTS AND CELERY WITH FENNEL SEEDS

(MAY BE PARTIALLY PREPARED UP TO 6 HOURS IN ADVANCE)

3 tablespoons unsalted butter
2 teaspoons fennel seeds
4 large celery stalks (about ½ pound), leaves trimmed
1 medium onion, thinly sliced
1½ pounds carrots, peeled
1 teaspoon sugar
½ teaspoon salt
Freshly ground black pepper
2 tablespoons minced fresh parsley

In a 12-inch skillet, preferably one with a nonstick surface, melt 2 tablespoons of the butter over low heat. Add the fennel seeds and toast for about 3 minutes, stirring occasionally.

With a vegetable peeler, scrape off any tough strings from the celery stalks. Cut the celery in julienne strips, about ¼ by 3 inches. Add them and the onion to the fennel seeds. Sauté, stirring occasionally, until both are soft, about 5 minutes. Remove the skillet from the heat and reserve.

Cut the carrots into julienne strips about ½ by 3 inches. Place them, with the sugar, in a saucepan filled two-thirds full with salted water. Bring to a boil, lower the heat, and cook until just barely tender, about 7 to 12 minutes. Drain and refresh under cold water. Drain again and pat dry with paper towels.

Add the carrots to the skillet with the celery and onion. Season with salt and pepper and toss to mix. Cover the skillet with its lid or loosely with plastic wrap to prevent the vegetables from drying out, and set it in a cool spot in the kitchen until final preparation.

TIME ALLOWANCE FOR FINAL PREPARATION: 10 MINUTES

Dot the vegetables with the remaining tablespoon of butter. Reheat them, uncovered, over moderate heat, tossing frequently, until very hot. Transfer them to a heated serving dish and garnish with the minced parsley.

SERVES 8

LAYERED APRICOT MOUSSE

(MAY BE PARTIALLY PREPARED UP TO 24 HOURS IN ADVANCE;
MUST BE PARTIALLY PREPARED AT LEAST 6 HOURS IN ADVANCE)

2 (16-ounce) cans unpeeled apricot halves in heavy syrup
3/4 cup sugar
3 envelopes unflavored gelatin
1/2 teaspoon almond extract
1/4 teaspoon salt
3 tablespoons apricot brandy (optional)
1 (2 1/2-ounce) package sliced almonds
1 1/2 cups heavy cream, whipped
1 (10-ounce) package frozen strawberries, thawed

Drain the apricots, reserving 1 cup of the syrup. (Discard the rest.) Pour the reserved syrup into a small saucepan and mix in 1/2 cup of the sugar. Sprinkle the gelatin over the surface, let it soften for 5 minutes, then warm the syrup over low heat, stirring until the sugar and gelatin have dissolved. Set aside.

Place the apricots in the bowl of a food processor fitted with a steel blade, and puree until very smooth, about 20 seconds. Add the almond extract, salt, apricot brandy if desired, and the gelatin syrup. Whirl until well blended. Transfer the mixture to a large mixing bowl and refrigerate it until it just begins to jell and has the consistency of raw egg whites. Wash and dry the food processor bowl.

Meanwhile, place the almonds in a nonstick skillet and toast them over moderately low heat, shaking the pan frequently, until they just start to brown.

Place them in the bowl of the food processor and whirl until they are nicely ground. Add the remaining ¼ cup sugar and whirl to mix.

When the apricot mixture has achieved the right consistency, gently fold in the whipped cream. Spoon half the mixture into a 9 × 5-inch loaf pan that has been rinsed out with cold water. Using a tablespoon, sprinkle the ground almonds over the mousse, distributing them as evenly as possible. Spoon the remaining mousse over the almonds, cover the loaf pan with plastic wrap, and refrigerate until firm, about 3 hours, or until time for final preparation.

TIME ALLOWANCE FOR FINAL PREPARATION: 10 MINUTES

Place the strawberries in the bowl of a food processor fitted with a steel blade, and whirl until pureed. Transfer to a sauceboat to serve with the mousse.

Run a knife around the edge of the loaf pan to loosen the mousse. Set the pan in a bath of hot water for 1 minute. Remove it from the water and invert a serving dish over the pan. Turn over the pan and dish, give a firm shake, and the mousse should slip out. (If not, repeat the procedure.)

Cut the mousse crosswise into slices and serve them accompanied by the strawberry puree.

SERVES 8

A CLASSIC CHICKEN STEW FOR EIGHT

Coq au Vin

Boiled Potatoes

Sautéed Green Beans with Toasted Almonds

Hot French Bread

Individual Flourless Chocolate Souffles

Coq au Vin, or chicken in red wine, is a classic from Burgundy, one of the great wine-producing provinces of France. An exception to the rule that only white wine should be used with chicken, Coq au Vin is traditionally made with a fruity red Burgundy—preferably the same wine drunk later with the stew. (This may be a little hard on the budget, considering the price of French wines today. I wouldn't oppose breaking with tradition and using a nice Australian Cabernet Sauvignon for both cooking and drinking. Who but a purist would know the difference?)

Hearty Coq au Vin is no harder to prepare than any other stew. Making it a day or two in advance only improves the dish, allowing its many flavors to blend and mellow.

Since Coq au Vin is such a traditional French dish, I suggest serving the traditional accompaniments: boiled potatoes and green beans. I have spruced up the green beans a bit by adding toasted, buttered almonds; it's amazing what the little extra step of toasting the nuts in butter does for them and the beans.

The dessert, a flourless chocolate souffle with just a hint of orange, is two desserts in one. It can be baked, producing a puffy and moist souffle, or, after 3 hours chilling in the refrigerator, be served uncooked as a rich, dense mousse.

COQ AU VIN

(MAY BE PARTIALLY PREPARED UP TO 2 DAYS IN ADVANCE)

1 frying chicken (about 3 to 4 pounds), plus 2 additional whole chicken legs
1 cup flour
1½ teaspoons salt
Freshly ground black pepper
½ cup vegetable oil
1 tablespoon minced garlic
2 cups coarsely chopped onions
3 cups dry red wine, preferably a red Burgundy
1 tablespoon tomato paste
1 teaspoon dried thyme
1 (6-ounce) ham steak, cut in ½-inch dice
1 to 2 cups chicken stock
4 tablespoons butter
1 (12-ounce package) white mushrooms, quartered
½ pound pearl onions, peeled
1 teaspoon sugar
¼ cup minced fresh parsley

Cut the chicken into small serving pieces by severing the wings from the body, cutting the breasts in four sections, and separating the thighs from the legs. You should have 14 pieces (2 wings, 4 breast pieces, 4 thighs, and 4 legs).

In a shallow bowl, combine the flour, ½ teaspoon of the salt, and a generous sprinkling of freshly ground pepper. With your fingers, stir to mix well. Dredge the chicken pieces in the seasoned flour and shake off any excess.

In a large (14-inch) frying pan, preferably one with high sides, heat the vegetable oil over moderately high heat. Add enough chicken parts to cover the bottom of the pan without crowding. Sauté the chicken, turning the pieces several times, until they are golden brown on all sides. When they are done, transfer them to a 6- or 8-quart flameproof casserole. Repeat until all the chicken pieces are browned.

Lower the heat under the frying pan. Add the garlic and onions and sauté, turning frequently, until they are soft. Add the wine, tomato paste, thyme, remaining 1 teaspoon of salt, and another generous grinding of pepper, and stir to mix. Bring the wine to a boil.

Distribute the pieces of ham evenly around the chicken in the casserole. Pour the wine and onion mixture over the pieces of meat. Add just enough chicken stock to cover. Stir to blend. Place the casserole over high heat and bring the liquid to a boil. Then lower the heat, cover the casserole, and simmer the chicken 35 minutes, or until the meat feels tender when pierced with the tip of a knife.

With a slotted spoon, transfer the chicken parts to a large bowl. Cover the bowl tightly with plastic wrap and refrigerate until 1 hour before final preparation.

Meanwhile, raise the heat under the casserole and bring the liquid to a boil. Boil vigorously for 10 to 15 minutes, or until it has been reduced by half and has thickened considerably. Allow it to cool, then transfer the contents of the casserole to a mixing bowl and refrigerate. When the fat on the surface has solidified, scrape it off and discard. Cover the surface with plastic wrap and refrigerate until 1 hour before final preparation.

TIME ALLOWANCE FOR FINAL PREPARATION: 30 MINUTES

In a medium-size skillet, melt 2 tablespoons of the butter over moderate heat. Add the quartered mushrooms and sauté them, stirring frequently, for 3 to 4 minutes, or until they are barely cooked. Remove them from the heat and reserve.

Place the onions in a pot of cold water. Bring the water to a boil. Boil 1 minute, then drain the onions in a colander. Melt the remaining 2 tablespoons butter in another medium-size skillet, add the onions, and toss to coat them well with the butter. Sprinkle with the sugar and sauté for 10 minutes over moderate heat, stirring occasionally, or until the onions are nicely caramelized. Set aside and reserve.

Pour the sauce into a flameproof casserole large enough to contain the chicken and vegetables. Add the reserved chicken, cover, and reheat the chicken over moderately high heat for 10 minutes, turning the pieces occasionally. Add the reserved mushrooms and onions and heat 5 more minutes, or until the contents of the casserole are steaming hot.

Sprinkle with the minced parsley and serve immediately.

SERVES 8

SAUTÉED GREEN BEANS WITH TOASTED ALMONDS

(MAY BE PARTIALLY PREPARED UP TO 8 HOURS IN ADVANCE)

2½ pounds green beans, ends trimmed
Salt
3 tablespoons butter
2 ounces (about ½ cup) sliced almonds

Drop the beans into a nonreactive saucepan full of boiling salted water. Bring them to a boil, partially cover, and cook over moderate heat for 5 minutes, or until they are barely cooked and still bright green.

Immediately drain the beans and refresh them under cold water. Drain again and transfer them to a colander lined with paper toweling. Cover with more toweling and set aside in a cool corner of the kitchen until time for final preparation.

Meanwhile, melt 1 tablespoon of butter in a medium-size skillet, preferably one with a nonstick surface. Add the almonds and toast them over moderate heat, stirring frequently, until they are golden brown. Set them aside on paper toweling and reserve.

TIME ALLOWANCE FOR FINAL PREPARATION: 8 MINUTES

Melt the remaining 2 tablespoons of butter in a large skillet. When it is foaming, add the beans, cover, and sauté over moderate heat, tossing them frequently, until they are heated through. Take care not to overcook or they will lose their bright green color. Transfer the beans to a heated vegetable dish and sprinkle them with the reserved toasted almonds. Serve immediately.

SERVES 8

INDIVIDUAL FLOURLESS CHOCOLATE SOUFFLES

(MAY BE PARTIALLY PREPARED UP TO 6 HOURS IN ADVANCE)

8 ounces (6 squares) semisweet chocolate
1¼ cups sugar
⅔ cup light cream
¼ teaspoon plus a pinch of salt

6 egg yolks, beaten
¼ cup Cointreau or Grand Marnier (orange liqueur)
7 egg whites
1 cup heavy cream

In the top of a double boiler, over simmering water, combine the chocolate and half of the sugar. Cook over moderately low heat, stirring occasionally, until the chocolate and sugar have melted. Add the light cream and salt. Stir to blend thoroughly. Remove the top of the double boiler from the hot water and allow the chocolate to cool.

When the chocolate is no longer hot to the touch, beat in the egg yolks and the liqueur. Cover the pan with its lid or plastic wrap, and set it aside in a cool corner of the kitchen until final preparation.

TIME ALLOWANCE FOR FINAL PREPARATION: 30 MINUTES

Preheat the oven to 375 degrees. Generously butter and coat with sugar eight individual souffle dishes (¾-cup each) and shake out any excess sugar.

In a large mixing bowl, beat the egg whites with a pinch of salt until frothy. While continuing to beat, gradually add the remaining sugar. Beat until the whites are stiff but still shiny. Mix one-fourth of the whites into the chocolate mixture to lighten it, then gently fold the chocolate into the remaining whites, mixing only until no trace of white is visible.

Divide the mixture among the souffle dishes. Set them on a rack in the middle of the oven and bake for 15 to 20 minutes, or until the surface of the souffles is resilient to the touch. Do not overbake or the souffles will dry out.

Serve at once, accompanied by a pitcher of cream.

SERVES 8

NOTE: The recipe is equally successful when served, uncooked, as a mousse. Prepare the recipe as described, but instead of baking the souffles, refrigerate them, uncooked, for 3 hours before serving. Garnish with mounds of unsweetened whipped cream.

A PLEASING POLENTA
FOR EIGHT

Polenta with Gingered Shrimp

*Braised Fennel with Parmesan
Cheese*

*Hot Italian Bread with Garlic
Butter*

Daiquiri Chiffon Pie

Americans, unless they are of Italian extraction, generally don't know anything at all about polenta, which is ironic when one considers that corn, the primary ingredient of polenta, is one of our biggest crops.

Along with rice, polenta is the staple of northern Italy and is served all over that area in any number of forms. I first encountered it in Venice, in a small restaurant tucked out of sight behind the Rialto. It looked rather peculiar to my uninitiated eye: a pie-shaped wedge appearing to be cast in solid plastic foam. Actually, it was a solidified, memorable mass of cornmeal mush, hot from the oven and smothered with thin slices of calf's liver and onions. A few days later in Florence I was served another variety: a crisp pan-fried slice, infused with cheese, which accompanied most delectably a succulent grilled *poussin*, or baby chicken. And before my trip was over, I must have eaten polenta in ten different guises.

It didn't take me long, after such a marvelous indoctrination, to get on the Polenta Trail, and this menu's Polenta with Gingered Shrimp is the result of some intensive experimentation. Try the dish. There will be some polenta left over. Experiment yourself, and you'll be amazed at how many other entrees couple well with polenta. Forget rice. Forget potatoes. You'll have a new favorite soon.

Braised fennel is a European favorite, and now that this anise-flavored cousin of celery is so widely available in the United States, I think it should be served more often. Raw or cooked, it is truly distinctive.

Daiquiri Chiffon Pie, in a chocolate crust, is a light but satisfying, ethereal culmination to the meal. Of course, I am partial to daiquiris, but, then, I hardly think I'm alone with this predilection.

POLENTA WITH GINGERED SHRIMP

◆

(POLENTA MAY BE PARTIALLY PREPARED UP TO 2 DAYS IN ADVANCE;
SHRIMP MAY BE PARTIALLY PREPARED UP TO 6 HOURS IN ADVANCE)

POLENTA

7 cups water
2 cups yellow cornmeal, preferably stone-ground
2 teaspoons salt
3 tablespoons olive oil

To prepare the polenta: Pour 2 cups of the water into a mixing bowl. Pour the remaining 5 cups into a 2- to 3-quart saucepan and bring it to a boil over high heat. Add the cornmeal to the water in the mixing bowl and stir until well combined.

When the water in the saucepan is boiling, add the salt. With a rubber spatula, scrape in the moist cornmeal and any residue of liquid. Add the olive oil. With a hand-held electric mixer—taking care not to immerse the machine in the liquid—or a large wooden spoon, immediately start beating the cornmeal vigorously. This is the most important period in cooking the polenta; do not stint on the beating. Continue nonstop beating until the mixture returns to a boil.

Lower the heat to moderate and cook the polenta, stirring with a wooden spoon frequently but not necessarily constantly, until the mixture becomes very thick and comes away easily from the sides of the saucepan. This will take about 45 minutes for the stone-ground cornmeal (about 25 minutes for regular cornmeal). If in doubt abut the timing, drop a small amount of the polenta on a clean surface and allow it to cool. If it adheres to itself nicely, it is done. It should be a soft but compact mass.

Pour the still-hot mixture into a 9-by-5-inch loaf pan that has been rinsed with water but not dried. As the polenta cools, it will solidify. Cover the loaf pan with plastic wrap and refrigerate until 1 hour before final preparation.

GINGERED SHRIMP

6 tablespoons unsalted butter
4 teaspoons minced garlic
¼ cup minced, peeled gingerroot
2 cups finely chopped onions
1½ cups finely chopped celery
1½ cups finely chopped green pepper
½ pound mushrooms, thinly sliced
2 (28-ounce) cans Italian plum tomatoes, drained and coarsely chopped
3 pounds large shrimp, shelled and deveined
1 teaspoon salt
Freshly ground black pepper
¾ cup minced fresh cilantro (or substitute parsley)

To prepare the shrimp: In a 14-inch skillet, preferably one with high sides, melt the butter over moderate heat. Add the garlic, ginger, onions, celery, and green pepper. Cook, stirring frequently, until the vegetables are just softened, about 5 minutes. Immediately add the mushrooms and sauté them, stirring, for 3 minutes. Mix in the tomatoes, lower the heat, and simmer the vegetables, partially covered, for 15 minutes.

Remove the skillet from the heat. When it has cooled to room temperature, cover it tightly, and set it aside in a cool corner of the kitchen until final preparation.

TIME ALLOWANCE FOR FINAL PREPARATION: 25 MINUTES

Preheat the oven to 300 degrees.

Run a knife around the sides of the loaf pan to loosen the polenta. Giving it a good shake, turn it out onto a wooden cutting board. With a serrated knife, cut eight ½-inch-thick slices crosswise from the polenta loaf.

Lightly butter a cookie sheet or jellyroll pan. Lay the polenta slices down on the pan, and warm them in the oven for 20 minutes.

Ten minutes before the polenta is done, return the vegetable-filled skillet to the range. Turn the heat to moderately high, and warm the vegetables. When they are steaming hot (about 5 minutes), add the shrimp. Cook, tossing the shrimp, just until they turn opaque, about 5 minutes. Add the salt, pepper, and cilantro.

Place one slice of heated polenta on each of eight dinner plates. Spoon the Gingered Shrimp on top and serve immediately.

SERVES 8

BRAISED FENNEL WITH PARMESAN CHEESE

(MAY BE PARTIALLY PREPARED UP TO 8 HOURS IN ADVANCE)

4 whole fennel bulbs (about ¾ pound each), trimmed
¼ cup thinly sliced scallions (white parts only)
2 cups chicken stock
4 tablespoons unsalted butter, cut in small pieces
Freshly ground black pepper
½ cup freshly grated Parmesan cheese

Preheat the oven to 375 degrees.

Trim the fennel bulbs of all stalks and spidery leaves. Cut each bulb in half from stalk end to the "heart" at the base.

Place the fennel halves, cut sides up, in an ovenproof baking dish large enough to hold them all in one layer. Scatter the scallions on top. Pour the chicken stock over the fennel. Dot with the butter. Sprinkle generously with pepper.

Seal the baking dish tightly with aluminum foil. Bake the fennel in the oven for 1 hour. Remove the dish from the oven, loosen the foil, and reserve the fennel in a cool corner of the kitchen until final preparation.

TIME ALLOWANCE FOR FINAL PREPARATION: 50 MINUTES

Preheat the oven to 375 degrees.

Remove the aluminum foil from the baking dish.

Return the fennel to the oven and bake, uncovered, for 30 minutes. Sprinkle the fennel with the Parmesan cheese, allowing 1 tablespoon for each bulb. Bake 10 minutes longer, then place the dish under the broiler and broil until the surface is brown and bubbling (about 5 minutes).

Serve immediately, direct from the baking dish, spooning excess juices over each portion.

SERVES 8

DAIQUIRI CHIFFON PIE

◆

(MAY BE PREPARED UP TO 24 HOURS IN ADVANCE;
MUST BE PREPARED AT LEAST 4 HOURS IN ADVANCE)

CHOCOLATE PIE CRUST

1⅓ cups pulverized chocolate wafers (about 6 ounces)
¼ cup sugar
6 tablespoons unsalted butter, melted

To make the crust: Preheat the oven to 400 degrees.

In a mixing bowl, combine the pulverized chocolate wafers, sugar, and melted butter. Mix until the ingredients adhere to each other. Press the crumbs with your fingers or the back of a spoon into a 9-inch pie plate, covering the bottom and sides as evenly as possible.

Bake the crust for 8 minutes. Remove it from the oven and set it aside to cool.

DAIQUIRI FILLING

4 eggs, separated
¾ cup strained fresh lime juice
1½ cups sugar
1 envelope unflavored gelatin
Pinch of salt
1 teaspoon grated lime rind
½ cup golden rum
½ cup heavy cream
2 tablespoons coarsely grated sweet German chocolate

To make the filling: In the top of a large double boiler, beat the egg yolks and lime juice until they are just combined. Beat in 1 cup of the sugar. Sprinkle the gelatin and salt over the mixture and let it soften for 5 minutes.

Place the top of the double boiler over boiling water and cook, stirring constantly, until the mixture thickens like a custard, coating the back of a spoon (about 10 minutes). Remove the top of the double boiler from the boiling water, add the lime rind and rum, and stir until they are well mixed. Allow the custard to cool to room temperature, then place it in the refrigerator to thicken.

When the custard has achieved the consistency of mayonnaise (about 30 minutes), beat the egg whites in a large mixing bowl until soft peaks form. Gradually beat in the remaining ½ cup of sugar. Continue beating until the whites stand in stiff peaks.

In a chilled large mixing bowl, beat the cream until stiff. Fold the beaten egg whites into the cream.

Mix one-third of the cream mixture into the custard to lighten it, then fold the lightened custard into the remaining cream mixture.

♦

To assemble the pie: Spoon three-quarters of the filling into the reserved chocolate pie shell. Refrigerate the pie, along with the remaining filling, for 30 minutes, or until it just starts to firm. Mound the remaining filling in the center of the pie, swirling and smoothing it decoratively. (By filling the pie in two parts, you will be able to mound and mold it more attractively.) Sprinkle the surface of the pie with the grated chocolate.

Refrigerate the pie for at least 3 hours before serving so that it completely solidifies. However, if you are making the pie more than 6 hours before serving it, be sure to cover it carefully and well. It is so delicate that any aromas from other foods in the refrigerator can be absorbed and will detract from its quality.

YIELD: 1 9-INCH PIE

ENTERTAINING
LARGE
GROUPS

Entertaining large groups is hard work. There's no doubt about that. Everything about it is demanding. Lots of food has to be purchased and prepared. Lots of utensils have to be obtained one way or the other, whether they're borrowed, rented, or dug out of the depths of some remote closet. Lots of cleaning has to be done—both before and after. Lots of details have to be anticipated and attended to. And, most of the time, entertaining many folk in one go-round means spending lots of money. Even with a strict eye on the budget, food and beverages cost dearly today.

But let's look on the bright side of entertaining large numbers. Once it's done, it's done! You've paid back a slew of obligations. The risk factor—a dud of a party (and, unfortunately, that happens to all of us at least once in a lifetime)—is reduced simply because of the numbers. In a large group, there are bound to be compatible souls who will find each other and enliven the gathering. And, although the amount of cooking is greater, there are still only a handful of dishes to prepare. (If, instead of throwing a party for fifty, you gave five parties for ten, you'd be slaving over five times as many entrees, vegetables, and desserts. I consider that *much* more labor intensive.)

The chapter that follows has suggestions and menus for a variety of events in which ten or more people are involved. Some are for specific occasions that we all have to face at one time or another, such as rehearsal dinners, large birthday celebrations, or graduation lunches. Others are for rather nebulous, even prosaic, occasions such as brunches, lunches, and picnics. All are designed to inspire as well as guide. No menu should be read as being carved in stone, or its recipes interpreted as the *only* dishes to serve at that particular occasion. Some, in fact, are appropriate for many different types of occasions, so feel free to borrow from one menu for another, or substitute one recipe for another.

The most important thing to remember, as in all manner of entertaining—whether for large groups or small—is that you, as host or hostess, enjoy yourself by organizing and preparing ahead. That way, it's a sure thing that your guests will have a great time too. It's a rule that never fails.

AN ELEGANT FRESH HAM ROAST DINNER FOR EIGHTEEN

*Avocados with Herb Vinaigrette**

Roast Fresh Ham with Red Currant Sauce

Sandy Delnickas's Potato Casserole Supreme

Broccoli Molds filled with Sautéed Cherry Tomatoes

Profiteroles with Hot Chocolate Sauce

A roast fresh ham is an elegant and different entree, and inexpensive to boot. If you like pork, you'll love this roast: it's lean, tender, and flavorful, and it is actually the same cut as a smoked ham without the smoking. Only beware: It's not always in your butcher's case, so be sure to allow a couple of extra days for special ordering.

Fresh hams are sizable roasts; they range from eight to eighteen pounds, so they can feed a large group nicely. Their cost is considerably lower per pound than a loin of pork. In spite of their large size, they do not demand much attention while in the oven, a blessing for the busy host. This recipe calls for basting the last hour or so with a piquant barbecuelike sauce, which gives the meat a dramatic glaze. (The same glaze is also the basis for the accompanying red currant sauce.) Since this dinner should be served sitting down, and you will be eighteen at the table, I suggest carving the ham in the kitchen and presenting it sliced, on a preheated platter. Carve it as you would a smoked ham: on a slight angle, perpendicular to the bone. Although it's very dramatic to carve a large roast at the table, by the time you would be ready to serve the last guest at the meal for eighteen, the first would be eager for seconds—and you wouldn't have eaten a morsel.

Start the meal off with avocado halves filled with herb vinaigrette dressing. Then with the roast, I suggest serving delicately flavored broccoli molds, brightened with sautéed cherry tomatoes, accompanied by a cheese-and-scallion-enlivened potato casserole. The ham and vegetables are visually very appealing together and, from a flavor viewpoint, very compatible.

Profiteroles with Hot Chocolate Sauce are an old favorite, popular with all ages.

* Make five times the recipe for Avocados with Herb Vinaigrette, page 40.

Who can resist a crisp casing, an interior of luscious ice cream, and a topping of chocolate sauce? With such desserts, the ice cream parlor was born; it's obvious they're going to remain with us for a long, long time.

ROAST FRESH HAM WITH RED CURRANT SAUCE

◆

(MUST BE PREPARED 5 TO 7 HOURS BEFORE SERVING)

There is no true "do-ahead" preparation for fresh ham. However, since it requires a long, slow period of cooking before the final glazing, it can almost be forgotten while other chores, even last-minute marketing, are accomplished.

> 1 whole fresh ham (about 14 to 16 pounds)
> 1½ teaspoons salt
> ¼ teaspoon freshly ground black pepper
> 3 tablespoons unsalted butter
> 1½ cups chopped onions
> 1 (10¾-ounce can) tomato puree
> ½ cup water
> ¼ cup honey
> 2 tablespoons Worcestershire sauce
> 1 tablespoon ground ginger
> 1 teaspoon dry mustard
> 1 cup red currant jelly

Preheat the oven to 325 degrees. Calculate a rough cooking time allowance for the ham of 23 minutes per pound. If you own a meat thermometer, however, please rely on an internal temperature of 160 degrees for doneness, rather than a time/weight calculation. Your ham should take between 5 and 6 hours to roast, plus 20 minutes for resting after it is removed from the oven.

Place the ham on a rack in a large roasting pan. Sprinkle its surface with 1 teaspoon of the salt and the pepper. Roast, undisturbed, for 4 hours.

Meanwhile, make the sauce for the glaze by melting the butter in a 2- to 3-quart saucepan over moderately high heat. Add the onions and cook them until they just begin to brown, stirring occasionally. Add the tomato puree, water, honey, Worcestershire sauce, ginger, dry mustard, and the remaining ½ teaspoon salt. Blend well. Bring the sauce to a boil, stirring frequently, then lower the heat and simmer it for 30 minutes. Strain the sauce, pressing down on the solids to extract all their juices. Set it aside until ready to use.

When the ham has roasted for 4 hours, remove it from the oven, but leave the oven turned on. Carefully cut off and discard all the fat. Discard all the fat that has accumulated in the roasting pan. With a pastry brush, generously coat the surface of the ham with the sauce. Return the ham to its rack in the roasting pan and continue to roast it, coating it every 15 minutes with the sauce, until a meat thermometer inserted in the center reads 160 degrees.

Transfer the ham to a heated platter, cover it loosely with aluminum foil, and allow it to rest for 20 minutes before carving.

Add the currant jelly to any sauce that remains and heat the mixture until it boils, stirring until the jelly has melted. Serve the sauce in a sauceboat to accompany the ham.

SERVES 18

NOTE: The National Pork Producers Council recommends cooking pork to an internal temperature of 155 to 160 degrees, considerably below the old guideline of 170 degrees. Trichinae are rarely found in hogs today, and even if they are present, cooking to these temperatures will safeguard against infection. Do not be afraid to serve moist, slightly pink pork.

SANDY DELNICKAS'S POTATO CASSEROLE SUPREME

(MAY BE PARTIALLY PREPARED UP TO 2 DAYS IN ADVANCE;
MUST BE PARTIALLY PREPARED 12 HOURS IN ADVANCE)

6 pounds new potatoes, peeled
1½ cups unsalted butter, melted
6 cups grated sharp Cheddar cheese (about 1 to 1 ½ pounds)
¾ cups sliced scallion, including the green leaves
3 pints sour cream
1½ teaspoons salt
½ teaspoon freshly ground black pepper

Cook the potatoes in boiling salted water until they are tender when pierced with a knife. Drain, cover, and refrigerate overnight or for at least 12 hours.

Coarsely shred the potatoes into a large mixing bowl. Add the butter, cheese, scallions, sour cream, salt, and pepper, and beat until all the ingredients are well mixed.

Divide the potato mixture among two 2-quart, shallow baking dishes. Cover with plastic wrap and refrigerate until 1 hour before final preparation.

TIME ALLOWANCE FOR FINAL PREPARATION: 40 MINUTES

Preheat the oven to 350 degrees.

Bake the potatoes for 30 to 35 minutes, or until they are bubbly and golden brown.

SERVES 18

BROCCOLI MOLDS FILLED WITH SAUTÉED CHERRY TOMATOES

(MAY BE PARTIALLY PREPARED UP TO 6 HOURS IN ADVANCE)

6 pounds broccoli
8 eggs
2 cups heavy cream
1/2 teaspoon freshly grated nutmeg
1 teaspoon salt
1/2 cup unsalted butter
2 pounds cherry tomatoes, stems removed
1 teaspoon sugar
1/4 cup minced fresh parsley

Fill a 6- to 8-quart saucepan to within 3 inches of its rim with salted water. Bring the water to a boil. Cut off the broccoli flowerets where they branch out above the thick stems; reserve them. Cut off a 3-inch length of each thick stem and cut it into 1/2-inch-thick slices. Discard the lower end of the stalks. Drop the stem slices into the boiling water and boil for 5 minutes. Add the flowerets and boil them an additional 5 minutes. Do not overcook the broccoli, or it will lose its bright green appearance.

Drain the broccoli and refresh it under cold water. Pick out 4 cups of flowerets and reserve. Place the remaining broccoli in a food processor fitted with a steel blade. Whirl until coarsely chopped. Add the eggs, cream, nutmeg, and salt. (If you have a small processor, you may have to do this in 2 batches.) Whirl for 2 minutes, or until the mixture is quite smooth.

Meanwhile, chop the reserved broccoli flowerets quite fine. Add them to the puree and stir by hand until well distributed. Generously butter two 2-quart ring molds. Divide the broccoli mixture evenly between them. Cover the molds with plastic wrap and refrigerate them until 1 hour before final preparation.

TIME ALLOWANCE FOR FINAL PREPARATION: 45 MINUTES

Preheat the oven to 325 degrees. Bring 2 kettles of water to a boil.

Place each mold in a baking dish. Pour boiling water into the dishes until it comes halfway up the sides of the molds. Bake for 30 minutes, or until the broccoli custards are set.

About 8 minutes before the broccoli is finished, melt the butter in a large 14-inch skillet, preferably one with high sides. When it is foaming, add the tomatoes. Sprinkle them with the sugar and keep tossing them over high heat for about 3 to 4 minutes. Do not cook them too long or they will burst.

To serve: Run a knife around the inside edges of the broccoli molds. Invert a round platter or serving dish over each ring mold. Turn the ring mold and platter over and give a firm shake. The broccoli mold should slip out easily. If not, run the knife around the edges again and repeat the procedure.

Divide the tomatoes evenly between the centers of the broccoli molds and sprinkle them with the parsley. Serve immediately.

SERVES 18

PROFITEROLES WITH HOT CHOCOLATE SAUCE

◆

(PROFITEROLES MAY BE PREPARED UP TO 2 WEEKS IN ADVANCE AND FROZEN;
SAUCE MAY BE PREPARED UP TO 2 WEEKS IN ADVANCE AND REFRIGERATED)

Making the "pâte à choux" dough for the profiteroles requires a fair amount of heavy beating with a strong arm. Therefore, it is easier to make the recipe in three batches, although the baking can be done all at once. The amounts given below for the pastry are for one batch; it should be repeated two more times in order to have enough to serve 18.

PROFITEROLES
1 cup water
½ cup unsalted butter
1 cup flour
1 teaspoon sugar
¼ teaspoon salt
4 eggs

To make the profiteroles: Preheat the oven to 400 degrees. Lightly butter a jellyroll pan or cookie sheet.

Combine the water and butter in a 1- to 2-quart saucepan and bring them to a boil. In a small bowl, mix the flour, sugar, and salt. Add them to the butter mixture all at once. With a wooden spoon, beat briskly over medium heat until the mixture comes away from the sides of the pan and forms a ball. Remove the saucepan from the heat and add the eggs, 1 at a time, beating until each is totally incorporated before adding the next.

Mound the dough, which will be thick and somewhat sticky, by the heaping serving-spoonful on the baking sheet. Place the pan in the oven and bake for 5 minutes. Reduce the heat to 350 degrees, and bake the pâte à choux rounds for 30 more minutes. Remove them from the oven and split them in half horizontally with a serrated knife. Return them to the oven for 5 more minutes to dry out. The puffs should be golden and dry. Pull away and discard any damp dough clinging to the insides. Allow the puffs to cool completely before filling.

(Repeat the recipe two more times in order to have a total of about 20 to 22 profiteroles.)

FINAL ASSEMBLY
2 quarts vanilla or chocolate ice cream, slightly softened

Place a large scoop of ice cream in the bottom half of each puff. Top each puff with its matching half. Place the filled puffs on cookie sheets and put them in the freezer. When they are frozen solid, transfer them to plastic bags, sealing them well.

HOT CHOCOLATE SAUCE

1 cup unsweetened cocoa
1 cup white sugar
1 cup firmly packed dark brown sugar
2 cups light corn syrup
1 cup heavy cream
2/3 cup unsalted butter
1/4 teaspoon salt
1/4 teaspoon ground cinnamon
2 teaspoons vanilla

To make the sauce: In a 2- to 3-quart saucepan, combine the cocoa, white and brown sugars, corn syrup, cream, butter, salt, and cinnamon. Over moderate heat, bring the mixture to a boil and stir continuously until the ingredients are dissolved and well mixed. Boil the syrup for 5 minutes.

Remove the pan from the heat and stir in the vanilla. Cool.

Transfer the sauce to a glass jar equipped with a tight-fitting lid. Cover and refrigerate until 1 hour before final preparation.

YIELD: ABOUT 5 CUPS

TIME ALLOWANCE FOR FINAL PREPARATION: 15 MINUTES

Remove the profiteroles from the freezer and arrange them on individual serving dishes or a platter. Allow them to thaw for at least 10 minutes, so that they will not be too hard to eat.

Transfer the chocolate sauce to a saucepan and bring it to just under a boil over moderately low heat.

Ladle generous amounts of the sauce over the profiteroles, or serve it separately in a sauceboat.

SERVES 18

KAFFEE KLATSCH FOR TWENTY

Freshly Brewed Coffee and Tea

Citrus Squares

Miniature Sticky Buns

Apple Cake

Morning meetings over coffee seem to be one of the most popular settings for informal discussions of local issues. Groups gather in the early hours to make plans for a school fair, to raise money for a hospital or museum, or to meet candidates for political office. And more often than not, the coffee proffered is bitter, and the doughnuts are the relatively tasteless commercial kind purchased from a market down the street.

But you can reverse this trend. When it's your turn to host the gathering, offer good coffees, brewed from freshly ground beans—Mocha Java or Columbia Excelso or Hawaiian Kona. You only need to offer two kinds of coffee but make certain one is decaffeinated, preferably by the water process (a nonchemical secret method patented by a Swiss company). Don't skimp on the teas, either. There are a lot of eager tea drinkers out there. Keep them happy with a scented Earl Grey or an aromatic cinnamon or mint blend.

And forget the doughnuts! Offer one, two, or all three of the nibbles I'm suggesting here: tart, delightful Citrus Squares, nutty sticky buns, or a moist apple cake—all of which can be made in advance. Your meeting cannot fail to produce the desired results. The way to *everyone's* heart is through his or her stomach.

CITRUS SQUARES

(MAY BE PREPARED UP TO 2 MONTHS IN ADVANCE AND FROZEN,
OR UP TO 2 DAYS IN ADVANCE AND KEPT AT ROOM TEMPERATURE)

CRUST

1 cup unsalted butter, cut in pieces
½ cup confectioners' sugar

2 cups flour
¼ teaspoon salt

To make the crust: Place the butter pieces, sugar, flour, and salt in the bowl of a food processor fitted with a steel blade. Pulse 10 or 12 times to cut and distribute the butter, then whirl until the mixture just forms a soft ball. (Do not overprocess or the dough will toughen.)

Pinch off pieces of the dough and pat them onto the bottom of a jellyroll pan approximately 10 by 15 inches in size. Try to keep the crust the same thickness all over. Place the pan in the refrigerator for 30 minutes for the butter to harden.

Preheat the oven to 350 degrees.

Prick the crust all over with the tines of a fork. Bake the crust for 25 minutes. Cool it on a rack before covering it with the topping. Do NOT turn off the oven.

TOPPING

4 eggs
2 cups sugar
6 tablespoons cornstarch
¼ cup grated lemon rind
2 tablespoons grated orange rind
½ cup strained fresh lemon juice
Pinch of salt
Confectioners' sugar

To make the topping: In a mixing bowl, beat the eggs until frothy. Gradually beat in the sugar and continue beating until the mixture is very light in color. Beat in the cornstarch, lemon and orange rinds, lemon juice, and salt. Beat for 1 minute to make certain the cornstarch has been absorbed.

To assemble: When the crust is cool, spread the topping evenly over its surface.

Return the pan to the oven and bake the pastry for 25 minutes. Cool on a rack. With a wet knife, cut the pastry into 1½-inch squares.

Just before serving, dust the top with confectioners' sugar.

YIELD: APPROXIMATELY 75 SQUARES

MINIATURE STICKY BUNS

(MAY BE PARTIALLY PREPARED UP TO 4 DAYS IN ADVANCE;
MUST BE PARTIALLY PREPARED 12 HOURS IN ADVANCE)

1 package dry yeast
½ cup lukewarm water
12 tablespoons unsalted butter
½ cup milk
¾ cup sugar
1 egg
3½ cups unbleached flour
½ cup brown sugar
2 tablespoons dark corn syrup
½ cup chopped pecans
1 tablespoon ground cinnamon
½ cup chopped seedless raisins

Sprinkle the yeast over the lukewarm water and allow it to rest for 10 minutes until it starts to foam. Meanwhile, in a small saucepan, combine 2 tablespoons of the butter, the milk, and ¼ cup of the sugar. Stir until the sugar has dissolved and the butter has melted. Set aside to cool.

Transfer the milk mixture and the yeast to a food processor fitted with a steel blade. Add the egg and whirl briefly to mix. Add the flour and whirl for 2 minutes. A ball will form and the dough will be well kneaded. Butter a small mixing bowl and place the dough in it; turn the dough around several times until it is completely coated with a thin layer of butter on all sides. Cover the bowl with plastic wrap and refrigerate the dough for at least 12 hours or overnight, or up to 4 days.

TIME ALLOWANCE FOR FINAL PREPARATION: 1½ TO 2¼ HOURS

In a small saucepan, over moderate heat, mix together the brown sugar, corn syrup, 8 tablespoons of the butter, and chopped pecans. Stir until the sugar and butter have melted. With a rubber spatula, scrape the mixture into a greased jellyroll pan, about 10 by 15 inches in size, and spread it as evenly as possible over the bottom of the pan. It will be sticky, particularly as it hardens, but it will melt and redistribute as the buns bake.

Combine the remaining ½ cup sugar with the cinnamon. Blend well. Melt the remaining 2 tablespoons butter. Have the chopped raisins close at hand.

Remove the dough from the refrigerator and punch it down with your fist. Knead the dough a few times on a floured surface and pat it into a rectangular shape. With a rolling pin, roll the dough into a 10-by-16-inch rectangle. Brush its surface with the melted butter, then sprinkle it evenly with the cinnamon-sugar and chopped raisins. Cut the dough lengthwise and crosswise in half so that you have four pieces, each approximately 5 by 8 inches. Beginning at the wide side, roll up each piece tightly, sealing the edges well and pushing the raisins back in if they slip out. Cut each roll into 1-inch segments. Place the pieces in the prepared pan, not too close together. (They will spread out as they undergo the second rising.) Cover the buns loosely with plastic wrap and let them rise in a draft-free place until they have doubled in volume, about 1 to 1½ hours.

Preheat the oven to 375 degrees.

Remove the plastic and bake the buns for 20 to 25 minutes.

While the buns are still warm, turn them out on a serving platter. Scoop up any topping remaining in the pan and spread it over the buns.

YIELD: ABOUT 40 MINIATURE BUNS

NOTE: If you prefer, you may bake the buns up to 24 hours in advance. After they have cooled, cover them tightly with plastic wrap or aluminum foil and set them aside. Reheat them in a 300-degree oven for 20 minutes before serving.

APPLE CAKE

(MAY BE PREPARED UP TO 2 DAYS IN ADVANCE)

4 large Golden Delicious apples (about 1½ pounds), peeled, cored, and chopped
1 cup coarsely chopped walnuts
1 cup seedless golden raisins
1 tablespoon grated orange rind
2 cups sugar
3 cups flour
1 teaspoon baking soda
1 teaspoon ground cinnamon
1 teaspoon salt
3 eggs
1 cup vegetable oil
2 teaspoons vanilla

In a mixing bowl, combine the apples, walnuts, raisins, orange rind, and sugar. Toss thoroughly. Set the mixture aside for 1 hour, stirring it occasionally. During this time the apples will release their juices, thus providing the liquid that is essential to the recipe.

Preheat the oven to 350 degrees. Generously butter a 9-inch tube pan.

Sift together the flour, baking soda, cinnamon, and salt into another bowl. In a separate bowl, beat the eggs until thick; then, continuing to beat, add the oil and vanilla. Pour the flour mixture into the eggs and mix thoroughly. The batter will be lumpy and rather sticky. Add the apples and walnuts. Blend well. Spoon the batter into the prepared tube pan. Rap the pan sharply on a solid surface to eliminate any air bubbles.

Bake the cake for 1¼ hours, or until a knife inserted in the center comes out clean. Cool the cake on a rack. To release the cake from the tube pan, run a knife around its edges to loosen it before inverting it onto a serving platter.

If you are baking the cake well in advance, wrap it tightly in aluminum foil and refrigerate it until 2 hours before serving.

YIELD: 1 9-INCH TUBE CAKE

SUMMER LUNCHEON FOR TEN

Chilled Borscht with Sour Cream

Stroganoff Salad

Herbed Corn Sticks

Strawberry Pie

"Summertime and the Livin' is Easy...." warbles the familiar Gershwin tune.

It's a nice idea, but all too often the livin' is not easy when it comes to summer entertaining. During those balmy days, when the temperature is in the 90s, it is a real struggle to cook joyously. If the range isn't radiating heat, the oven is, and any delight in feeding hungry guests declines as precipitously as the temperature outside has elevated.

Planning and cooking ahead helps, as do cold menus. But as we all know, not every day is a killer in the summer, and some of the best-laid plans can go awry. If we plan a cold evening meal for a hot summer's night, it inevitably is sweater weather. If the forecast seems to promise cool breezes and we go for broke with a hot meal, we melt in the process of presenting it. Grilling out-of-doors is a good solution, but it's hardly feasible for the apartment dweller.

Luncheon menus in the summer are not as risky to plan as dinners. Appetites are programmed for cold midday meals, even if there's a deluge outside. And cold meals, even for a large group, are very simple to plan, prepare, and present.

This menu for a summer luncheon is a veritable breeze. The Borscht (beet soup) does not have to be made. A very creditable bottled version can be found at your local supermarket (buy two 32-ounce jars to feed ten) and spark up each serving with a dollop of sour cream. The Stroganoff Salad can be prepared up to two hours in advance and dressed at the last moment. (All the cutting can be done well ahead if the ingredients are properly wrapped and sealed.) It's a host's delight; it's hearty enough to please any voracious appetite around, or, minus a few spoonfuls, it will prove equally satisfactory to a dainty eater. The Herbed Corn Sticks can be made a day earlier and still be as crisp and crunchy as if they came straight from the oven. Slathered in sweet butter, they are impossible for any but the most determined dieter to resist.

But even dieters won't be able to forego the Strawberry Pie, which also can be made well in advance. Piled high with berries, and glazed with a shimmering strawberry puree, it is every bit as delectable as it is stunning to behold.

STROGANOFF SALAD

◆

(SALAD MAY BE PARTIALLY PREPARED UP TO 6 HOURS IN ADVANCE;
DRESSING MAY BE PREPARED 24 HOURS IN ADVANCE,
BUT IT MUST BE PREPARED AT LEAST 4 HOURS IN ADVANCE)

1 medium head escarole, washed, dried, and torn into bite-size pieces
1 medium head Boston lettuce, washed, dried, and torn into bite-size pieces
2 bunches watercress, washed, dried, and tough stems discarded
1 small red cabbage (about 1½ pounds), coarsely shredded
1 yellow pepper (about ½ pound), cored, seeded, and cut in julienne strips
1 pound mushrooms, thinly sliced
6 cups thinly sliced and julienned tender, rare beef (such as eye of the round, about 3 pounds)
2 cups thinly sliced and julienned imported Gruyère cheese (about ½ pound)
½ pound cherry tomatoes, stems removed
3 tablespoons minced fresh chives

To make the salad: Place the escarole, Boston lettuce, watercress, cabbage, and pepper in a very large salad bowl lined with paper toweling. Toss with your hands or a salad fork and spoon until the vegetables are well mixed. Cover with more sheets of paper toweling and refrigerate until time for final preparation.

Prepare the mushrooms, beef, and cheese, and wrap them separately with plastic wrap. Refrigerate until final preparation.

STROGANOFF DRESSING

½ cup sour cream
½ cup plain yogurt
⅔ cup mayonnaise
3 tablespoons strained fresh lemon juice
⅓ cup finely sliced scallions (white parts only)
2 tablespoons prepared horseradish, drained
2 teaspoons Dijon-style mustard
¼ teaspoon freshly ground black pepper

To make the dressing: Combine the sour cream, yogurt, mayonnaise, and lemon juice in a mixing bowl. Mix until completely blended with a rubber spatula or large wooden spoon. Stir in the scallions, horseradish, mustard, and pepper. Transfer to a jar and seal with a tight-fitting lid or plastic wrap. Refrigerate until time for final preparation.

YIELD: ABOUT 2¼ CUPS DRESSING

TIME ALLOWANCE FOR FINAL PREPARATION: 10 MINUTES

Give the salad dressing a final stir or two. Remove the paper toweling from the salad. Add the mushrooms, beef, and cheese, and mix thoroughly. Pour the dressing over the salad and toss until all the ingredients are well coated. Arrange the cherry tomatoes decoratively around the edge of the bowl, and sprinkle the chives on top.

SERVES 10

HERBED CORN STICKS

◆

(MAY BE PREPARED UP TO 24 HOURS IN ADVANCE)

1½ cups cornmeal, preferably stone-ground
½ cup flour
2 tablespoons sugar
1 tablespoon baking powder
1 teaspoon salt
2 eggs
1½ cups buttermilk
1 teaspoon dried rosemary, crushed
1½ tablespoons unsalted butter, melted

Preheat the oven to 400 degrees.

Sift the cornmeal, flour, sugar, baking powder, and salt into a large mixing bowl.

In a separate bowl, beat the eggs lightly with a whisk. Add the buttermilk and mix thoroughly. Pour this mixture into the dry ingredients and stir until the batter is smooth. Mix in the rosemary.

Place two cast-iron corn-stick pans in the oven for 5 minutes to heat. Carefully remove them, one at a time, and brush the corn-stick molds with melted butter. Fill the molds almost to the rim with the batter. Bake for 30 minutes, or until the corn sticks are golden brown and crisp. While they are still hot, unmold the sticks and cool them on a rack. If you have extra batter left, immediately brush the hot molds with any remaining melted butter, fill them with batter, and bake.

When the corn sticks are cool, store them in a plastic bag, securely tied. (Refrigerate them if holding them longer than 6 hours.)

Serve them at room temperature, or briefly reheat them in a 300-degree oven. Serve them with plenty of butter.

YIELD: ABOUT 20 CORN STICKS

STRAWBERRY PIE

◆

2 (3-ounce) packages cream cheese, softened
2 tablespoons light cream
1 tablespoon strained fresh lemon juice
1 10-inch prebaked pie shell, cooled
2 quarts strawberries, hulled and washed
½ cup water
3 tablespoons cornstarch
1¼ cups sugar
¼ teaspoon salt
1 tablespoon unsalted butter, melted
1½ cups heavy cream

In a small bowl, using an electric mixer, whip the cream cheese with the light cream and lemon juice until smooth and light. Using a rubber spatula, spread the mixture over the bottom of the pie crust. Mound 6 cups whole strawberries on top.

There should be between 2 and 3 cups of strawberries remaining. Whatever the amount, puree the berries in a food processor fitted with a steel blade.

Pour the water, cornstarch, sugar, and salt into a medium-size saucepan, and bring to a boil, stirring until dissolved. Add the strawberry puree, return the mixture to a boil, lower the heat, and simmer 4 minutes, stirring occasionally. Press the mixture through a sieve, extracting all the juice. Discard the pulp. Stir the butter into the juice and mix well. Spoon the mixture over the whole strawberries in the pie shell, distributing it as evenly as possible and coating all the berries. Refrigerate, loosely covered with plastic wrap, for at least 1 hour, or as long as 6 hours to firm the glaze.

TIME ALLOWANCE FOR FINAL PREPARATION: 5 MINUTES

Whip the cream until it stands in soft peaks. Transfer it to a serving bowl. Cut the pie into wedges and serve it with generous spoonfuls of the whipped cream.

SERVES 10

SHERRIED SEAFOOD BUFFET FOR EIGHTEEN

Salmon and Lobster Newburg

Steamed Rice with Toasted Coconut

Italian Garden Salad

Black Currant and Chocolate Cheesecake

Buffets, as has been said before, demand easy eating. That is, the food must be bite-size and knives unnecessary. There is nothing worse than a stand-up buffet where the guests have to balance plates and glasses while struggling to sever a piece of beef into a manageable mouthful. No one yet has been born with three or four arms, which would come in very handy at such an event.

This buffet's menu for eighteen has been designed especially for simple serving and eating. (I trust you have hotplates, or can borrow a couple, to keep the food warm. I hate to see food cool unnecessarily when there are a good number of guests helping themselves at a leisurely pace.) The Salmon and Lobster Newburg is a variation on an old and splendid theme: succulent morsels of lobster bathed in a rich, sherry-enhanced sauce. To keep the budget somewhat intact as the cost of lobster escalates, and to provide some variety, salmon has been incorporated in the dish. Not only does this beautiful pink fish add color, it also offers a pleasant contrast in texture.

The Newburg sauce calls out for rice as an accompaniment to absorb its delicate flavor. I first enjoyed this rice dish with toasted coconut in India, and it seems the perfect foil for the Newburg. However, if you would prefer plain steamed rice (thus avoiding the chore of grating a fresh coconut), by all means substitute it. The Italian Garden Salad is a real winner. All my guests rave whenever I serve it. It's pretty and crunchy and packs a lot of colorful vegetables. And what is particularly nice, it can be entirely prepared a couple of hours before the evening begins.

There's no way to describe adequately the Black Currant and Chocolate Cheesecake. It is a unique combination of flavors. I've always enjoyed experimenting with cheesecakes; they're so versatile. But I went rather wild with this one, and, I must confess, I found myself rather nervous when I first brought it to the table. (My guests come prepared for anything!) Happily, it worked, and even my children—my most severe critics—request it time and time again.

SALMON AND LOBSTER NEWBURG

(MAY BE PARTIALLY PREPARED UP TO 6 HOURS IN ADVANCE)

1 cup minced shallots
4 pounds salmon steaks, each about 1½ inches thick
6 cups dry white wine
3 to 4 cups water
3 bay leaves
3 pounds cooked lobster meat, cut into bite-size pieces
12 tablespoons unsalted butter
1½ pounds medium-size mushrooms, trimmed and quartered
½ cup flour
4 cups light cream
2 egg yolks, beaten
½ cup dry sherry
Salt and freshly ground pepper to taste
½ cup minced fresh dillweed

Sprinkle ½ cup of the shallots on the bottom of a 14-inch skillet (equipped with high sides) or a flameproof roasting pan. Arrange the salmon steaks side by side, but not overlapping, in the pan. Pour the wine over the steaks, then add between 3 to 4 cups water, or just enough to cover the fish. Drop in the bay leaves. Bring the liquid just to a boil, then immediately lower the heat and simmer, partially covered, for 15 minutes, or until the fish flakes easily when pierced with the tip of a knife. Using a slotted spatula, transfer the steaks to a platter.

Return the skillet to a high heat and reduce the liquid in the pan until there are 8 cups. Strain and reserve the fish stock.

When the steaks are cool enough to handle, remove the skin and carefully pull the meat off the bones. Cut the meat into bite-size pieces. (Be careful to remove all small bones as well.) Discard the skin and bones. Combine the salmon with the lobster meat in a large mixing bowl, tossing to mix well. Reserve.

In a large skillet, melt 4 tablespoons of the butter. Add the remaining ½ cup shallots and the mushrooms. Sauté them over moderately low heat until just tender, tossing them occasionally. Remove from the heat and cool. Add the mushrooms and shallots to the salmon and lobster mixture and reserve.

In a 4- to 6-quart saucepan, melt the remaining 8 tablespoons butter over low heat. Add the flour, stir until well combined, and continue cooking for 2 minutes to eliminate any raw taste. Slowly add the 8 cups of reserved fish stock, stirring well after each addition so that no lumps form. Increase the heat to moderate and add the cream, a cupful at a time. Stir briskly. When the mixture has thickened and has just come to a boil, remove the pan from the heat. Beat ½ cup of the sauce into the egg yolks, then return the egg mixture to the sauce and blend well. Mix in the sherry. Taste for seasoning, and add salt and pepper to taste. Return the pan to moderate heat, and bring the sauce to just below the boiling point, stirring constantly. Remove the pan from the heat, and cool.

When the sauce is no longer warm, pour it over the salmon and lobster mixture and stir to blend. Cover the bowl with plastic wrap and refrigerate until 1 hour before final preparation.

TIME ALLOWANCE FOR FINAL PREPARATION: 20 MINUTES

With a rubber spatula, scrape the seafood and sauce into a 6- to 8-quart flameproof casserole. Stir once or twice to blend. Place the casserole over moderately low heat. Slowly heat the ingredients, stirring constantly, being careful that the sauce does not scorch. Cover the casserole and simmer, stirring occasionally, until the seafood and sauce are steaming hot, about 15 to 20 minutes. Sprinkle the dillweed over the top and serve immediately.

SERVES 18

STEAMED RICE WITH TOASTED COCONUT

(MAY BE PARTIALLY PREPARED UP TO 12 HOURS IN ADVANCE)

3 cups coarsely grated fresh coconut (see directions on page 146)
½ cup unsalted butter
4 cups long-grain rice
2 teaspoons salt
8½ cups water

Preheat the oven to 325 degrees.

Spread the coconut out on a shallow baking pan, such as a jellyroll pan. Toast it in the oven, stirring occasionally, until golden brown, about 15 minutes. Remove it from the oven and cool. Pour it into a plastic bag, seal it tightly, and reserve until final preparation.

In a flameproof 4- to 6-quart casserole, melt the butter over moderately low heat. Add the rice and stir to coat all the kernels. Add the salt and water. Stir to mix. Raise the heat and bring the water to a boil. Immediately cover the casserole, lower the heat, and simmer the rice for 20 minutes. Remove it from the heat and allow it to rest, covered, for 10 minutes. Stir once or twice, re-cover, and hold it in a cool corner of the kitchen until final preparation.

TIME ALLOWANCE FOR FINAL PREPARATION: 30 MINUTES

Preheat the oven to 325 degrees.

Fluff the rice. Fold in 2½ cups of the reserved coconut and mix well. Cover the casserole and place it in the oven. Heat the rice for 20 minutes, or until it is steaming. Just before serving, fluff the rice again and sprinkle the surface with the remaining ½ cup coconut.

SERVES 18

ITALIAN GARDEN SALAD

◆

(SALAD AND DRESSING MAY BE PREPARED UP TO 6 HOURS IN ADVANCE;
THEY MUST BE PREPARED AT LEAST 2 HOURS IN ADVANCE)

CREAMY ITALIAN DRESSING

¼ cup tarragon vinegar
2 teaspoons Dijon-style mustard
½ teaspoon garlic salt
2 egg yolks, beaten
⅔ cup fruity, imported olive oil
2 tablespoons mayonnaise
½ teaspoon freshly ground black pepper

To make the dressing: Pour the vinegar into a small bowl. Add the mustard and garlic salt, and beat with a whisk until they are dissolved. Whisk the egg yolks into the mixture. Slowly add the oil and continue beating until the dressing is well emulsified. Finally beat in the mayonnaise and pepper, mixing until well blended and smooth.

YIELD: 1 CUP DRESSING

SALAD

2 red peppers, cored and seeded
2 yellow peppers, cored and seeded
2/3 cup thinly sliced red onion
6 small zucchini (about 2 pounds), ends trimmed, cut in 1/4-inch slices
3 cups broccoli flowerets
2 large fennel bulbs, ends trimmed, cut in half, and sliced thin
3/4 cup minced fresh dillweed
1 (8-ounce) can medium, pitted ripe olives, drained

To make the salad: Cut the red and yellow peppers into 1-inch pieces. Combine them, the onion slices, zucchini rounds, broccoli flowerets, sliced fennel, and dillweed in a large salad bowl. Toss well to distribute evenly all the ingredients. Pour the Creamy Italian Dressing over the vegetables and toss until they are thoroughly coated. Cover the bowl with plastic wrap and refrigerate for at least 2 hours, or as long as 6 hours.

TIME ALLOWANCE FOR FINAL PREPARATION: 5 MINUTES

Remove the salad from the refrigerator. Toss a few times to redistribute the dressing. Add the olives, toss again, and serve immediately.

SERVES 18

BLACK CURRANT AND CHOCOLATE CHEESECAKE

(MAY BE PREPARED UP TO 2 DAYS IN ADVANCE;
MUST BE PREPARED AT LEAST 6 HOURS IN ADVANCE)

CRUST

3/4 cup butter, melted
4 cups finely crushed vanilla wafers (about 1 1/2 11-ounce boxes)
2 ounces white chocolate, finely grated

To make the crust: Pour the butter over the crushed wafers and grated chocolate in a mixing bowl. With a fork, mix until well blended and all the crumbs are covered with butter. Divide the mixture between two 9-inch ungreased spring-form pans, and press it as evenly as possible over the bottoms and 2 inches up the sides of each pan. The crusts should be quite thin. Chill for at least 1 hour or until ready to fill.

FILLING

5 (8-ounce) packages cream cheese, at room temperature
2 cups sugar
¾ cup Crème de Cassis (black currant liqueur)
½ teaspoon salt
7 eggs
6 ounces white chocolate, finely grated

Preheat oven to 375 degrees.

To make the filling: Cream the cream cheese with the sugar with an electric mixer, or by hand, until very soft. Beat in the Crème de Cassis and salt. Add the eggs, one at a time, mixing well after each addition. Beat in the white chocolate.

Pour the batter, evenly divided, into the chilled crusts. Bake the cheesecakes in the center of the oven for 50 to 60 minutes, or until their centers have solidified. Remove the cheesecakes from the oven and cool for 15 minutes. Reduce the oven temperature to 350 degrees. While the cheesecakes are cooling, make the topping.

FINAL ASSEMBLY

3 cups sour cream
½ cup sugar
2 tablespoons Crème de Cassis
2 ounces semisweet dark chocolate, shaved

Combine the sour cream, sugar, and Crème de Cassis, and mix until well blended. Spread this topping, evenly divided, over the surfaces of the two cheesecakes. Return them to the oven and bake another 10 minutes. Remove them from the oven and cool. Place the cheesecakes in the refrigerator and chill them for at least 4 hours.

Just before serving, release the springform sides, transfer the cheesecakes to platters, and garnish with the chocolate shavings.

YIELD: 2 9-INCH CHEESECAKES

A KEBAB PICNIC FOR TWELVE

Curried Chicken Kebabs

Vegetable Kebabs

Diane Nottle's Tortellini Salad al Pesto

Sliced Watermelon

Almond Carrot Cake Squares

Assorted Soft Drinks and Ice Tea

Sangria

Picnics have to be one of the nicest forms of warm-weather eating. Appetites are stimulated by the out-of-doors, and food cooking over the charcoal grill seduces us further with its intensely smoky odor. There's always a group playing softball or throwing a frisbee somewhere that sometimes threatens the safety of the food while adding excitement to the meal. Occasionally there are bugs to harass us, or an unexpected shower attempts to dampen our spirits, but nobody—at a picnic—really seems to mind too much.

I like to serve finger food, or bite-size food, at picnics. While I adore grilled steak and the like, attempting to cut a piece on a paper plate requires fortitude and dexterity, if not downright luck. My vehemence is perhaps due to the fact that my mother was a great one for barbecuing steaks on the beach near our summer home in Massachusetts. While the evenings were wonderful and evoke great nostalgia for the past, they also bring back not-so-fond memories of my teeth crunching through seemingly endless, sand-encrusted morsels, eloquent testimony to the hazards of steak-on-the-beach.

This picnic's menu is one I have devised to avoid all of that. And it's a good picnic even if you live far from sandy beaches but like to eat out-of-doors. (Please, though, remember to take adequate precautions for holding the food cold. Buy yourself well-insulated containers and picnic bags, and be generous with the freezer packs. Food spoils rapidly in warm weather, and we should never underestimate such a danger.) The chicken, in bite-size pieces on a kebab, is pleasantly assertive with its use of spices. The Vegetable Kebabs, also in easy-to-eat size, are a prime example of just how good fresh vegetables can be when grilled. The charring seems to bring out their best. The pasta salad, for whom my friend Diane Nottle is justly famed, is piquant with cheese and basil. And the cinnamon-infused, almond-spiked carrot cake is a delightful conclusion to an edible, movable feast.

CURRIED CHICKEN KEBABS

◆

(MAY BE PARTIALLY PREPARED UP TO 12 HOURS IN ADVANCE;
MUST BE PARTIALLY PREPARED UP TO 8 HOURS IN ADVANCE)

¼ cup curry powder
2 tablespoons ground cardamon
1 teaspoon ground ginger
1 teaspoon ground allspice
1 teaspoon ground cinnamon
¼ teaspoon garlic salt
1 cup vegetable oil
¼ cup strained fresh lime juice
2 (8-ounce) containers plain yogurt
4 to 5 pounds boned and skinned roasting-size chicken breasts, cut in 1½-inch
  cubes
2 small eggplants (1 pound each), stems cut off
1 cup olive oil
Mango chutney

In a large glass or enamel-lined baking dish, combine the curry powder, cardamon, ginger, allspice, cinnamon, garlic salt, oil, and lime juice. Stir to mix thoroughly. Add the yogurt and blend well. Drop in the chicken and toss until all the pieces are coated with the marinade. Cover the dish with plastic wrap and allow the chicken to marinate in the refrigerator for at least 8 hours, or as long as 12 hours, tossing occasionally to redistribute the marinade. Remove the chicken from the refrigerator 1 hour before final preparation.

TIME ALLOWANCE FOR FINAL PREPARATION: 30 MINUTES
PLUS TIME TO PREPARE THE COALS

Prepare the charcoal grill. The coals should be red-hot but not flaming when you begin to grill the kebabs.

Without peeling them, cut the eggplants into 1-inch-thick slices. Then cut each slice into 1-inch cubes. Place the olive oil in a large mixing bowl, add the eggplant cubes, and toss to coat them on all sides with the oil.

Alternate the chicken and eggplant pieces on metal or wooden skewers, packing them tightly together. If you have 10- to 12-inch skewers, allow one per person. If you have shorter ones, you will want at least two per person.

Place the skewers about 5 inches above the red-hot coals, cover the grill with a lid but keep the vents open, and grill for 7 to 8 minutes. Turn the kebabs and grill them another 8 minutes.

(If your grill is not equipped with a lid, turn the kebabs frequently and watch for flaming. If the coals should flame, sprinkle them with water.)

Serve immediately, accompanied by mango chutney.

SERVES 12

VEGETABLE KEBABS

◆

(MAY BE PARTIALLY PREPARED UP TO 6 HOURS IN ADVANCE;
MUST BE PARTIALLY PREPARED AT LEAST 2 HOURS IN ADVANCE)

6 cloves garlic, peeled and quartered lengthwise
1½ cups olive oil
24 white onions (about 3 pounds)
3 10-inch-long zucchinis (about ¾ pound each)
3 red peppers (about ½ pound each), cored and seeded
36 large cherry tomatoes
Salt and freshly ground black pepper to taste

Drop the garlic pieces into a shallow bowl filled with the olive oil. Allow them to remain for at least 2 hours, or as long as 6 hours, so that the garlic flavors the oil.

Place the onions in a saucepan full of boiling salted water set over high heat. Bring the water to a boil again and boil 1 minute. With a slotted spoon, remove the onions from the water. When they are cool enough to handle, trim the ends and slip off their outer skin. Return the onions to the same water and boil them for 8 minutes to cook them partially. Drain them, place them in a plastic bag, and refrigerate.

Trim the ends off the zucchinis and cut each one crosswise into eight 1-inch rounds, for a total of 24 pieces. Cut each pepper into eight 1½-inch squares, for a total of 24 pieces. Place the zucchini and pepper pieces separately in plastic bags and refrigerate until final preparation.

TIME ALLOWANCE FOR FINAL PREPARATION: 30 MINUTES
PLUS TIME TO PREPARE THE COALS

Prepare the charcoal grill. The coals should be red-hot but not flaming when you begin to grill the kebabs. Place the rack 5 inches above the coals.

To assemble the kebabs: Remove the pieces of garlic from the olive oil and discard them. Immerse a cherry tomato briefly into the olive oil and slip it on a skewer. Follow the tomato with an onion, a round of zucchini, and a square of pepper, all dipped into the oil. Repeat the pattern one more time, ending with one last tomato. (There will be a total of 3 tomatoes, 2 onions, 2 pieces of zucchini, and 2 pieces of pepper.) Repeat on eleven other skewers, using up all the vegetables.

Lay the skewers side by side across the grill. Sprinkle with salt and pepper to taste. Cover the grill with its lid, leaving the vents fully open, and cook the vegetables for 10 minutes. Brush with any remaining oil, turn the skewers over, and grill, covered, another 5 minutes. (If your grill is not equipped with a lid, turn the kebabs frequently and watch for flaming. If the coals begin to flame, sprinkle them with water.)

Slide the vegetables off the skewers onto heated plates and serve immediately.

SERVES 12

DIANE NOTTLE'S TORTELLINI SALAD AL PESTO

(SALAD MAY BE PARTIALLY PREPARED UP TO 6 HOURS IN ADVANCE;
PESTO DRESSING MAY BE PREPARED UP TO 3 DAYS IN ADVANCE)

4 (9-ounce) packages green and yellow dried cheese tortellini
⅓ cup fruity, imported olive oil
¾ pound Black Forest ham, cut in 1-by-¼-inch strips
2 cups frozen peas, thawed
1 red pepper, cored, seeded, and cut in 1-by-¼-inch strips
Cherry tomatoes
Basil leaves

To make the salad: Cook the tortellini in boiling salted water according to the package's directions. Cook until it is *al dente,* being careful not to overcook. Drain it in a colander and stop the cooking by running it briefly under cold water. Drain it again, then transfer it to a large mixing bowl.

Immediately toss the tortellini with the olive oil until all the pieces are well coated. Add the ham, (uncooked) peas, and pepper, and mix well. Cover with plastic wrap and reserve in a cool corner of the kitchen until final preparation.

PESTO DRESSING

12 walnuts, shelled
2 tablespoons pine nuts (pignoli)
1 teaspoon salt
6 peppercorns
3 cloves garlic, peeled
4 tablespoons unsalted butter, softened
2 cups loosely packed fresh basil leaves (about 1 large bunch)
1 to 2 cups Parmesan cheese, freshly grated
1½ cups fruity, imported olive oil

To make the dressing: Place the walnuts, pine nuts, salt, peppercorns, garlic, and butter in a food processor fitted with a steel blade. Whirl until a thick paste forms. Add the basil leaves and whirl until well mixed. Add 1 cup of cheese and whirl until blended. Finally, pour the olive oil through the feed tube while the motor is running, and whirl until the pesto is smooth and creamy. Taste, and add more cheese if you like. Cover and refrigerate until ready to use.

YIELD: ABOUT 2 CUPS DRESSING

NOTE: If this recipe makes more than you need to coat the tortellini, cover the remainder with a thin layer of olive oil and refrigerate it until needed.

TIME ALLOWANCE FOR FINAL PREPARATION: 10 MINUTES

Pour the Pesto Dressing over the tortellini and toss until all the pasta is well coated. Transfer the salad to a clean bowl and garnish it with cherry tomatoes and basil leaves.

SERVES 12

ALMOND CARROT CAKE SQUARES

(MAY BE PREPARED UP TO 24 HOURS IN ADVANCE)

CAKE

1½ cups vegetable oil
2 cups sugar
4 eggs
1 teaspoon salt
1 tablespoon ground cinnamon
2 cups flour
2 teaspoons baking soda
1 teaspoon vanilla
1½ cups sliced almonds
3 cups grated carrots (about 1½ pounds)

To make the cake: Preheat the oven to 325 degrees. Generously butter a 10-by-12-inch baking pan.

In a large mixing bowl, with an electric mixer or a wooden spoon, blend the oil and sugar together. Add the eggs, one at a time, beating thoroughly after each addition.

Sift the salt, cinnamon, flour, and baking soda. Add the dry ingredients to the egg mixture, beating until they are well blended. Add the vanilla and mix well. Coarsely chop 1 cup of the almonds. Beat the carrots and chopped almonds into the batter, mixing until they are completely incorporated. Using a rubber spatula, scrape the batter into the prepared baking pan and bake it for 1 to 1¼ hours, or until a straw inserted in the center comes out clean.

Set the pan on a rack to cool completely.

CREAM CHEESE FROSTING

1 (8-ounce) package cream cheese, softened
¼ cup unsalted butter, melted
2 tablespoons vanilla
1 (1-pound) box confectioners' sugar

To make the frosting: With an electric mixer, beat the cream cheese until it is light and fluffy. Gradually add the melted butter, beating until it is completely absorbed. Add the vanilla and the sugar, beating well after each addition. Continue beating until the frosting is smooth.

To assemble: When the cake is cool to the touch, run a knife around the edge of the pan to loosen it. Leave it in the pan as you spread the frosting generously over the surface of the cake.

Cut the cake into 2-inch-square portions. Garnish the top of the cake with a sprinkling of the sliced almonds.

Cover the pan with aluminum foil to protect it until serving time. When you are ready to serve the cake, remove the portions carefully, using a narrow spatula.

YIELD: 30 (2-INCH-SQUARE) PIECES

NOTE: If you are serving this cake at home, instead of on a picnic, remove the squares from the pan after icing the cake and transfer them to an attractive serving platter.

SANGRIA

◆

(MAY BE PREPARED UP TO 24 HOURS IN ADVANCE;
MUST BE PREPARED AT LEAST 6 HOURS IN ADVANCE)

1 cup sugar
2 cups water
4 limes, thinly sliced
4 oranges, thinly sliced, seeds removed
2 (750-milliliter) bottles dry red wine, chilled
8 ounces Cognac
1 (10-ounce) bottle club soda, chilled

Combine the sugar and water in a 2-quart stainless steel saucepan over medium heat. Stir until the sugar dissolves. When the mixture starts to boil, remove it from the heat. Add 2 of the sliced limes and 2 of the sliced oranges, and stir to mix. Allow the fruit to macerate in the syrup at least 6 hours, but as long as 24 hours.

Fill a 1-gallon insulated jug with the red wine, brandy, and club soda. Strain the fruit-flavored syrup into the wine mixture. Discard the old fruit. Add the remaining sliced limes and oranges and stir well.

When you are ready to serve, pour the Sangria into 8-ounce tumblers filled with ice.

YIELD: ABOUT 18 5-OUNCE DRINKS

A BUFFET BRUNCH FOR TWELVE

Susan's Fruit Drink

Mai Tais from Scratch

Frittata Florentina

Tomato-Tarragon Salad

Marmalade Bread

Cold Strawberry Souffle

While I may have trouble defining exactly what "brunch" is, I am the first to admit that it is generally an easy and relaxed form of entertaining. My favorite time to hold a brunch is in the summer, on leisurely Sundays, when the warm sunlight filters through the trees, and the breezes are sweet with the scent of flowers. But a brunch doesn't have to be held in the summer. Any season will do, provided your friends have time to gather early and stay late. The goal is to have a convivial mix of people, to whom you serve fruit-based, not-too-heady beverages, while seductive aromas emanate from the kitchen, holding the promise of the best of breakfast and luncheon combined.

I like to offer fruity drinks, alcoholic or otherwise, at brunch. After all, for a few people, brunch IS breakfast, and many do not want to face hard liquor so early in the day. For this brunch, I suggest offering both a nonalcoholic fruit shake—which is wonderfully smooth, thick, and creamy and was developed by my niece, Susan Gibson—and insidiously delicious citrus-laced Mai Tais from Scratch, a fine lesson in how inferior to the Real Thing mixes can be.

I always feel that brunches call for eggs of one sort or another, and frittatas, like quiches, are a splendid half-lunch, half-breakfast compromise with all manner of components besides eggs. The Tomato-Tarragon Salad, with its sweet-sour dressing, marries beautifully with the Frittata Florentina. Further, the dressing so enhances the tomatoes that I will reverse my age-old stand and say that even the pale, insipid hothouse species taste remarkably good in this salad, although fresh, local tomatoes will always win hands down.

The dessert—Cold Strawberry Souffle—not only looks delectable but also is the perfect finale to the meal: pretty, light, and sweetly redolent of strawberries. No one will need to go home and sleep this brunch off. It's filling enough to be satisfying, and satisfying enough to energize even the Sunday-laziest.

SUSAN'S FRUIT SHAKE

(MAY BE PARTIALLY PREPARED UP TO 24 HOURS IN ADVANCE;
MUST BE PARTIALLY PREPARED AT LEAST 12 HOURS IN ADVANCE)

3 medium-size bananas
*1½ (32-ounce) jars natural (unsweetened) papaya juice nectar (available in
health food stores)*
1½ cups cran-raspberry juice
3 (12-ounce) packages frozen whole unsweetened raspberries
3 (8-ounce) containers plain yogurt
Sugar to taste
Mint leaves

Peel the bananas and wrap them individually in plastic wrap. Place them in the
freezer to freeze for at least 12 hours.

Chill the papaya and cran-raspberry juices in the coldest section of the
refrigerator. Keep the raspberries frozen and the yogurt chilled.

When all the ingredients are either thoroughly chilled or frozen, make the
shake in three batches, transferring it, as it is done, to large plastic or glass
containers or pitchers.

For each batch: Pour 2 cups papaya juice and ½ cup cran-raspberry juice into
a blender. Break 1 banana into three pieces and drop them into the blender. Add
1 package frozen raspberries and 1 container yogurt. Whirl the mixture at medium
speed until smooth, stopping occasionally to stir the ingredients as they are being
pureed. Taste for sweetness, adding sugar if desired.

Repeat two more times. Store the fruit shake in the refrigerator until time for
final preparation.

TIME ALLOWANCE FOR FINAL PREPARATION: 5 MINUTES

If the shake has separated, stir it briskly with a large spoon. Pour ¾-cup
servings of the shake into twelve (10-ounce) red wine glasses and float a mint leaf
on top of each. Serve chilled.

SERVES 12 (WITH SECONDS)

MAI TAIS FROM SCRATCH

(MAY BE PREPARED UP TO 24 HOURS IN ADVANCE)

2 cups sugar
2 cups water
2 cups strained fresh lemon juice (about 9 lemons)
1 (fifth) bottle gold Jamaican or Barbadian rum
¾ cup Cointreau or Curaçao liqueur
½ cup Crème de Noyaux (almond cream liqueur)
Fresh pineapple spears
Orange slices

Combine the sugar and water in a 2-quart saucepan and stir over moderate heat until the sugar has dissolved. Set the pan aside and let the syrup cool.

When it is no longer warm, pour the syrup into a 2-quart jar. Add the lemon juice, rum, Cointreau, and Crème de Noyaux, and stir until the ingredients are well combined.

Taste, and adjust proportions if desired.

Store in the refrigerator, tightly covered, until ready to serve.

TIME ALLOWANCE FOR FINAL PREPARATION: 10 MINUTES

Fill twelve (8- or 10-ounce) wine glasses with crushed ice. Pour ⅓ cup Mai Tai mix over the ice. Garnish each glass with a pineapple spear and an orange slice.

SERVES 12 (WITH SECONDS)

FRITTATA FLORENTINA

(MAY BE PARTIALLY PREPARED UP TO 3 HOURS IN ADVANCE)

This recipe will make 1 large Frittata, or 12 pieces, sufficient to feed 12. If you anticipate having hungry guests, it might be advisable to make the recipe twice, so that second helpings are available for all.

¼ cup olive oil
1 teaspoon minced garlic
¾ cup chopped onions

½ pound mushrooms, ends trimmed, thickly sliced
1 teaspoon dried basil
1 (10-ounce) package frozen chopped spinach, thawed and drained
⅓ pound sliced Black Forest ham, cut in ½-inch dice
8 eggs, at room temperature
⅓ cup light cream
1 teaspoon salt
Freshly ground black pepper
¾ cup freshly grated Parmesan cheese
1 cup shredded mozzarella cheese

In a large skillet, over moderate heat, warm the oil. Add the garlic and onions. Sauté them, stirring occasionally, until they are soft, about 5 minutes. Add the mushrooms and basil and cook 5 minutes longer, stirring occasionally. Remove the skillet from the heat.

With your hands or a wooden spoon, squeeze the spinach to remove any remaining moisture. Add the spinach and the diced ham to the skillet, and stir to mix the ingredients. Hold the skillet in a cool corner of the kitchen until final preparation.

Place the eggs in a mixing bowl and beat until frothy. Add the cream, salt, pepper, and Parmesan cheese, and mix well. If you are not proceeding with the recipe immediately, cover the bowl with plastic wrap and refrigerate the egg mixture until 30 minutes before final preparation.

TIME ALLOWANCE FOR FINAL PREPARATION: 40 MINUTES

Preheat the oven to 350 degrees.

Generously butter the bottom and sides of a 9-by-13-inch baking pan.

With a rubber spatula, scrape the mushroom and spinach mixture into the eggs, and mix well. Pour the frittata mixture into the prepared pan, sprinkle the mozzarella cheese evenly over the surface, and bake the frittata for 30 minutes, or until the eggs are set and the cheese is bubbling.

Serve the frittata either hot, or at room temperature, cut into 3-by-4-inch pieces.

SERVES 12 (WITHOUT SECOND HELPINGS)

TOMATO-TARRAGON SALAD

(MAY BE PREPARED UP TO 6 HOURS IN ADVANCE;
MUST BE PREPARED 2 HOURS IN ADVANCE)

8 tomatoes (about 4 pounds), peeled
2 English cucumbers, cut in ¼-inch slices
1½ cups thinly sliced scallions, including 4 inches of green leaves
1 green pepper, cored, seeded, and cut into julienne strips
¾ cup tarragon vinegar
½ cup minced fresh tarragon leaves
2 tablespoons sugar
⅔ cup water
1 tablespoon celery salt
¾ cup fruity, imported olive oil
Salt and freshly ground pepper to taste
½ cup minced fresh parsley

Cut the peeled tomatoes into quarters, and cut each quarter in half crosswise. Place them in a bowl with the cucumber slices, scallions, and pepper strips, and toss to distribute the vegetables evenly.

In a small nonreactive saucepan, combine the vinegar, tarragon, sugar, water, and celery salt. Bring the mixture to a boil over moderately high heat, and boil it vigorously for 2 minutes or until it is reduced by one-half. Remove the pan from the heat. When the liquid is cool, whisk in the olive oil. Immediately pour the dressing over the vegetables, tossing them well to coat them evenly. Taste, and add salt and pepper as desired.

Loosely cover the salad and set it aside in a cool corner of the kitchen to let the vegetables marinate for at least 2 hours, or as long as 6 hours. Toss the vegetables occasionally as they marinate.

TIME ALLOWANCE FOR FINAL PREPARATION: 5 MINUTES

Sprinkle the vegetables with the parsley. Toss to mix.
Transfer the salad to a salad bowl and serve it at room temperature.

SERVES 12

MARMALADE BREAD

◆

(MAY BE PREPARED UP TO 2 DAYS IN ADVANCE)

3 cups cake flour
1 tablespoon baking soda
½ teaspoon salt
¼ cup unsalted butter, melted
¾ cup sugar
1 egg
2 tablespoons grated orange rind
½ cup marmalade, melted and softened
1 cup buttermilk
½ cup coarsely chopped pecans
Cream cheese, softened

Preheat the oven to 350 degrees. Butter and flour a 9-by-5-inch loaf pan.

Combine the cake flour, baking soda, and salt in a sifter or strainer, and sift them twice into a large mixing bowl.

Pour the butter into a small mixing bowl and beat in the sugar with an electric mixer. Add the egg and beat well. With the mixer still running, add the orange rind, marmalade, and buttermilk. Mix until thoroughly blended.

With a rubber spatula, scrape the buttermilk mixture onto the flour. Stir until the ingredients are just blended. Add the pecans and mix until the nuts are evenly distributed throughout the batter. Scrape the batter into the prepared loaf pan.

Place the pan in the center of the oven and bake the bread for 60 minutes, or until a straw inserted in the center comes out clean. Allow the bread to cool in the pan for 10 minutes, then turn the bread out on a rack to cool completely.

Wrap the bread in aluminum foil and refrigerate until 1 hour before serving.

TIME ALLOWANCE FOR FINAL PREPARATION: 10 MINUTES

Cut the bread into thin slices and serve accompanied by cream cheese. (Or spread the cheese on the slices before serving.)

YIELD: 1 2-POUND LOAF

COLD STRAWBERRY SOUFFLE

◆

(MAY BE PARTIALLY PREPARED UP TO 24 HOURS IN ADVANCE;
MUST BE PARTIALLY PREPARED AT LEAST 4 HOURS IN ADVANCE)

2 (10-ounce) packages frozen strawberries, thawed
2 envelopes unflavored gelatin
½ cup strained fresh orange juice
8 eggs, separated
1 cup sugar
¼ teaspoon salt
Red food coloring (optional)
2 cups heavy cream, chilled
1 pint fresh strawberries
1 tablespoon strained fresh lemon juice

Generously butter a 2½-quart souffle dish. Tear off a length of wax paper 6 inches longer than the circumference of the bowl. Fold the wax paper in half lengthwise and butter one side of it. Wrap the wax paper around the outside of the souffle bowl, buttered side in, making a "collar," and secure it with kitchen string.

In a food processor fitted with a steel blade, puree the frozen strawberries. Sprinkle the gelatin over the orange juice and set it aside to soften.

Place the egg yolks, ½ cup of the sugar, and the salt in a small saucepan set over very low heat. Whisking constantly, beat the yolks until the sugar has dissolved and the mixture has thickened slightly, about 5 minutes. Remove the pan from the heat and cool. Stir in the gelatin and strawberry puree and blend well. (Add 6 to 8 drops of red food coloring if you want a very pink souffle, and mix well.) Transfer the puree to a mixing bowl and refrigerate it until it has thickened to the consistency of mayonnaise, about 30 minutes.

Beat the egg whites until they hold a soft shape. Gradually add ¼ cup of the sugar and continue beating until the whites are stiff. Mix one-quarter of the whites into the strawberry puree to lighten it, then fold in the remaining whites.

Beat the cream until stiff. Pile the cream on top of the souffle mixture, and very gently fold it in until no traces of white remain. Pour the souffle into the prepared bowl and refrigerate until firm, about 3 hours, or up to 24 hours.

TIME ALLOWANCE FOR FINAL PREPARATION: 10 MINUTES

Pick out 5 of the most perfect strawberries from the pint box. Halve them. Place the remaining berries, the lemon juice, and the remaining ¼ cup of sugar into the bowl of a food processor fitted with a steel blade, and puree until smooth. Transfer the sauce to a sauceboat.

Remove the cold souffle from the refrigerator. Cut the piece of string, carefully peel off the wax paper "collar," and discard. Garnish the top of the souffle with the 10 strawberry halves.

Serve the souffle accompanied by the strawberry sauce.

SERVES 12

A CARIBBEAN BUFFET DINNER FOR THIRTY

Picadillo (Boiled Beef in Spicy Tomato Sauce)

Griots (Pork Braised in Citrus Juices)

Moros y Cristianos (Black Beans and Rice)

Cucumber, Fennel, and Radish Salad

Pungent Ginger Roll

This Caribbean buffet menu is the direct result of a Caribbean cruise my husband and I took a few years ago, during which our large, luxurious (but rather boring) liner deposited us each day at a different island, each offering different and often spectacular cuisines. I became so entranced with the variety of Caribbean foods that at our next large dinner I decided to give my guests something to talk about and savor, food that presumably few had tasted before.

It is always a risk to present really foreign foods to innocent friends. For that reason I chose to offer two meat dishes; the *Picadillo* from Cuba is quite spicy, while the *Griots* from Haiti is quite unusual with its blended citrus sauce. That way, my guests could pick and choose, and, if they wanted, stick entirely with the one they preferred. Because I assumed that few friends would have two full-size helpings, I made quantities of each sufficient to serve twenty-four, not thirty, thus ensuring that there would be enough to go around . . . but not so much that I would be inundated with leftovers. Of course, there *was* the small risk that all thirty guests would like only one of the two meat dishes, and I would not have made enough! But let me hasten to add that such a calamity did not occur.

The Black Beans and Rice (*Moros y Cristianos*, literally "Moors and Christians") originates in Cuba too. It is well suited as a foil for both meats, as is the soothing yogurt-bathed salad.

You will note that this menu is for a large party where, in all probability, some of the guests will be eating standing up, plate clasped in hand. For this reason, the meats can be handled with a fork alone. A knife is not necessary.

Ginger is a component in many Caribbean foods. The Ginger Roll seems the appropriate ending for the meal. It is light and very fragrant with ginger—both powdered and crystallized. As a matter of fact, it really is too good to be relegated only to Caribbean meals.

PICADILLO

◆

(MAY BE PARTIALLY PREPARED UP TO 2 DAYS IN ADVANCE)

12 pounds boneless shoulder of beef, cut into 2-inch cubes
2 tablespoons salt
¾ to 1 cup oil
¼ cup minced garlic
½ to 1 cup minced hot chili peppers, according to taste
18 green peppers (about 6 pounds), cored, seeded, and coarsely chopped
6 (28-ounce) cans Italian-style peeled tomatoes, drained and chopped (about 12 cups)
1 tablespoon ground cloves
1 teaspoon freshly ground black pepper
1½ cups pimiento-stuffed olives
1½ cups seedless raisins
¾ cup distilled white vinegar

Place the cubes of beef in an 8-quart kettle. Add 1 tablespoon of the salt and enough water to cover the meat by 2 inches. Bring the water to a boil over high heat, skimming off any foam that forms. Reduce the heat to low, partially cover, and simmer for 1 hour. Drain the beef and reserve the broth. (Use the broth when you are making Black Beans and Rice, or any other dish calling for beef stock.) When the beef is cool enough to handle, chop it coarsely. Transfer it to a container, cover it tightly, and refrigerate until 1 hour before final preparation.

In an 8- to 10-quart flameproof casserole (the larger, the better), heat ¾ cup oil, or enough to coat the bottom of the pan by a ¼ inch. Add the garlic, ½ cup hot chili peppers, and the onions. Cook over moderate heat, stirring frequently, until the vegetables are soft, about 10 minutes. (If you like your food spicy and hot, add more chili peppers. The heat of chili peppers varies according to variety.) Add the peppers, toss to mix, and cook another 10 minutes until they are wilted. Mix in the tomatoes, cloves, the remaining tablespoon of salt, and the pepper. Increase the heat to moderately high and cook until most of the liquid in the pan has evaporated and the mixture is thick, about 30 minutes. Stir the mixture frequently to prevent any scorching of the vegetables.

Add the olives, raisins, and vinegar, and stir to mix. Remove the casserole from the heat, cool, cover, and refrigerate until 1 hour before final preparation.

TIME ALLOWANCE FOR FINAL PREPARATION: 20 MINUTES

Place the casserole, covered, over moderate heat. Bring the vegetables slowly to a boil, stirring occasionally. Drop in the chopped beef, mix well, and cover. Cook for 10 or 15 minutes, or until the dish is steaming hot.

SERVES 24 AS A SINGLE ENTREE OR 30 AS A DUAL ENTREE

GRIOTS

(MAY BE PARTIALLY PREPARED UP TO 2 DAYS IN ADVANCE)

12 pounds boneless fresh ham (or substitute loin of pork), cut in 1-inch cubes
1 cup vegetable oil
3 tablespoons minced garlic
6 cups coarsely chopped onions
3 tablespoons cumin seeds
1½ teaspoons dried thyme
3 to 5 cups strained fresh orange juice
1 cup pineapple juice
1 cup strained fresh lime juice
1 cup water
2 teaspoons salt
¾ teaspoon freshly ground black pepper
½ cup minced fresh cilantro (or parsley)

Pat the pork cubes dry with paper toweling. In your largest skillet, preferably a 14-inch one, with 4-inch-high sides, heat ¼ cup of the oil over moderately high heat until it is very hot. Add the pork cubes in batches so that they are not crowded and sauté them, turning frequently, until they have browned on all sides. When they are done, transfer them with a slotted spoon to an 8-quart flameproof casserole. Add more oil as needed. Repeat until all the pork has been browned.

Add the garlic and onions to the oil remaining in the skillet. Cook them over moderate heat, stirring frequently, until they are wilted, about 8 to 10 minutes. Add the cumin and the thyme and cook for 1 or 2 minutes.

Transfer the onions to the casserole with the pork and toss to mix well. Pour 3 cups orange juice, the pineapple and lime juices, and the water over the pork. The liquid should barely cover the meat. If it does not, add more orange juice until it does. (The amount of juice depends on the size and shape of your casserole.) Add the salt and pepper. Stir the pork to blend the juices and seasonings. Bring it to a boil over high heat, cover the pan, lower the heat, and simmer for 30 minutes, turning once or twice.

Remove the casserole from the heat and allow to cool. Cover and refrigerate until 2 hours before final preparation.

TIME ALLOWANCE FOR FINAL PREPARATION: 30 TO 40 MINUTES

Uncover the casserole and place it over high heat. Stirring frequently to prevent the meat from sticking, briskly cook the pork and its liquid for approximately 30 minutes, or until the sauce has reduced substantially and has thickened to a syrupy glaze.

Sprinkle the minced cilantro over the meat and serve immediately.

SERVES 24 AS A SINGLE ENTREE OR 30 AS A DUAL ENTREE

MOROS Y CRISTIANOS

(MAY BE PARTIALLY PREPARED UP TO 24 HOURS IN ADVANCE)

1 (16-ounce) package black beans, washed
3 teaspoons salt
2 cloves garlic, peeled and smashed
4 tablespoons butter
1 tablespoon minced garlic
¼ cup coarsely chopped onions
4 cups long-grain converted rice
9 cups beef stock (or water)

Place the beans in a 4- to 6-quart kettle. Add enough water to cover them by 3 inches. Bring the water to a boil. Boil the beans for 2 minutes. Turn off the heat and let the beans soak for 1 hour.

Drain the beans, return them to the kettle, and cover them by 3 inches with water. Add 1 teaspoon of the salt and the 2 smashed garlic cloves. Stir. Bring the water to a boil, lower the heat, and simmer, partially covered, for 1½ hours, or until the beans are tender but still intact. Drain the beans and refresh under cold water. Discard the garlic. Set the beans aside.

Melt the butter in a 4- to 6-quart kettle. Add the minced garlic and onions and sauté over low heat until soft, about 5 minutes. Add the rice and the remaining 2 teaspoons salt, and stir until all the kernels are coated with the butter. Pour in the beef stock or water and stir to mix. Bring the liquid to a boil, stir the rice, lower the heat, and simmer, covered, for 20 minutes. Remove the kettle from the heat and let the rice stand, still covered, for another 10 minutes.

Uncover the rice and let it cool to room temperature. Generously butter a 6- to 8-quart ovenproof casserole equipped with a tight-fitting lid. Combine the rice and reserved beans in it, tossing them until they are evenly mixed. Cover the casserole. If you have prepared the casserole more than 4 hours in advance, refrigerate it until 2 hours before the final preparation. Otherwise, set it in a cool corner of the kitchen and reserve.

TIME ALLOWANCE FOR FINAL PREPARATION: 40 MINUTES

Preheat the oven to 300 degrees.

Set the covered casserole on a rack in the center of the oven and reheat the beans and rice for 30 minutes, or until steaming hot.

SERVES 30

CUCUMBER, FENNEL, AND RADISH SALAD

(MAY BE PREPARED UP TO 8 HOURS IN ADVANCE;
MUST BE PREPARED AT LEAST 2 HOURS IN ADVANCE)

4 English cucumbers
2 teaspoons salt
6 fennel bulbs (about ¾ pound each)
6 (6-ounce) packages radishes
3 cups thinly sliced scallions, including 4 inches of green leaves
3 tablespoons grated lime rind
1 cup strained fresh lime juice
6 cups plain yogurt
1 cup plus 2 tablespoons minced fresh cilantro (or parsley)
1 teaspoon freshly ground black pepper

With a sharp paring knife, cut the cucumbers into paper-thin slices. Place them in a colander and sprinkle them with 1 teaspoon of the salt. Toss to mix thoroughly. Set the colander over a bowl or in the sink and allow the cucumbers to drain for 30 minutes.

Meanwhile, prepare the other vegetables. Trim and discard the ends of the fennel bulbs. With a swivel-blade parer, peel off the coarse strings on the outer leaves. Cut the bulbs in half lengthwise. Cut each half crosswise into paper-thin slices. Transfer the slices to a large mixing bowl. Trim and discard the ends of the radishes. Slice the radishes paper-thin. Add them to the fennel. Toss in the sliced scallions.

Transfer the cucumbers to paper toweling and pat dry. Add them to the other vegetables and toss to mix well.

In another mixing bowl, combine the lime rind, lime juice, remaining 1 teaspoon salt, yogurt, 1 cup cilantro, and pepper. Stir until well blended. With a rubber spatula, scrape the dressing over the vegetables and toss until they are all well coated. Cover the bowl with plastic wrap and refrigerate for at least 2 hours, or up to 8 hours, until final preparation.

TIME ALLOWANCE FOR FINAL PREPARATION: 5 MINUTES

Toss the salad briefly. Transfer it to a large salad bowl. Sprinkle the surface with the remaining 2 tablespoons minced cilantro.

SERVES 30

PUNGENT GINGER ROLL

(ROLL MAY BE PREPARED UP TO 24 HOURS IN ADVANCE;
ROLL MAY BE FILLED UP TO 4 HOURS IN ADVANCE)

This recipe will make one Pungent Ginger Roll, sufficient to feed 16. It is necessary to make a second one in order to have enough to serve 30.

GINGER ROLL

3 eggs, at room temperature
½ cup sugar
Pinch of salt
¼ cup molasses
¾ cup cake flour
2 teaspoons baking powder
1 teaspoon ground cinnamon
2 teaspoons ground ginger
½ teaspoon freshly grated nutmeg
½ teaspoon ground allspice
2 tablespoons finely chopped crystallized ginger

To make the roll: Preheat the oven to 375 degrees.

Generously butter an 11-by-16-inch jellyroll pan. Cut a length of wax paper 11 by 24 inches. Line the pan with the wax paper, allowing a 4-inch overlap at each end, and butter the wax paper.

Break the eggs into the bowl of an electric mixer and beat them until frothy. With the motor running, gradually add the sugar and the salt. Continue beating for 5 minutes, or until the eggs are very thick and light. Beat in the molasses.

In a sifter or strainer set over a large mixing bowl, combine the cake flour, baking powder, cinnamon, ginger, nutmeg, and allspice. Sift them together. With a rubber spatula, gently fold the flour mixture into the eggs, mixing only until the flour is incorporated. Fold in the crystallized ginger. Pour the batter into the prepared jellyroll pan, spread it out into the corners, and bake the roll for 14 to 15 minutes, or until the surface of the roll holds its shape when gently prodded with a finger. Do not overcook it, as crisp edges will prevent the cake from rolling easily.

Remove the pan from the oven and set it on a wire rack to cool for 10 minutes.

Dampen a kitchen towel with water and wring it out well. Spread it out on a kitchen counter. Run a knife along the edges of the roll to loosen it from the pan. Using the wax paper "handles," lift the roll out of the pan and set it, wax paper down, on the towel. Roll up the cake and its wax paper lining lengthwise into a compact cylinder. Wrap the towel around the cake and let it cool thoroughly. If you are not proceeding to fill the roll at this point, cover the roll and towel tightly with plastic wrap or aluminum foil, and refrigerate. (It can hold in the refrigerator up to 1 day.)

FINAL ASSEMBLY

1½ cups heavy cream, chilled
⅓ cup sugar
¼ teaspoon vanilla
2 tablespoons finely chopped crystallized ginger

Pour the cream into a chilled mixing bowl. Beat it until it starts to thicken. Gradually add the sugar and continue beating until the cream is stiff. Beat in the vanilla.

Remove the plastic wrap and toweling from the roll. Carefully unroll it. With a rubber spatula, spread two-thirds of the whipped cream over the surface of the roll, leaving a 1-inch edge free of all cream. Using the wax paper as a guide, reroll the cake, peeling the paper away as you progress. Do not be concerned if the cake should crack in the rolling process; it will be covered with more whipped cream and any flaws will be hidden.

Transfer the ginger roll to a serving platter. Discard the wax paper. Cover the top of the roll with the remaining whipped cream, swirling it around decoratively. Sprinkle the crystallized ginger over the whipped cream. Refrigerate the ginger roll for no more than 4 hours before serving.

SERVES 16

A BUFFET LUNCHEON OF PACIFIC SALADS FOR TWENTY-FOUR

Potato, Bean Sprout, and Broccoli Salad

Spicy Chicken Salad with Coriander and Fennel Dressing

Hawaiian Ahi Poke (Marinated Raw Tuna Fish Salad)

Carrot and Celeriac Salad

Curried Pea and Cashew Salad

Sesame Shrimp Salad

Rebecca's Almond Plum Tart

Inform a gathering of men and women that they will be having salad for lunch, and the women will smile while the men, by and large, will grimace. Both sexes will conjure up images of crisp lettuce leaves with those assorted garnishes so familiar to all of us who have hovered over salad bars recently. For the women this kind of meal is generally agreeable; for most men, a salad luncheon is far too light.

This menu's salad luncheon is very different from the salad-bar types. It was inspired by a magnificent salad repast at the Hotel Hana-Maui, on the island of Maui, in Hawaii. For luncheon, this very luxurious, food-oriented hotel offered a choice of salads second to none, and unusual to boot. All of them were subtle in flavoring, beautiful in composition, and sumptuously satisfying.

The salads given in this menu are not those of the Hana-Maui hotel whose chef uses Pacific-related ingredients, which are, for the most part, not readily available on "the mainland." (The one exception is the Hawaiian *Ahi Poke*, or marinated raw tuna fish. This salad is found all over Hawaii, even in the supermarket fish sections. Since so many of us appreciate raw fish these days, and tuna is so widely available, I thought I would include my version.) But, in keeping with the Hana-Maui tradition, I tried to compose salads that would prove as unusual and as satisfying to the palate as theirs. Certainly no one will go home hungry after such a luncheon.

Not all these salads serve 24. Some are meant to serve as few as 18. But following the hotel's example, I visualized my guests taking a sample of each and helping themselves to more of their favorites. (You may only want to make a few of them.)

The dessert is a special plum tart, one for which I can take no credit. I had it at the home of a friend, Elaine Dunn, and was so impressed that I asked her for the recipe, which she happily gave me. Her only request was that I call it "Rebecca's Almond Plum Tart."

Now I don't know who Rebecca is, nor where she lives. But I certainly am grateful for her tart. As I am sure you will be.

POTATO, BEAN SPROUT, AND BROCCOLI SALAD

◆

(MAY BE PREPARED UP TO 24 HOURS IN ADVANCE)

4 pounds small red potatoes
2 pounds broccoli
2 cups thinly sliced scallions, including 4 inches of green leaves
1 pound bean sprouts, coarsely chopped
2 (6-ounce) packages radishes, ends trimmed, thinly sliced
6 hard-boiled eggs, shelled and coarsely chopped
1½ cups mayonnaise
1½ cups sour cream
2 tablespoons Dijon-style mustard
3 tablespoons strained fresh lemon juice
2 teaspoons salt
½ teaspoon freshly ground black pepper

Fill a large steamer with 3 inches of water. Set it over moderate heat and bring it to a boil.

Meanwhile, cut the potatoes into quarters lengthwise, then halve the quarters crosswise. Place them in the steamer, cover tightly, and let them steam for 15 minutes or until tender. (Do not let them overcook.)

While the potatoes are steaming, cut the flowerets off the broccoli stems and set them to one side. With a sharp paring knife, trim the stems into symmetrical cylinders and cut them crosswise into ⅛-inch-thick slices.

When the potatoes are tender, transfer them from the steamer to a colander to drain and cool. Immediately place the broccoli stems in the steamer and steam them about 5 minutes, or until barely tender. Transfer them to a colander or sieve to drain and cool. Finally, steam the broccoli flowerets for exactly 2 minutes, or until just tender and bright green. Rinse them quickly under cold water to refresh them, drain, and allow to cool.

Place the cooled potatoes in a large mixing bowl. Add the cooled broccoli stems, scallions, bean sprouts, radishes, and eggs. Toss to distribute all the ingredients evenly.

In another mixing bowl, combine the mayonnaise, sour cream, mustard, lemon juice, salt, and pepper, and blend well. Scrape the mixture over the vegetables and toss with a salad fork and spoon to thoroughly coat all the ingredients with the dressing. Cover the bowl tightly with plastic wrap and refrigerate until 1 hour before serving.

Loosely cover the broccoli flowerets with plastic wrap. Refrigerate them if you have prepared them more than 4 hours in advance of serving (if so, bring them to room temperature at least 30 minutes before serving). Otherwise, set them aside in a cool corner of the kitchen.

TIME ALLOWANCE FOR FINAL PREPARATION: 5 MINUTES

Transfer the potato salad to a large salad bowl. Place the broccoli flowerets decoratively around the edge of the bowl. If there are some left over, cluster them together in the center.

SERVES 18

SPICY CHICKEN SALAD WITH CORIANDER AND FENNEL DRESSING

(DRESSED SALAD MAY BE PREPARED UP TO 2 DAYS IN ADVANCE;
IT SHOULD BE PREPARED AT LEAST 1 DAY IN ADVANCE)

CORIANDER AND FENNEL DRESSING
2 tablespoons coriander seeds (available in health food stores)
1/2 cup rice wine vinegar
1/4 cup strained fresh lemon juice
3 tablespoons fennel seeds, pulverized in a mortar and pestle
1 1/2 teaspoons salt
1/2 teaspoon freshly ground black pepper
3/4 cup fruity, imported olive oil

To make the dressing: Grind the coriander seeds by emptying a pepper grinder and replacing the peppercorns with the coriander seeds. Grind the coriander onto a small saucer and reserve.

Pour the vinegar into a small mixing bowl. Add the lemon juice, fennel seeds, salt, pepper, and 2 teaspoons of the ground coriander seeds. Beat briskly with a whisk. Slowly add the olive oil, stirring constantly, until it is thoroughly emulsified. Taste for seasoning and adjust. Set aside while you prepare the salad.

YIELD: 1 1/2 CUPS DRESSING

CHICKEN SALAD

7 pounds boned, skinned chicken breasts
2 red peppers, cored, seeded, and cut in ¼-inch dice
4 to 8 jalapeño peppers (according to taste), cored, seeded, and minced
8 plum tomatoes (about 2 pounds)

To make the salad: Bring a large skillet of water to a boil over high heat. Reduce the heat and add the chicken breasts. (Depending upon the size of your skillet, you may have to do this in two batches.) Simmer the breasts for 10 minutes. Turn off the heat and let the breasts remain in the water another 10 minutes.

Drain the breasts and pat them dry with paper toweling. Cut the breasts crosswise into the thinnest possible slices. Cut the longer slices (from the center of the breast) in half so that the pieces are all uniform in size. Transfer the chicken to a large salad bowl. Add the red peppers and 4 minced jalapeño peppers.

Cut the plum tomatoes in half from stem to bottom. With a sharp knife, cut out the white core and seeds. Cut the halves into fine julienne strips. Add the tomato strips to the chicken. Toss the ingredients with a salad fork and spoon to mix them well.

Drizzle the Coriander and Fennel Dressing over the chicken and toss until all the ingredients are completely coated. (Unlike many salads, this one is sparsely dressed. Do not be concerned if the dressing is not visually discernible. It is the flavors of the coriander and fennel that are important.) Taste the salad and add more minced jalapeño peppers if you want.

Cover the salad bowl tightly with plastic wrap and refrigerate at least 24 hours, or as long as 48 hours, before serving to allow the flavors to develop. Remove the salad from the refrigerator 1 hour before serving and toss well to redistribute the dressing.

SERVES 18

HAWAIIAN AHI POKE

(MAY BE PREPARED UP TO 24 HOURS IN ADVANCE;
MUST BE PREPARED AT LEAST 4 HOURS IN ADVANCE)

4 tuna steaks, cut 1 inch thick (about 4 pounds)
2 cups finely chopped sweet Spanish or Vidalia onions
1½ cups light soy sauce

3 to 6 jalapeño peppers (according to taste), cored, seeded, and minced
¾ cup plus 1 tablespoon minced cilantro (or parsley)

This is a dish the Hawaiians make from scraps of raw tuna whose better cuts have already been used for *sushi* or *sashimi*. Tuna steaks that are about 1-inch thick are the easiest to transform into ½-inch cubes, or the approximation of scraps. Chop away as you see fit: uniformity is not of any particular importance. Transfer the cubes of tuna to a mixing bowl.

Add the onions, soy sauce, 3 minced jalapeño peppers, and the ¾ cup of cilantro. Toss well to mix the ingredients and coat them thoroughly with the soy sauce. Take a bite to see if the spiciness of the Poke is agreeable and add as many more jalapeño peppers as seems desirable.

Cover the mixing bowl tightly with plastic wrap. Refrigerate the Poke for at least 4 hours, or as long as 24 hours. Stir it occasionally as it chills. Remove it from the refrigerator 1 hour before serving.

To serve, transfer the Poke to a clean salad bowl and sprinkle the surface with the remaining tablespoon of cilantro.

SERVES 20

CARROT AND CELERIAC SALAD

(DRESSED SALAD MAY BE PREPARED UP TO 2 DAYS IN ADVANCE)

4 pounds carrots, peeled, ends trimmed
4 celeriacs (about ½ pound each), peeled
1 cup thinly sliced scallions, including 4 inches of green leaves
1 cup plus 2 tablespoons minced fresh dillweed
4 recipes Vinaigrette (see page 24)

Cut the carrots and celeriacs into fine julienne strips (about ⅛ inch square and 2 inches long) either by hand or by using a julienne disc in a food processor. (You may also finely grate the vegetables, but the texture won't be as nice.)

Transfer the vegetables to a large mixing bowl. Add the scallions and 1 cup dillweed and mix until all the ingredients are well distributed.

Drizzle the dressing over the salad and toss with a salad fork and spoon until the vegetables are well coated with the dressing. Cover the bowl with plastic wrap and refrigerate the salad until 1 hour before serving.

TIME ALLOWANCE FOR FINAL PREPARATION: 5 MINUTES

Toss the salad to redistribute the dressing. Transfer it to a salad bowl and garnish the surface with the remaining 2 tablespoons of dillweed.

SERVES 24

CURRIED PEA AND CASHEW SALAD

(SALAD MAY BE PARTIALLY PREPARED UP TO 8 HOURS IN ADVANCE; DRESSING MAY BE PREPARED UP TO 3 DAYS IN ADVANCE)

SALAD

3 (10-ounce) packages frozen baby peas
1½ cups thinly sliced scallions, including 4 inches of green leaves
1½ cups finely chopped celery (about 3 large stalks)
2 cups roasted cashews

To make the salad: Place the peas in a colander and set it in the sink to defrost and drain. Toss the peas every 10 minutes to accelerate the process.

When the peas are thoroughly defrosted and well drained, pour them into a salad bowl lined with paper toweling. Add the scallions and celery and mix well. Cover with a layer of paper toweling and refrigerate. Hold until 1 hour before final preparation.

CURRY DRESSING

1½ teaspoons curry powder
1 teaspoon Dijon-style mustard
1 tablespoon brown sugar
½ teaspoon salt
3 tablespoons tarragon vinegar
Freshly ground black pepper
½ cup vegetable oil

To make the dressing: Place the curry powder, mustard, brown sugar, salt, and vinegar in a jar with a tight-fitting lid. Stir until the mustard and sugar are dissolved. Add the pepper and oil, cover the jar tightly, and shake the dressing vigorously. Store the dressing in a cool corner of the kitchen until ready to use.

YIELD: ¾ CUP DRESSING

TIME ALLOWANCE FOR FINAL PREPARATION: 5 MINUTES

Remove the paper toweling from the salad. Add the cashews and toss to mix. Shake the Curry Dressing vigorously and pour it over the peas. With a salad fork and spoon, toss the vegetables until they are well coated with the dressing.

SERVES 18

SESAME SHRIMP SALAD

◆

(MAY BE PARTIALLY PREPARED UP TO 24 HOURS IN ADVANCE)

½ cup imported sesame oil
¼ cup vegetable oil
1 tablespoon minced garlic
¼ cup minced gingerroot
4 pounds large shrimp, shelled and deveined
¾ cup thinly sliced scallions, including 4 inches of green leaves
½ cup rice wine vinegar
6 Belgian endive heads, leaves separated
¾ cup toasted sesame seeds
½ pound large, very white mushrooms, sliced thin

In a very large skillet, over moderate heat, combine the sesame and vegetable oils. When they are hot, add the garlic and gingerroot. Stirring constantly, sauté until they are just soft, about 2 minutes. Immediately add the shrimp and cook, still stirring, until they just turn opaque, about 4 to 5 minutes.

With a slotted spoon, remove the shrimp from the skillet and transfer them to a mixing bowl. Add the scallions to the oil remaining in the skillet and cook them over moderate heat for 1 minute, stirring continuously. Pour in the vinegar and cook 1 more minute. Scrape the scallions and any residue of liquid over the shrimp and toss to mix. When the shrimp have cooled to room temperature, cover the bowl with plastic wrap and refrigerate until 1 hour before final preparation.

TIME ALLOWANCE FOR FINAL PREPARATION: 10 MINUTES

Line a large salad bowl with the endive leaves, standing them as nearly as possible on end, points up. Sprinkle the toasted sesame seeds over the shrimp and mix well. Spoon the shrimp into the salad bowl, taking care not to disturb the endive leaves. Arrange the mushroom slices in concentric circles on top of the shrimp, starting around the edge of the bowl.

SERVES 18

REBECCA'S ALMOND PLUM TART

(MAY BE PARTIALLY PREPARED UP TO 24 HOURS IN ADVANCE)

This recipe will make one 10-inch tart, sufficient to feed 8 or 10. It is necessary to make three tarts in order to have enough to serve 24. Make the pastry and almond filling in three separate batches, but bake all three tarts at the same time. You will need three 10-inch springform or tart pans for this.

SHORTBREAD PASTRY

1 cup flour
⅓ cup sugar
½ cup unsalted butter, softened and cut in pieces
¼ teaspoon salt
¼ teaspoon vanilla

To make the pastry: Preheat the oven to 400 degrees.

Place the flour and sugar in the bowl of a food processor fitted with a steel blade. Whirl for a second or two to mix. Add the butter, salt, and vanilla, and whirl until a smooth dough has been achieved.

Pat small pieces of the dough over the bottom of a 10-inch springform cake or tart pan until the bottom is completely covered. Distribute the dough as evenly as possible; it should be about ¼ inch thick. Do not build any dough up the sides of the pan.

Place the pan in the oven and bake the pastry 20 minutes, or until it is barely golden brown. Set the pan on a cake rack to cool.

ALMOND FILLING

1¼ cups sliced almonds
½ cup sugar
1 egg
½ teaspoon ground cinnamon

To make the filling: Place the almonds in the bowl of a food processor fitted with a steel blade. Whirl until the almonds are ground into small particles. Do not overblend or the almonds will become oily.

While the motor is running, add the sugar, egg, and cinnamon, and blend until a smooth paste has formed.

When the tart shell has cooled completely, spread the paste, which will be sticky, evenly over the pastry. Cover loosely with aluminum foil and, if not proceeding immediately, refrigerate until 1 hour before the final baking.

TIME ALLOWANCE FOR FINAL PREPARATION AND BAKING: 1 HOUR

PLUM TOPPING
18 to 24 Italian plums, cut in half and pitted
3 tablespoons sugar
2 tablespoons unsalted butter, softened
1 cup heavy cream, plain or whipped

To finish the tart: Preheat the oven to 400 degrees.

Arrange the halved plums, skin side up, in concentric circles on top of the almond filling. Sprinkle the plums with the sugar and dot with the butter.

Place in the oven and immediately reduce the temperature to 375 degrees. Bake for 45 to 50 minutes, or until the plums have softened and all their juices have been absorbed.

The tart may be baked up to 6 hours prior to serving. Serve warm or at room temperature, with or without cream.

YIELD: 1 10-INCH TART

A GRADUATION LUNCHEON FOR SIXTEEN

Jellied Madrilene with Sour Cream

Saint Patrick's Roast Veal

Italian Gnocchi with Cheese and Chives

Spinach Salad with Mango Chutney Dressing

Rolled Baklava

Graduation from high school is truly a cause for celebration! It's the culmination of many years of study and the beginning of a new life—often away from home—for the student. The parents are proud; college acceptances have (hopefully) been received and their child is on the brink of adulthood. Everybody feels good! What better reason to throw a party?

For a graduation held in the morning, a formal, sit-down luncheon is a natural corollary to the event. Proud relatives have presumably journeyed from near and far to witness the festivities, and, while all they really want to see is one young person receive his diploma, they have to sit through speeches and watch all the other graduates receive those important pieces of paper—a process that, as many of us know, takes a long, long time. A lovely luncheon with the beaming graduate in tow is a fitting reward to all that's been endured. The graduate won't be around long; in the evening, he'll undoubtedly be with his pals, celebrating in his far-rowdier fashion.

The meal begins with a jellied madrilene straight out of a can to simplify things, topped with a dollop of sour cream. It progresses to the main course, which centers around a sweet and succulent roast of veal, bathed in a delicate sauce of cream and pureed leaks (legend hath it that Saint Patrick miraculously created leeks out of rushes, hence the name "Saint Patrick's Roast Veal"). The veal is accompanied by cheese-encrusted Italian gnocchi and a tangy spinach and mushroom salad with a novel chutney dressing. None of the food is heavy. Even the dessert—a feathery, crisp baklava—is light. And all except the veal (with a wonderful self-basting chicken-skin topping to prevent its drying out during its roasting) and its simple sauce can be prepared well in advance so that no one has to miss the excitement of the graduation exercises.

SAINT PATRICK'S ROAST VEAL

(MAY BE PARTIALLY PREPARED UP TO 4 HOURS IN ADVANCE)

1 (5- to 6-pound) boneless top round or top sirloin of veal
6 tablespoons unsalted butter
3 large leeks, roots and green leaves trimmed, thoroughly washed and cut in
  ¼-inch slices (about 3 cups)
1½ cups dry white wine
½ teaspoon salt
Freshly ground black pepper
¼ pound mushrooms, ends trimmed, coarsely chopped
½ cup heavy cream
¼ cup Marsala wine
¼ cup minced fresh parsley

When you order your veal roast, which is a relatively fat-free cut of meat, ask your butcher to cover its surface with chicken skin before tying it up. Most butchers will cover veal with pork fat, or lard it with salt pork, but the fat from the skin of a chicken is much more delicate in flavor and will act as a self-basting device as the veal cooks. Since butchers are constantly skinning and boning chicken breasts, they should have plenty of chicken skin on hand if properly forewarned.

Melt 4 tablespoons of the butter over low heat in the roasting pan in which you will be cooking the veal. Add the leeks and sauté them gently, stirring occasionally, until they are just softened but still bright green. Remove the pan from the heat. Pour the wine over the leeks, place the veal on top of them, and sprinkle it with salt and pepper. Cover the veal loosely with plastic wrap or aluminum foil and hold it in a cool corner of the kitchen until time for final preparation.

TIME ALLOWANCE FOR FINAL PREPARATION: 1¾ TO 2 HOURS

Preheat the oven to 450 degrees.

Place the veal in the oven and immediately lower the temperature to 350 degrees. Roast the meat without basting for 1½ hours for a 5-pound cut or 1¾ hours for a 6-pound cut. Remove the roast from the oven and transfer it to a warmed platter. Let it rest undisturbed for 15 minutes while you prepare the sauce.

In a small skillet, melt the remaining 2 tablespoons of butter over low heat. Add the mushrooms and sauté them, stirring occasionally, until they are barely tender. Turn off the heat and reserve.

With a rubber spatula, scrape the contents of the roasting pan into a food processor fitted with a steel blade. Whirl until the mixture is nearly smooth but retains a slight texture (or whirl until smooth, if you prefer). Pour the sauce back into the roasting pan and place it over moderately high heat on top of the stove. Add the cream, stir to blend, and reduce the sauce by one-half, or until it has thickened nicely. Pour in the Marsala, add the sautéed mushrooms, and cook 1 to 2 minutes, or until the sauce is bubbling hot. Remove the pan from the heat and stir in 2 tablespoons of the parsley.

Cut the strings binding the roast and remove and discard the chicken skin. Carve the roast into ¼-inch-thick slices. Arrange the slices, overlapping, on a preheated serving platter (or individual dinner plates). Ladle the sauce over the meat and sprinkle with the remaining 2 tablespoons of parsley.

SERVES 16

ITALIAN GNOCCHI WITH CHEESE AND CHIVES

(MAY BE PARTIALLY PREPARED UP TO 2 DAYS IN ADVANCE)

8 cups milk
1½ cups regular-style Cream of Wheat
½ cup plus 2 tablespoons unsalted butter
1½ cups freshly grated Parmesan cheese
1 teaspoon salt
½ cup minced fresh chives

Pour the milk into a 3- to 4-quart saucepan and bring it to a boil over moderately high heat. When it is boiling, add the Cream of Wheat so gradually that the milk does not stop boiling. Beat continuously so that no lumps form. Watch for scorching and lower the heat if necessary.

When the Cream of Wheat is very thick and comes away from the sides of the pan as you are stirring it (about 5 to 8 minutes), remove the saucepan from the heat. Beat in ½ cup butter, 1 cup of the cheese, the salt, and the chives, and continue beating until they are all well incorporated.

Generously butter a 10-by-14-inch baking dish (or the equivalent). Using a rubber spatula, scrape the Cream of Wheat mixture into the dish, spreading it out evenly. Set it aside to cool.

When it is cool and hard, cut the Cream of Wheat into rounds with a 2-inch cookie cutter or a small glass. With careful cutting you should be able to obtain 15 to 18 rounds. The rounds will be thick: cut each in half horizontally so that you then have 30 to 36 rounds. (Save the scraps for leftovers.)

Generously butter one or more ovenproof baking dishes (preferably ones that you can bring to the table). Arrange the gnocchi rounds in the dish or dishes, overlapping them slightly. Sprinkle the surface of the gnocchi with the remaining ½ cup of cheese and dot with the remaining 2 tablespoons of butter. Cover the baking dish or dishes with plastic wrap and refrigerate until 1 hour before final preparation.

TIME ALLOWANCE FOR FINAL PREPARATION: 30 MINUTES

Preheat the oven to 400 degrees.

Bake the gnocchi for 20 to 25 minutes, or until they are golden brown.

SERVES 16

SPINACH SALAD WITH MANGO CHUTNEY DRESSING

(SALAD MAY BE PARTIALLY PREPARED UP TO 6 HOURS IN ADVANCE; DRESSING MAY BE PREPARED UP TO 24 HOURS IN ADVANCE)

SPINACH SALAD
2 (10-ounce) packages spinach, stems discarded, torn into bite-size pieces
1 small red onion, peeled and thinly sliced
½ pound mushrooms, thinly sliced
12 strips bacon, fried, drained, and crumbled
2 (8-ounce) cans sliced water chestnuts, drained and patted dry on paper toweling
1 cup seasoned croutons

To make the salad: Line a salad bowl with paper toweling. Place the spinach, onion slices, mushrooms, bacon, water chestnuts, and croutons in the bowl. Toss with your hands to distribute the ingredients. Cover with a dampened linen towel and refrigerate until time for final preparation.

MANGO CHUTNEY DRESSING

¾ cup mango chutney (including its juices), finely chopped
¾ cup white wine vinegar
1 teaspoon minced garlic (optional)
3 tablespoons Dijon-style mustard
1 cup sour cream

To make the dressing: Place the chutney in a small mixing bowl. Using a whisk, beat in the vinegar, garlic (if desired), mustard, and sour cream and mix until well blended. Cover with plastic wrap and refrigerate until 1 hour before final preparation.

YIELD: 3 CUPS DRESSING

TIME ALLOWANCE FOR FINAL PREPARATION: 5 MINUTES

Remove the toweling from the salad. Stir the dressing briskly. With a rubber spatula, scrape 1 cup of dressing over the salad. With a salad fork and spoon, toss the salad until all the spinach leaves are completely coated with the dressing.

SERVES 16

ROLLED BAKLAVA

(MAY BE PARTIALLY PREPARED AND FROZEN UP TO 1 MONTH IN ADVANCE;
MAY BE PREPARED UP TO 24 HOURS IN ADVANCE)

1 (1-pound package) frozen fillo dough, thawed according to package directions
  (allow 12 hours)
1½ cups walnuts
1¾ cups sugar
1 tablespoon ground cinnamon
½ teaspoon freshly ground nutmeg
1 to 1½ cups unsalted butter, melted
1 cup honey
3 tablespoons strained fresh lemon juice

Because fillo dough dries out so rapidly, making it hard to work with, prepare the filling before assembling the Baklava rolls.

In the bowl of a food processor fitted with a steel blade, combine the walnuts, ¾ cup of the sugar, cinnamon, and nutmeg. Whirl until the walnuts are finely chopped. Transfer the mixture to a large bowl. Have a ¼-cup measuring cup at hand.

Remove the fillo dough from its package and gently unroll it, laying the sheets flat on a kitchen counter. Cover them with a dampened towel so that they do not dry out while you fill them. Spread a dry kitchen towel right next to the covered dough.

Lifting back the dampened towel, carefully peel off a fillo sheet from the stack of dough and lay it on top of the dry towel. Immediately recover the remaining dough with the damp towel. Fillo is paper-thin and tricky to work with. Do not become alarmed if you tear any of the sheets, although it is better not to. In this recipe, torn or damaged fillo sheets do not matter too much and are easily disguised. Working rapidly, lightly brush the entire surface of the single sheet with melted butter. Lay another fillo sheet on top of the first, fitting it corner to corner so that they stack evenly. Brush the second sheet with melted butter. Repeat with two more sheets until you have a stack of four sheets.

Scoop up a heaping ¼ cupful of the walnut mixture and sprinkle it evenly along one of the short ends of the pastry, leaving an inch at each side without any nuts. Fold this inch over on itself on each side. Starting at the filling end, roll up the sheets of dough jellyroll fashion. Place the roll, seam side down, on an ungreased cookie sheet or baking dish. Brush the surface of the roll with more butter.

Repeat until all the sheets of fillo have been buttered, filled, and rolled. You should have five rolls.

Refrigerate the rolls for 30 minutes. (Or wrap them separately and freeze for up to 1 month.)

Preheat the oven to 350 degrees.

Without breaking through to the base, cut each roll on the diagonal into four pieces. Transfer them to an ungreased baking dish and bake them for 40 minutes, or until they are puffed and delicately tanned.

While they are baking, prepare the syrup by combining the remaining 1 cup sugar, honey, and lemon juice in a 1- to 2-quart saucepan. Bring the mixture to a boil over moderately low heat, stirring until the sugar is dissolved. Lower the heat and simmer for 5 minutes. Watch carefully, for the mixture tends to boil over. Remove it from the heat.

When the baklava has finished baking, cut through the rolls and separate the pieces. With a slotted spoon, dip each piece into the warm honey mixture, turning it over to coat all sides. Transfer each piece to a serving platter. Repeat until all the pieces have been dipped.

If you are not serving the baklava within the next 2 hours, store the pieces in an airtight container to preserve their freshness.

YIELD: 20 PIECES

A REHEARSAL DINNER FOR TWENTY-FOUR

Chilled Sunflower Soup

Tournedos Chivry

Peas with Pignoli

Mixed Green Salad with Vinaigrette*

Almond Meringue Sundaes

One of my happiest recollections of my wedding was the lovely rehearsal dinner my aunt gave for the bridal party. Customarily this dinner is given by the groom's family, but often relatives of the bride will give it, particularly if the groom's parents live out of town—as they did in our case.

My aunt threw the party in her home, and we totaled, as I recall, about twenty-four—the same as this menu. She did all the work herself, and her love and effort permeated the whole affair. Somehow she got rid of her large dining room table and set up six card tables in its place, four in the dining room and two just beyond in the garden. She covered the tables with floor-length pastel cloths and centered a tiny bouquet in matching tones on each. She cooked the food herself, relying on a roast for ease of preparation, and had two people to help with the serving. Her two real extravagances for the evening were a continuous flow of champagne and an accordion player who hovered in the garden, regaling us with romantic songs. The informality and simplicity of the dinner generated a magical camaraderie.

I hope my menu for a rehearsal dinner is as successful for you as my aunt's was for me. The food is slightly more sophisticated, but in the sixties roast beef, roast potatoes, and peas were considered pretty elaborate dining. Most of my menu can be prepared in advance, leaving the hosts plenty of time to celebrate with the bridal party.

* Prepare six times the recipe on page 24.

The "sunflower" soup (named for its principal ingredient, Jerusalem artichokes or "sunchokes," which are actually sunflower tubers) will keep the guests guessing. The "tournedos" (for convenience of execution, thick slices of roast tenderloin, not steaks), with their piquant green sauce, will stimulate all appetites. The crunchy Almond Meringue Sundaes for dessert will give every member of the bridal party fortitude for the big day ahead.

Just don't forget the champagne—even if it's simply a sparkling wine—nor the toasts to go with it!

CHILLED SUNFLOWER SOUP

(MAY BE PARTIALLY PREPARED UP TO 2 DAYS IN ADVANCE;
MUST BE PARTIALLY PREPARED UP TO 3 HOURS IN ADVANCE)

3½ pounds Jerusalem artichokes ("sunchokes")
¼ cup unsalted butter
3 cups coarsely chopped onions
1½ teaspoons salt
1½ teaspoons dried thyme
8 cups chicken broth
¼ cup strained fresh lemon juice
½ to 1 teaspoon Tabasco sauce, or to taste
3 cups light cream
2 lemons

With a sharp paring knife, peel the Jerusalem artichokes, cutting off, as necessary, any small knobs (and discarding them) to facilitate the task. Cut each artichoke crosswise into ¼-inch slices. Immediately drop the slices into cold water to prevent discoloration.

In a 4- to 5-quart nonreactive saucepan, melt the butter over moderate heat. Add the onions and cook them, stirring occasionally, until they are soft, about 5 minutes. Add the sliced artichokes, salt, thyme, and chicken broth. Bring the liquid to a boil over high heat, then reduce the heat and simmer, partially covered, for 12 to 15 minutes, or until the artichokes are soft when pierced with the tip of a knife. Remove the saucepan from the heat and allow the soup to cool to room temperature.

Puree the soup in batches in a blender or a food processor fitted with a steel blade until all lumps have disappeared. Transfer the puree into a large mixing bowl. (If you prefer a very smooth consistency, strain the soup as you pour it into the mixing bowl.)

Add the lemon juice and ½ teaspoon of Tabasco sauce. Stir to mix well. Taste the soup and add Tabasco to taste, bearing in mind that the soup will be further diluted by the addition of cream. Cover the soup with plastic wrap and refrigerate it for at least 3 hours, or as long as 48 hours, until final preparation.

TIME ALLOWANCE FOR FINAL PREPARATION: 5 MINUTES

Pour the cream into the chilled soup. Stir to blend. Cut the lemons into 24 paper-thin slices.

Ladle the soup into 24 shallow bowls and float a lemon slice on top of each portion for garnish.

SERVES 24

TOURNEDOS CHIVRY

(CROUTONS MAY BE PREPARED UP TO 12 HOURS IN ADVANCE;
TENDERLOIN AND SAUCE MUST BE PREPARED JUST PRIOR TO SERVING)

Tournedos are steaks cut from a beef tenderloin. To facilitate the execution of this entree for 24 and avoid grilling so many individual steaks, roast the tenderloin whole, and simulate tournedos steaks by carving the roasts into steaklike slices.

CROUTONS
1 (18-inch) baguette, or loaf of French bread
¾ cup unsalted butter, softened

To make the croutons: Using a serrated knife, and slicing on a wide diagonal, cut the baguette into ½-inch-thick slices so that a long, oval piece of bread is obtained rather than a small round (to better fit the shape of the steak portions). You should be able to get about 28 slices from one 18-inch loaf.

Generously butter each slice on both sides with the butter.

Place the slices, in batches, in a heavy skillet and toast them on both sides over moderately low heat until golden brown. Cool the toasted slices on a plate.

Hold the croutons in a plastic bag until time to assemble the Tournedos Chivry.

TIME ALLOWANCE FOR FINAL PREPARATION: 45 MINUTES

CHIVRY SAUCE

¼ cup minced shallots
4 teaspoons dried tarragon
⅔ cup tarragon vinegar
8 egg yolks
2 cups unsalted butter, melted and cooled
1 teaspoon salt
¼ teaspoon freshly ground black pepper
1 cup packed watercress leaves, stems discarded

To make the sauce: Place the shallots, tarragon, and tarragon vinegar in a small nonreactive saucepan. Over moderate heat, cook the mixture until the shallots and tarragon are soft and the liquid has reduced to about 3 tablespoons. Remove the pan from the heat and strain the liquid into a 1-quart nonreactive saucepan, pressing down hard on the herbs to extract as much flavor as possible.

Return the pan to very low heat, add the egg yolks, and whisk vigorously until the yolks start to thicken. Start adding the melted butter, drop by drop, checking the heat of the pan constantly. If the bottom of the pan is too hot to touch, remove it from the heat until it cools, but continue whisking and adding the butter as you do so. Keep whisking in the butter, drop by drop, until it is completely incorporated and the sauce has thickened to the consistency of mayonnaise. Set the pan in a bowl filled with lukewarm—not hot—water to maintain its warmth.

Place the watercress leaves in the bowl of a food processor fitted with a steel blade and whirl until almost pureed. Scrape the mixture into the sauce and stir to blend.

TOURNEDOS

2 (6- to 7-pound) tenderloins of beef, well trimmed (roasting weight: 5 pounds
  each), tops covered with thin layer of suet, and tied at 2-inch intervals
Freshly ground black pepper
Watercress

To make the tournedos: Preheat the oven to 475 degrees.

Sprinkle the tenderloins lightly with pepper. Place the tenderloins, with some space separating them, on a rack in a roasting pan. Roast them in the middle of the oven for 25 minutes. Transfer the tenderloins to a warm platter and let them stand for 10 minutes before carving. (This will produce rare meat; cook them 5 to 7 minutes longer for medium.)

To assemble: Place the croutons on 24 preheated dinner plates. Carve the tenderloins into ½-inch-thick slices (thus resembling the tournedos steak-cut) and arrange a slice on top of each crouton. Top each slice with a generous spoonful of Chivry Sauce and garnish each plate with watercress. Serve immediately.

SERVES 24

PEAS WITH PIGNOLI

(MAY BE PARTIALLY PREPARED UP TO 6 HOURS IN ADVANCE)

1½ cups thinly sliced scallions, including 2 inches of green leaves
2 teaspoons sugar
3 cups chicken broth
6 tablespoons unsalted butter
1 cup pine nuts (pignoli)
3 tablespoons minced fresh rosemary (or 1 tablespoon dried rosemary, crushed)
6 (10-ounce) packages frozen peas
Salt and freshly ground black pepper to taste

In a 4- to 6-quart nonreactive saucepan, combine the scallions, sugar, and chicken broth. Bring the broth to a boil, then lower the heat and simmer, partially covered, for 5 minutes. Remove the pan from the heat and hold it in a cool corner of the kitchen until final preparation.

In a large skillet, melt the butter over moderately low heat. Add the pine nuts and rosemary, and, stirring frequently, cook the nuts until they are brown on all sides, about 10 minutes. (Be careful that they do not burn.) Remove the pan from the heat and hold it in a cool corner of the kitchen until final preparation.

TIME ALLOWANCE FOR FINAL PREPARATION: 10 MINUTES

Bring the chicken broth to a boil. Add the peas, cover, and cook for 5 minutes, stirring once or twice, or until the peas are just tender. Drain.

Briefly reheat the pine nuts. With a rubber spatula, scrape the nuts and the butter over the peas, and stir to mix. Season with salt and pepper to taste. Serve immediately.

SERVES 24

ALMOND MERINGUE SUNDAES

(MERINGUES MAY BE PREPARED UP TO 3 DAYS IN ADVANCE;
TOPPING MAY BE PREPARED 2 DAYS IN ADVANCE)

ALMOND MERINGUES
1 pound whole unsalted almonds
1½ cups sugar
¼ cup cornstarch
12 egg whites, at room temperature

To make the meringue: Preheat the oven to 325 degrees.

Drop the almonds into a saucepan full of boiling water and blanch them for 1 minute. Drain them immediately and run them under cold water to cool. Slip the almond skins off. Spread the almonds on a nonstick (or lightly buttered) baking sheet, and bake them, stirring occasionally, for 10 minutes or until they are lightly toasted. Do NOT turn the oven off.

Transfer the almonds to the bowl of a food processor fitted with a steel blade. Whirl them until they are finely grated. Add the sugar and cornstarch and whirl briefly to blend.

In a large bowl, beat the egg whites with an electric mixer until they are stiff. Sprinkle the almond mixture over the whites and gently fold the ingredients together with a rubber spatula.

Using a serving spoon, place a large mound of the almond meringue on a nonstick baking sheet (or a generously buttered and floured sheet). Rinse a dessert spoon in cold water, and press it, bowl side up, onto the mound of meringue, making a small depression. Repeat making the meringue mounds until all the meringue is used up. There should be enough for at least 24. (You will need to use two or three baking sheets, depending upon their size, but the meringues do not expand appreciably and can be baked quite close together.) Bake the meringues in the oven for 1¼ hours.

Remove the meringues from the oven and transfer them to racks to cool. Store the meringues in airtight containers until time for final assembly.

BUTTERSCOTCH TOPPING

2 cups light cream
¼ cup unsalted butter
1½ cups dark brown sugar
3 tablespoons dark corn syrup
2 tablespoons strained fresh lemon juice
¼ teaspoon salt
½ teaspoon vanilla
¼ cup confectioners' sugar

To make the sauce: In a 2-quart saucepan, combine the cream, butter, brown sugar, and corn syrup. Over moderate heat, bring the mixture to a boil, stirring frequently until the sugar dissolves and the butter melts. Then cook over low heat until the mixture is thick and smooth, about 8 to 10 minutes. Remove the saucepan from the heat and stir in the lemon juice, salt, and vanilla.

When the sauce is cool, sift in the confectioners' sugar. With a whisk, beat to blend. Pour the sauce into a jar.

Tightly cover the suace and refrigerate up to 2 weeks.

FINAL ASSEMBLY

3 quarts vanilla ice cream, slightly softened
2 (4-ounce) packages slivered almonds, toasted

Transfer the Butterscotch Topping to a saucepan and bring it to a boil over moderate heat.

Center the meringues on 24 dessert plates. Place 1 large or 2 medium scoops of ice cream in the depression of each meringue. Ladle a generous portion of hot Butterscotch Topping over the ice cream and sprinkle a teaspoonful of toasted slivered almonds on top. Serve immediately.

SERVES 24

A FIFTIETH BIRTHDAY PARTY FOR FIFTY

Seafood Creole

Brown and Wild Rice Casserole

Asparagus and Corn Salad with Herb Dressing

Assorted Scoops of Ice Cream

Birthday Cupcakes with Chocolate Glaze

It's a little formidable to plan a dinner party for fifty, but the occasion of someone special's fiftieth birthday prompts us to rise to the occasion.

For this fiftieth birthday party, the largest portion of the preparation can be done ahead of the party, with only reheating and last-minute presentation to worry about. Furthermore, it's a menu that is as festive as possible while taking into account the financial burdens of feeding such a vast number. The Seafood Creole and the Brown and Wild Rice Casserole are both compromises. The Seafood Creole is my lower-budget version of that spicy New Orleans favorite, Shrimp Creole. Instead of containing only shrimp, my recipe calls for Japanese surimi (also known as sea legs or imitation crab, a manmade extrusion of crab-flavored pollock, which costs about one-third as much as shrimp). Because it has a rich and flavorful sauce, the dish does not suffer from my substitution. Nonetheless, if money's no object, make the dish a hundred percent shrimp.

Similarly, I made a financially oriented compromise on the rice casserole. Instead of being all wild rice, a very costly grain, it's half brown and half wild rice. (Don't substitute a boxed mix, though. This recipe is easy and tastes much better with its far higher proportion of wild rice than you'd find in a mix. The only inconvenience, and it's a small one, is starting the brown rice ten minutes earlier than the wild.)

The greatest problem with this whole birthday meal, to be perfectly frank, is finding big enough pots. The average household just isn't equipped for feeding fifty. If you have a friend in the restaurant business, see if you can borrow a couple of giant kettles from him. Or try to rent them. Some of the rental businesses actually have large-scale kitchen equipment. Another alternative is to round up all your friends' big pots and casseroles and make the recipes in smaller portions. Or, I suppose, you could go to a restaurant supply store and buy some large cooking utensils.

Once you solve this not-inconsiderable hurdle, the rest of the party will be smooth sailing. Just make certain, though, you have someone on hand to help you light the fifty-one candles! That's the next biggest problem!

SEAFOOD CREOLE

◆

(MAY BE PARTIALLY PREPARED UP TO 4 DAYS IN ADVANCE)

1 cup vegetable oil
12 cups finely chopped onions
8 cups finely chopped celery
4 large green peppers, cored, seeded, and finely chopped (about 6 cups)
3 tablespoons minced garlic
4 bay leaves
2 tablespoons salt
1 teaspoon freshly ground black pepper
2 teaspoons Tabasco sauce
1 tablespoon crushed dried red pepper
3 tablespoons dried basil
¼ cup fresh thyme
2 (8-ounce) jars clam juice
8 (28-ounce) cans Italian-style peeled tomatoes, drained and chopped (about 16 cups)
4 (13-ounce) cans tomato sauce (about 6 cups)
3 tablespoons sugar
8 pounds large shrimp, peeled and deveined
4 pounds Japanese surimi (also known as sea legs or imitation crab)

In a 14- to 16-quart kettle, warm the oil over moderate heat. Add the onions, celery, peppers, and garlic. Stirring frequently, cook until the vegetables are soft, about 10 minutes. Add the bay leaves, salt, pepper, Tabasco, crushed red peppers, basil, and thyme, and mix well.

Pour in the clam juice, chopped tomatoes, tomato sauce, and sugar, and stir to blend. Bring to a boil over high heat. Reduce the heat to low, partially cover, and simmer for 30 minutes, stirring occasionally. Remove from the heat and cool.

When the sauce is cool, refrigerate it, tightly covered, until 1 hour before final preparation.

TIME ALLOWANCE FOR FINAL PREPARATION: 30 MINUTES

Pick out and discard the bay leaves. Set the kettle over moderately high heat and bring the sauce to a boil. Add the shrimp and surimi, stir to mix, and bring the sauce to a boil once more. Immediately turn off the heat, cover the kettle, and let the seafood rest in the hot sauce until the shrimp are opaque, about 5 to 10 minutes. Serve immediately.

SERVES 50

BROWN AND WILD RICE CASSEROLE

(MAY BE PARTIALLY PREPARED UP TO 24 HOURS IN ADVANCE)

4 cups brown rice, rinsed
4 cups wild rice, rinsed
8 large carrots, peeled
1 cup unsalted butter
2 pounds mushrooms, ends trimmed, thinly sliced
2 teaspoons salt
Freshly ground black pepper
2 cups light cream

Fill an 8- to 10-quart kettle to within 4 inches of its rim with salted water. Place it over high heat and, when the water boils, add the brown rice, stirring once or twice to separate the kernels. Boil the brown rice for 10 minutes, then add the wild rice, stirring briefly. When the water returns to a boil, lower the heat to moderate, partially cover the kettle, and boil the rice for 30 minutes. Turn off the heat and let the rice rest in the water for 5 additional minutes. Drain the rice in a large strainer and cool them under cold running water.

While the rice is cooking, cut the carrots on the diagonal into ¼-inch-thick slices. Bring a large saucepan of salted water to a boil and parboil the carrots for 3 minutes. Drain and refresh them under cold water.

Melt the butter in a large skillet over moderate heat. Add the mushrooms and sauté them for 2 to 3 minutes, or until barely tender. Remove the pan from the heat.

Transfer the rice to a very large ovenproof casserole (or divide it among several smaller ones). Add the carrots, mushrooms, salt, pepper, and cream, and toss to mix thoroughly. Cover the casserole and refrigerate until 1 hour before final preparation.

TIME ALLOWANCE FOR FINAL PREPARATION: 45 MINUTES

Preheat the oven to 325 degrees.

Place the casserole, covered, in the oven and bake it for 30 to 40 minutes, or until steaming hot. (Smaller casseroles will take less time to reheat.)

SERVES 50

ASPARAGUS AND CORN SALAD WITH HERB DRESSING

(SALAD AND DRESSING MAY BE PARTIALLY PREPARED UP TO 10 HOURS IN ADVANCE;
THEY MUST BE PARTIALLY PREPARED AT LEAST 4 HOURS IN ADVANCE)

HERB DRESSING
1¼ cups strained fresh lemon juice
3 tablespoons Dijon-style mustard
2 tablespoons dried sweet basil
3 tablespoons sugar
1 tablespoon paprika
4 egg yolks, beaten
4½ cups fruity, imported olive oil
2 teaspoons salt
½ teaspoon freshly ground black pepper
6 cloves garlic, peeled and crushed

To make the dressing: In a mixing bowl, combine the lemon juice, mustard, basil, sugar, and paprika. Beat with a whisk until the ingredients are well blended. Whisk in the egg yolks. Gradually beat in the olive oil, whisking continuously until it is completely emulsified. Add the salt, pepper, and garlic, and blend well. Taste and adjust the seasonings, adding more herbs or salt if you prefer a stronger flavor. Set aside as you prepare the salad.

YIELD: 6 CUPS DRESSING

ASPARAGUS AND CORN SALAD
5 pounds asparagus, ends trimmed
5 (10-ounce) packages frozen corn, thawed

10 large carrots, peeled
12 large stalks celery, strings peeled
5 red peppers, cored, seeded, and cut in ¼-inch-dice
3 pounds mushrooms, ends trimmed, sliced thin
1½ cups minced fresh dillweed
3 cups thinly sliced scallions, including 6 inches of green leaves
3 to 4 heads Boston lettuce (or any other lettuce of your choice), washed and
*   dried*
3 cups seasoned croutons
1 cup freshly grated Parmesan cheese

To make the salad: Fill a large nonreactive skillet with salted water to within 1 inch of its rim. Bring it to a boil. Add the asparagus. When the water returns to a boil, cook them for exactly 2 minutes. Drain the asparagus and refresh them under cold water, then drain again. Pat them dry with paper toweling. Cut them on the diagonal into 1-inch lengths. Transfer them to a very large mixing bowl.

Fill a 4- to 5-quart saucepan with salted water and bring it to a boil over high heat. Drop in the corn. When the water returns to a boil, immediately drain the corn and refresh it under cold running water. Spread the kernels out on paper toweling to dry completely. Add the corn to the asparagus.

Cut the carrots and celery on the diagonal into very thin slices. Add them and the peppers, mushrooms, dillweed, and scallions to the asparagus and corn. Toss to distribute the vegetables well.

Pour approximately 4 cups of the Herb Dressing over the vegetables and toss until they all are well coated. Cover the salad with plastic wrap and refrigerate at least 4 hours, or as long as 10 hours, to permit the flavors to blend. Cover and refrigerate the remaining dressing. Remove the salad and dressing from the refrigerator 30 minutes before final preparation.

TIME ALLOWANCE FOR FINAL PREPARATION: 10 MINUTES

Line a very large salad bowl (or bowls) with the lettuce. Toss the vegetables a few times to redistribute the dressing. Heap the vegetables in the center of the bowl and sprinkle the croutons on top. Drizzle the remaining 2 cups of dressing over the lettuce and vegetables. Sprinkle the surface with the cheese.

SERVES 50

BIRTHDAY CUPCAKES WITH CHOCOLATE GLAZE

(CUPCAKES MAY BE BAKED AND GLAZED 24 HOURS IN ADVANCE)

CUPCAKES

6 cups cake flour
2 tablespoons baking powder
1 teaspoon salt
2½ cups unsalted butter, softened
4½ cups sugar
10 eggs, at room temperature
2 cups milk
4 teaspoons vanilla

To make the cupcakes: Preheat the oven to 350 degrees. Set out as many 2½-inch-cup muffin tins as you have, and position 2½-inch paper baking cups in them. Select your largest glass or porcelain custard cup and generously butter it. Lightly flour it and shake out any excess.

Sift the cake flour, baking powder, and salt together two times. Set aside.

In a large mixing bowl, with an electric mixer, cream the butter until it is very soft. Slowly add the sugar and continue beating until the mixture is light and fluffy. Beat in the eggs, 1 at a time.

In batches, stir the flour into the egg mixture alternately with the milk, beginning and ending with the flour. Add the vanilla and beat the batter until it is smooth.

With a cup or a large kitchen spoon, scoop up approximately one-third cup of batter and pour it into a baking cup. (The cup should be two-thirds full.) Repeat until all the baking cups are filled. Fill the custard cup two-thirds full with batter. Rap the custard cup and muffin tins sharply on the counter to expel any bubbles in the batter. Bake the cupcakes in the center of the oven for 30 minutes, or until they have just started to turn golden. (The larger cupcake in the custard cup may take up to 5 minutes longer. Check it with a straw for doneness.)

Remove the cupcakes from the muffin tins and set them on a rack to cool. Carefully remove the larger cupcake from the custard cup and cool it. Continue baking the cupcakes until all the batter has been used up. (But do not make any more cakes in the custard cup; that one is for the birthday person.)

CHOCOLATE GLAZE

4 ounces unsweetened chocolate, cut into small pieces
1 cup sugar

¾ cup heavy (not whipping) cream, chilled
⅓ cup sour cream
2 tablespoons unsalted butter, softened
¼ teaspoon salt
Pinch of ground cinnamon
1 teaspoon vanilla

To make the glaze: Place the chocolate and sugar in the bowl of a food processor fitted with a steel blade. Whirl exactly 1 minute. The chocolate will have broken down into grains the size of the sugar.

Add the cream, sour cream, and butter. Blend in the food processor for 10 to 15 minutes, or until the chocolate has thickened slightly and turned a rich and shiny dark brown. (Do not get discouraged if this seems hopeless at first; just keep blending.) Add the salt, cinnamon, and vanilla, and blend a few seconds longer.

Scrape the chocolate glaze into a large mixing bowl.

FINAL ASSEMBLY

50 small white birthday cake candles
1 larger blue or pink birthday cake candle
White miniature carnations

Cover your largest tray with aluminum foil so that you have transformed it into a "silver" tray. Place paper doilies on top of the foil.

Dip the top of the large cupcake into the chocolate glaze. Swirl it slightly to completely coat its top. Place it, right side up, in the center of the tray. Repeat with all the remaining cupcakes, arranging them decoratively around the central cupcake.

Center the large blue or pink candle in the large cupcake and the smaller white candles in the smaller cakes. Loosely cover the tray with aluminum foil and set it aside in a cool corner of the kitchen.

(If there is any chocolate glaze left over, save it. It is delicious heated up and poured over ice cream.)

TIME ALLOWANCE FOR FINAL PREPARATION: 10 MINUTES

Tuck the miniature carnations around the edges of the tray. Light the candles, starting in the center, and present the Birthday Cupcakes to the birthday person!

YIELD: 55 TO 65 CUPCAKES

COCKTAILS AND GRAVLAX FOR FIFTY

Annie B's Gravlax with Mustard and Dill Sauce

Fillo Spring Rolls

Teriyaki Sausage

Chicken Puffs

Ham and Cream Cheese "Snails"

Steamed Vegetables with Marianne's Tuna Dip

Assorted Beverages

Cocktail parties can be very iffy. They can be smashing successes, or simply ho-hum. To be good, they require a lot of organization and work, and much fussing over small details. If they are planned meticulously, however, leaving nothing to chance, nine times out of ten you can throw a real winner.

To achieve those heights of hosting, bear in mind the following rules: Select your guests carefully, with an eye to compatibility and mutual interests. Be certain that each guest in a large party of fifty knows at least two or three others in order to have a sense of security. Arrange to have an abundant and varied supply of beverages, something to please everyone, with nothing running in too short supply. (Most liquor stores will take back unopened bottles.) Secure the help you will need for the party so that things run smoothly. Don't stint on hiring extra hands. You should be the all-present host, seeing to your guests' needs and making them feel comfortable. You are also The Great Introducer. And The Great Deliverer, saving those poor souls who might get stuck with The Town Bore. You should NOT be Bartender and Waiter too.

Above all, plan your food well. Choose a focal point, a special treat. It might be a smoked turkey, a gorgeous ham, slices of pale pink tenderloin, a seductively large bowl of shrimp or even caviar. Place this treat in the center of your buffet and allow people to help themselves. To its side, set alternate choices of delectables. At the same time, so that the buffet doesn't look like a crowded cafeteria, have your help pass the smaller food items. Scatter bowls of nuts and olives on small tables. Always consider circulation, and simplify the availability of food and beverages.

In this menu, my eye-catcher is *Gravlax,* the Scandinavian dill-and-brine version of smoked salmon. (And, in its own way, every bit as delicious.) The recipe comes from my Danish stepmother, Annie B, and it is different from traditional gravlax in that it calls for the inclusion of salami during the marinating, which imparts a slightly smoky flavor to the fish.

The other recipes given for this cocktail party are all somewhat "different." I don't think you will have encountered any of them before. Besides being tasty, their real plus for the host or hostess is that they can be partially prepared in advance, thus releasing them for the many other chores that will fall their way. (I have included quite a number of recipes for this one event. You don't have to serve them all. But don't worry; if you do, undoubtedly they'll get eaten.)

As I have said before: Sit back, or rather, stand up and enjoy your guests. Cocktails and Gravlax should prove to be one of the winners!

ANNIE B'S GRAVLAX WITH MUSTARD AND DILL SAUCE

(GRAVLAX MAY BE PARTIALLY PREPARED UP TO 1 WEEK IN ADVANCE OR MUST BE PARTIALLY PREPARED TO 2 DAYS IN ADVANCE; SAUCE MAY BE PREPARED UP TO 1 WEEK IN ADVANCE)

GRAVLAX
2 matching fillets of Norwegian salmon, cleaned, scaled, and all bones removed (about 5 to 6 pounds)
1/2 cup salt (preferably kosher)
1/3 cup sugar
1 teaspoon freshly ground white pepper
2 bunches fresh dillweed, root ends trimmed
1/4 pound smoky Genoa-type salami, cut in 1/8-inch-thick slices
Thinly sliced bread, buttered

To make the gravlax: Place one of the salmon fillets (which will measure approximately 16 inches in length), skin side down, in a large glass or stainless steel baking dish. Arrange the second fillet, skin side down, on a piece of paper toweling.

In a small bowl, combine the salt, sugar, and white pepper, and stir to mix well. Spoon half of this mixture over each fish fillet, rubbing it well into the flesh. Cover the fillet in the pan with the dill and lay the slices of salami on top of it. (Do not overlap the slices.) Place the remaining salmon fillet, skin side up, aligned head to head and tail to tail, on the dill-and-salami-covered fillet.

Cover the fish with heavy-duty aluminum foil and set a platter on it. Weight the platter down with several cans or five-pound bags of sugar or flour. Allow the salmon to marinate in the refrigerator for at least 2 days, or as long as 3 days. Turn the fish over every 12 hours, basting the inside and outside with the liquid that has accumulated. Replace the plates and weights each time.

When the gravlax has finished marinating, scrape off and discard the dill, salami, and any residue of the salt mixture. Pat the fillets dry with paper toweling. If you are not serving them immediately, wrap them well in aluminum foil and refrigerate for up to 5 days. Remove the fillets from the refrigerator 1 hour before serving to bring them to room temperature.

MUSTARD AND DILL SAUCE

2 egg yolks
4 tablespoons Dijon-style mustard
2 teaspoons dry mustard
4 tablespoons sugar
4 tablespoons tarragon vinegar
2/3 cup vegetable oil
1/4 teaspoon salt
Freshly ground white pepper
1/4 cup minced fresh dillweed

To make the sauce: In a small bowl, combine the egg yolks, mustards, and sugar. Beat with a whisk until the mixture is shiny and thick. Beat in the vinegar. Slowly beat in the oil until it forms a mayonnaiselike emulsion. Add the salt, pepper, and dillweed and stir to mix.

If you are not serving the sauce immediately, transfer it to a jar equipped with a tight-fitting lid and refrigerate until 1 hour before serving time. Whisk it once or twice just before serving.

YIELD: 1 CUP SAUCE

TIME ALLOWANCE FOR FINAL PREPARATION: 15 MINUTES PER GRAVLAX FILLET

Place one gravlax fillet, skin side down, on a wooden carving board. (Reserve the other in the kitchen.) Slice it as thinly as possible on the diagonal, detaching the slices from the skin.

Transfer the sauce to a small serving bowl and place it on the serving table next to the gravlax. Serve the gravlax on slices of buttered bread, topped with a small dollop of the Mustard and Dill Sauce. (When the first salmon fillet is finished, discard its skin and bring out the second.)

SERVES 50

FILLO SPRING ROLLS

(MAY BE PARTIALLY PREPARED AND FROZEN UP TO 1 MONTH IN ADVANCE;
MAY BE PARTIALLY PREPARED UP TO 24 HOURS IN ADVANCE)

*1 (1-pound) package frozen fillo dough, thawed according to package directions
(allow 12 hours)*

3 tablespoons imported sesame oil

2 tablespoons vegetable oil

3 tablespoons finely chopped gingerroot

2 teaspoons minced garlic

¾ pound bean sprouts

1 pound shrimp, shelled, deveined, and coarsely chopped

1 (8-ounce) can sliced water chestnuts, finely chopped

¾ cup finely sliced scallions, including 4 inches of green leaves

½ cup chopped carrots (about 1 medium)

2 teaspoons cornstarch

5 tablespoons soy sauce

1 cup unsalted butter, melted

3 tablespoons dry mustard

1 tablespoon water

1 tablespoon dry vermouth

Because fillo dough dries out so quickly, making it very hard to work with, prepare the filling for the Fillo Spring Rolls first.

Pour the sesame and vegetable oils into a wok or large skillet, preferably one with high sides. Over moderately high heat, sauté the ginger and garlic, stirring constantly, for 1 minute, or until soft. Add the bean sprouts, shrimp, water chestnuts, scallions, and carrots and, continuing to stir, fry for 3 to 4 minutes, or until the shrimp have become opaque and the vegetables are somewhat wilted.

In a small bowl, mix the cornstarch with 3 tablespoons of the soy sauce, stirring until the cornstarch is completely dissolved. Pour it over the shrimp mixture and mix until the sauce has thickened. Remove the shrimp mixture from the heat and set it aside to cool.

Remove the thawed fillo dough from its package and gently unroll the sheets, laying them flat on a kitchen counter. Using the point of a sharp knife, cut the stack of sheets in half crosswise. Dampen a kitchen towel with water, wring it out well, and place it over the dough to prevent it from drying out as you work with it. Spread a dry kitchen towel out on the kitchen counter, right next to the stack of fillo sheets.

Remove the damp towel from the fillo dough and carefully lift off one of the halved sheets. Transfer it to the dry towel. (Immediately re-cover the remaining sheets.) Fold over one short end of the fillo sheet, transforming its rectangular shape into a square. Lightly brush the entire surface of the square with melted butter. Arrange the square so that one corner is facing you. Place a heaping tablespoon of the shrimp mixture an inch from that corner. Fold the corner over the shrimp mixture, then fold it over again. Fold the left and right flaps of the pastry over on themselves, toward the center. Then, starting at the filled end, roll up the pastry to form a compact cylinder about 2 inches long and ¾ inch thick. Transfer the roll, seam side down, to an ungreased baking sheet and brush its surface with more of the melted butter. Repeat until all the pieces of fillo dough are filled and rolled. At this point, the rolls may be frozen and held up to 1 month before final preparation, or refrigerated, covered with plastic wrap, until 30 minutes before final preparation.

TIME ALLOWANCE FOR FINAL PREPARATION: 30 MINUTES

Preheat the oven to 350 degrees.

Bake the Fillo Spring Rolls for 20 to 25 minutes, or until they are brown and crisp.

While the rolls are baking, make the dipping sauce by placing the dry mustard in a small bowl. Add the remaining 2 tablespoons soy sauce, the water, and vermouth, and stir until smooth.

Set the rolls briefly on paper towels to drain. Serve hot, accompanied by the dipping sauce.

YIELD: 50 ROLLS

TERIYAKI SAUSAGE

(MAY BE PREPARED UP TO 24 HOURS IN ADVANCE)

3 pounds kielbasa sausage, casings removed
¾ cup light soy sauce
1 cup sugar
⅓ cup dry vermouth
2 tablespoons minced, peeled gingerroot

Cut the sausage into ¼-inch-thick slices. Place them in a saucepan and cover them with water. Bring the water to a boil over high heat, and boil the sausage for 5 minutes. Drain the sausage into a colander.

Make the teriyaki sauce by combining the soy sauce, sugar, vermouth, and gingerroot in a 2-quart nonreactive saucepan. Place the pan over moderate heat and cook, stirring constantly, until the sugar has dissolved. Add the sausage slices and bring the teriyaki sauce to a boil. Lower the heat and simmer the sausage, partially covered, for 20 minutes. Stir occasionally.

If you are not serving the sausage immediately, transfer the slices and the sauce to a bowl, cover them tightly with plastic wrap, and refrigerate until time for final preparation.

TIME ALLOWANCE FOR FINAL PREPARATION: 10 MINUTES

Return the sausage slices and teriyaki sauce to a saucepan, and reheat over moderate heat for 5 minutes. Transfer the slices and the sauce to a chafing dish and keep hot. Serve with toothpicks.

YIELD: 400 ¼-INCH SLICES

CHICKEN PUFFS

◆

(PUFFS MAY BE PREPARED UP TO 2 WEEKS IN ADVANCE AND FROZEN;
FILLING MAY BE PREPARED UP TO 24 HOURS IN ADVANCE;
PUFFS MAY BE FILLED UP TO 2 HOURS IN ADVANCE)

PÂTE À CHOUX
1 cup water
½ cup unsalted butter
1 cup flour
¼ teaspoon salt
4 eggs

To make the puffs: Preheat the oven to 400 degrees. Lightly butter two cookie sheets or jellyroll pans.

Combine the water and butter in a 1- to 2-quart saucepan and bring them to a boil. When the butter has melted, add the flour and salt all at once. With a wooden spoon, beat briskly over medium heat until the mixture comes away from the sides of the pan and forms a ball. Remove the saucepan from the heat and add the eggs, one at a time, beating until each is totally incorporated before adding the next.

Using either a pastry sleeve with a half-inch nozzle, or two teaspoons, mound rounds of the dough about 1 inch in diameter on the baking sheets.

Place the pans in the oven and bake for 5 minutes. Reduce the heat to 350 degrees and bake the puffs for 25 minutes longer. Remove them from the oven and cut off the top third of each with a serrated knife. Return the puffs to the oven for 5 more minutes to dry out. Set the puffs aside to cool.

When the puffs are cool enough to handle, dig out and discard any damp dough left clinging to the insides. Either freeze the puffs or store them in plastic bags until final preparation. (The puffs may be filled up to 2 hours before serving without danger of becoming soggy.)

CHICKEN FILLING

¾ pound skinned and boned chicken breasts
2 tablespoons mayonnaise
4 teaspoons Dijon-style mustard
2 teaspoons honey
2 tablespoons chopped mango chutney

To make the filling: Place the chicken breasts in a skillet and cover them with water. Bring the water to a boil, lower the heat, cover the pan, and simmer the chicken for 10 minutes. Remove the skillet from the heat and let the breasts cool in the liquid, still covered, for 10 minutes. With a slotted spoon, remove them from the liquid and transfer them to a platter to cool.

When they are no longer warm to the touch, coarsely chop the meat.

In a mixing bowl, combine the mayonnaise, mustard, honey, and chutney, and mix until well blended. Add the chicken and toss to coat on all sides with the dressing.

If you are not filling the puffs immediately, cover the bowl and refrigerate until time to fill.

TIME ALLOWANCE FOR FINAL PREPARATION: 15 MINUTES

Using a demitasse spoon, fill the base of each puff with ½ teaspoon of chicken filling. Set the tops back on and transfer the puffs to a serving platter.

YIELD: 48 PUFFS

HAM AND CREAM CHEESE "SNAILS"

◆

(MAY BE PARTIALLY PREPARED AND FROZEN UP TO 2 WEEKS IN ADVANCE;
MUST BE PARTIALLY PREPARED AND FROZEN UP TO 2 HOURS IN ADVANCE)

1 (8-ounce) package cream cheese, softened
2 tablespoons minced fresh chives
1 tablespoon prepared horseradish, drained
¼ cup finely chopped dill pickles
1 pound Black Forest ham, sliced

In a food processor fitted with a steel blade, combine the cream cheese, chives, horseradish, and pickles, and whirl until blended.

Spread a heaping tablespoon of the cheese mixture over each slice of ham. Roll the slices lengthwise into tight cylinders. Repeat until all the slices are used up. As you make them, transfer the rolls to a tray. Freeze them for at least 2 hours, or for as long as 2 weeks. (Rolls frozen for more than 2 hours should be wrapped tightly in plastic and sealed.) Do NOT thaw the rolls before final preparation.

TIME ALLOWANCE FOR FINAL PREPARATION: 30 MINUTES

Trim the ends off each roll. Cut each roll into ¼-inch slices. Place the slices, or "snails," on a platter and allow them to thaw for 15 minutes before serving.

YIELD: ABOUT 150 "SNAILS"

STEAMED VEGETABLES WITH MARIANNE'S TUNA DIP

◆

(VEGETABLES AND DIPPING SAUCE MAY BE PARTIALLY PREPARED
UP TO 12 HOURS IN ADVANCE)

STEAMED VEGETABLES

1 pound sugar snap peas, trimmed
2 (12-ounce) packages baby carrots, trimmed and peeled
1 pound asparagus, ends trimmed, peeled
¾ pound broccoli flowerets, trimmed
¾ pound small Brussel sprouts, trimmed
4 bunches scallions, roots and tips of green leaves trimmed

To prepare the vegetables: On a steaming rack set in a kettle over boiling water, steam the peas, carrots, string beans, broccoli, Brussels sprouts, and scallions, one variety at a time. Steam them until they are just tender but still vivid in color and slightly crunchy. The time allowances for steaming are: peas, 1 minute; carrots, 7 or 8 minutes; asparagus, 5 minutes; broccoli, 3 or 4 minutes; Brussels sprouts, 4 minutes; scallions, 2 minutes.

After the vegetables are steamed, transfer them to a bath of cold water to stop their cooking. Dry them with paper toweling. If you are not serving them immediately, wrap each vegetable separately in plastic wrap and refrigerate until final preparation.

MARIANNE'S TUNA DIP
1 (8-ounce) package cream cheese, softened
3 tablespoons horseradish
¼ cup minced shallots
1 (6 ½-ounce) can light meat tuna, preferably Italian
¼ cup minced cilantro leaves (or substitute dillweed)

To make the Tuna Dip: In the jar of a food processor fitted with a steel blade, combine the cream cheese, horseradish, shallots, and tuna, and whirl until smoothly pureed. Add the minced cilantro and pulse once or twice to mix.

Scrape the tuna mixture into a small bowl. Tightly cover and refrigerate until 1 hour before serving time.

TIME ALLOWANCE FOR FINAL PREPARATION: 10 MINUTES

Pat the vegetables once again with paper toweling to remove any excess moisture. Arrange them attractively in groupings on a serving platter with the Tuna Dip placed in a shallow bowl in the center.

SERVES 50

Liver, Calf's, Venetian Style, 26
Lobster
  in Paella, 149
  Salmon and, Newburg, 218

M

Macaroons
  in Trifle à la Milano, 106
Mai Tais from Scratch, 232
Mango
  Chutney Dressing, 257
  Cream, 116
Marianne's Tuna Dip, Steamed Vegetables with, 281
Marinades
  for Curried Chicken Kebabs, 224
  for Grilled Caribbean Chicken, 41
  for Grilled Pork Loin, 59
  for Indonesian Pork Saté, 46
  for Mustard-Coated Grilled Lamb, 153
  for Roast Leg of Lamb Instanbul, 113
  for Teriyaki Flank Steak, 129
Marmalade Bread, 235
Mayonnaise Mustard, 174
Meringue(s)
  Almond, 265
  Pie, Chocolate Almond, 100
Miniature Sticky Buns, 210
Minted Carrot Puree, 51
Mint "Sauce" Jelly, 154
Mocha Sauce, Bittersweet, 162
Moros y Cristianos, 240
Mousse
  Individual Flourless Chocolate, 190
  Layered Apricot, 185
  Lemon, Crêpes, 139
Mushroom(s)
  and Barley Soup, 89
  Creamed Spinach and, 94
  Salad with Raspberry Vinaigrette, 47
  Sautéed, and Cherry Tomatoes, 82
  Sautéed, with Scallions, 18
  and Spinach Salad with Vinaigrette, 78
  Steamed Haddock with, and Sauce Madeleine, 30

Mussel Sauce, Linguine with, 103
Mustard
  -Coated Grilled Lamb, 153
  and Dill Sauce, 275
  Mayonnaise, 174

N

Newburg, Salmon and Lobster, 218
Noodles, Oriental, with Chinese Cabbage, 130

O

Orange
  Chicken, 93
  -Ginger Coffee Cake, 166
  Jelly, 72
  in Griots, 239
  in Marmalade Bread, 235
  Pound Cake, 177
Oriental Noodles with Chinese Cabbage, 130
Oven-Fried Potatoes, 94
Oven-Steamed Carrots with Tarragon, 171

P

Paella, 149
Pasta
  Diane Nottle's Tortellini Salad al Pesto, 226
  Linguine with Mussel Sauce, 103
  Spaghetti with Fresh Tomato Sauce, 55
Pastry, Puff
  in Apple Tart, 127
  in Apple Turnovers, 91
  in Upside-Down Pear Pie, 121
Pastry, Shortbread, 252
Pâte à Choux
  in Chicken Puffs, 279
  in Profiteroles, 206
Peaches, Hot Gingered, 28
Pea(s)
  Curried, and Cashew Salad, 250
  with Pignoli, 264